Also by Paula Deen

By Paula Deen with Martha Nesbit

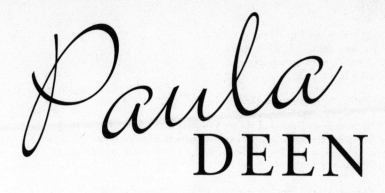

Paula DEEN

It Ain't All About the Cookin'

Paula Deen

with Sherry Suib Cohen

Simon & Schuster Paperbacks

New York London Toronto Sydney

Simon & Schuster Paperbacks
A Division of Simon & Schuster, Inc.
1230 Avenue of the Americas
New York, NY 10020

First Simon & Schuster trade paperback edition November 2009

SIMON & SCHUSTER PAPERBACKS and colophon are registered
trademarks of Simon & Schuster, Inc.

For information about special discounts for bulk purchases,
please contact Simon & Schuster Special Sales at
1-866-506-1949 or business@simonandschuster.com.

The Simon & Schuster Speakers Bureau can bring authors
to your live event. For more information or to book an event,
contact the Simon & Schuster Speakers Bureau at
1-866-248-3049 or visit our website at www.simonspeakers.com.

Designed by C. Linda Dingler

Manufactured in the United States of America

10 9 8 7 6 5 4 3 2 1

The Library of Congress has cataloged the hardcover edition as follows:

Deen, Paula H.
    Paula Deen : it ain't all about the cookin' / by Paula Deen, with Sherry Suib
Cohen.
        p.   cm.
    1. Deen, Paula H., 1947– 2. Cooks—Biography. 3. Cookery,
Southern. I. Cohen, Sherry Suib. II. Title. III. Title: Paula Deen : it ain't
all about the cookin'.
TX715.2.S68D438 2007
641.5092—dc22
[B]   2006053501

ISBN 978-0-7432-9285-6
ISBN 978-1-4391-6335-1 (pbk)
ISBN 978-1-4165-3968-1 (ebook)

Acknowledgments

First of all, thanks to my darlin' Michael, always Michael, my handsome, sexy, funny husband, who always makes me laugh so hard, I think I'm gonna bust. And thanks to my precious family who come along for the excitin' ride every day—Bobby, Jamie, and Brooke; Aunt Peggy Ort and Aunt Trina; my baby brother and partner, Bubba Hiers, and his new partner, Dawn Woodside, and her sons, Iain and Trevor; my beautiful niece, Corrie, and cute nephew, Jay; and, of course, the great Groover kids, Anthony and Michelle, and Michelle's new husband, Daniel Reed. I love and am so grateful for my brother-in-law, spiritual advisor, and Cajun connection, Father Hank Groover. My husband's baby brother, Nick Groover, the unwillin' subject of Captain Michael's childhood taunts, is not only part of my extended dear family, not only our neighbor, but also the contractor of the beautiful home Michael and I enjoy so much; Nick's wife, Jodi, and their adorable children, Jordan and Lauren, are in my life forever now.

My lovin' appreciation goes to my collaborator and newest friend, writer Sherry Suib Cohen, who helped me find the words I needed to tell my story. Sherry leaves Savannah talkin' Southern (she thinks) and with an educated view of butter.

What would I do without Team Paula, which includes my

never-forgets-anything, inspirational executive assistant, Theresa Luckey; my fabulously creative, witty, and indispensable right-hand man, Brandon Branch; the accomplished and devoted Michelle White, who wears so many hats—among them extraordinary graphic designer; Cassie Aimar, my talented personal assistant; and my favorite accountant on the planet, Karl Schumacher, for their never-ending efforts to make sure the details of my personal and professional life work smoothly. My agent, Barry Weiner, is the closest thing I've had to a father since my real father died; he's always there for cheerleading and wise words. I love you, Barry Cuda—you're my hero. My literary agent, Janis Donnaud, is endlessly loyal and helpful and always in my corner. My attorney, Peter Smith—well, I just adore him; he's one of the finest men I have ever met.

My Lady & Sons restaurant family is also the absolute best! Dora Charles has been there from the start, makin' me look good and keepin' me sane. I couldn't do without Rance Jackson, my number one kitchen manager; Dustin Walls, my general manager; and Scott Hopke, who is our executive kitchen manager. Cookie Espinoza is our office manager, and she manages to keep everyone happy and on track. The entire staff, from the bussers to the waitpeople, from the hostesses to the dishwashers—each and every one of them is so important to The Lady & Sons, and I'm forever grateful for this team we've formed.

My Simon & Schuster publishing family feels like real family to me. I'm immensely grateful to the following people who have turned my memories and ideas into this beautiful book. I love them all, but best of all I love my brilliant editor, Sydny Miner, who lavished such care, thought, and creativity on each page, you'd think this book was her real-life baby. I'm so beholden to Syd, my dream editor, and also to her personal assistant, Michelle Rorke, who has been marvelous and responsive throughout the whole publishing process. Linda Dingler and Jaime Putorti worked beautifully and imaginatively on the interior design, and I am really happy with Jackie Seow's cover design. I also lucked out because Arden Ward took the cover photograph—don't y'all agree? Thanks are also surely due to Randee Marullo and Sybil Pincus, the copy editors who diligently combed this book to make it the best it could be.

I'm also so pleased that David Rosenthal, the enlightened and extraordinary publisher of Simon & Schuster, leads my book team, and that Deb Darrock and Aileen Boyle are the fine associate publishers of the best publishing house in America. Deep gratitude goes to Tracey Guest, director of publicity, and her staff for telling the world about *Paula Deen: It Ain't All About the Cookin'*, and the biggest hug to everyone else at S&S who made this very personal memoir possible.

Thank you, thank you, thank you to a remarkable woman who's recently come into my life and given me a new focus and such joy. She is Phyllis Norton Hoffman, the publisher and president of Hoffman Media, LLC. Phyllis had the foresight to spot a powerful connection between me and the women in America—not just Southern women—and she offered me my very own stunning magazine, *Cooking with Paula Deen*. I was just astonished when she approached me—who would ever read such a thing?—but today, the magazine is sold on newsstands internationally. The magazine is about cookin', naturally, but also about entertaining and decorating and quaint little towns, and business and beauty and the color of eggs and—oh, just about everything that's on the minds of women like me.

My gratitude goes to four new and fabulous business partners who support me wonderfully: Pete Booker, Larry Pope, Jim Schloss, and Joe Luter III. Welcome aboard, all of you!

I'm forever grateful to the Food Network and my producer, the wild and wonderful Gordon Elliott, who have literally changed my life and have made me, Paula Deen, into a television star—I can hardly believe it! Judy Girard, Brooke Johnson, and Bob Tuschman of the network are deep in my heart forever. My two shows, *Paula's Home Cookin'* and *Paula's Party,* have given me a chance to share a love of makin' good meals and havin' fun with my terrific fans, who are always challenging me to cook better, tell more secrets, and show my stuff . . . even when my stuff ain't so perfect. I relish every moment of my life journey and I can't wait to see what happens next! Think of it: I'm a sixty-year-old, grey-haired, overweight woman and I'm still employed. Life is a beauty-ful thing.

So many thanks are due to Melanie Votaw, who transcribed every interview for this book, and from about a hundred tapes put my words down on paper with meticulous accuracy. And a huge thank-you to Nancy Assuncao, my personal publicist.

This book would not be complete without acknowledging the man with whom I spent twenty-seven years, Jimmy Deen. We had our differences, but he's a good person, a kind man, and together we made the most handsome, wonderful sons imaginable.

Finally, I want to give thanks for my beloved momma and daddy, Corrie and Earl Hiers, and to my Grandparents Paul and my Grandparents Hiers, who left life much too early. They molded me and had such a great influence on my life because they offered me the steady confidence, support, and love every little girl needs—especially a little girl who knew, deep inside, it ain't just about the cookin'—it's about surviving, and then love and laughter and living well, Southern style.

*T*his book is for Jack Deen, perfect grandbaby of my heart, and littlest cook. I've waited so long for you, child. In your precious self, our family past and future meet. I fell in love with you, tiny Jackpot, even before you were born, and already I know I will cherish the man you will become.

You're gonna come to like fried chicken, baby boy: it's in your genes.

Contents

Contents

Paula
DEEN

Foreword

I never call myself a chef. Never went to Chef School. Never made a Blanquette de Veau. Never met a boxed cake mix I didn't like.

I'm a cook. Learned at my grandmomma's stove. But I can cook, honey, cook rings around those tall-white-hatted chefs. My fried chicken, my grits—oh my stars, you'll think you died and went to heaven.

Like everyone else on this earth, there's a story behind the cook, behind the recipes, behind the woman.

So, y'all, here is what the publisher calls my memoirs.

How did they come about? Well, I've written five cookbooks, and after each one, I got thousands of letters from people asking about my personal life, not just my life with grits. Until now, I haven't been about ready to do that. Maybe if you heard the truth about Paula Deen, about the mistakes I made in my life, how bad my judgment's been at times, and how guilty I still feel because my mothering wasn't always so wonderful . . . well, maybe you wouldn't be quite as lovin' to me as you have been. And that would kill me.

If I could get back one wrong I did to my family, if I could choose some words I could take back and eat 'em down so they would never have seen the light, it would be the day I told my son

Jamie I hated him. I can barely write those words now. I love my sons more than life, but we were in the heat of the battle of starting a restaurant business, trying to get all those people fed, and I felt like Jamie was pulling against me, rather than with me. If I could only live that day over, oh, I would. You'd better believe I learned that the spoken word can never be taken back. Sure, you can apologize for it, but you and the person you hurt will never, ever forget. Forgive, maybe, if you're real lucky.

I've asked for a lot of forgiveness in my life and I've given it as well. You know what? In church, they always tell you to forgive your enemies. Seems to me it's even harder to forgive our loved ones and friends, but it's much more important to do so because it's the people we love who can hurt us the most. The terrible thing I said to Jamie taught me to speak with more care and try not to let my instinct for survival get me so mad I'll give pain to someone close to me. But can you imagine me, a mother who loves her boys beyond love, saying such a thing to her own child?

I'll tell you something else: in all the things that have been written about me, there's something that's been left out of the tellin'. I'm a smoker. There, I said it. Hardly anyone outside my family knows that, and it embarrasses me because it's an addiction I can't be quit of, though I try every day. They say Jackie Kennedy was a chain smoker, but she would never allow herself to be photographed with a cigarette—and I get that real well because I also try my damndest to see that no one takes my picture with one. I love my fans so much and I hate to disappoint them; to see me with such a weakness will surely upset them. I still need to walk into a room where they're waiting with my head up.

But suddenly, somehow, it's time to show and tell—warts and all. I plan to tell some hard secrets in these pages, but it's taken a long time to get up the nerve to do so. Try ten years. Maybe twenty.

Mostly, I want to share with you that I'm livin' proof that the

American dream is alive and well, that you can be an imperfect person and still end up with so much fun in your life you can hardly stand it. I'm prayin' that if even one of you out there gets some inspiration from the way my own American dream turned into reality, it'll be worth playing true confessions here.

You should know this: you gotta be willin' to work for that American dream—work for it, and feel the passion. You gotta truly be in love with what you do. If you have a wild hair to fly a circus trapeze, to chug out to sea on a tug, to own a restaurant when you haven't much more than a dime to your name, or to search for true love even when you're no spring chicken—go for it. Sure, luck plays a part, but here's the thing: the harder I work, the luckier I get.

A warning: you may be a little shocked at some of the language in this book, and that's another weakness of mine. I tell people who come to my cooking class that sometimes I can be a little bawdy and I sure hope that don't upset them. But I'm my father's daughter, and I'm banking on one thing, and I'm not budging on this: my God has a sense of humor even if what I say has a four-letter word in it. I think He'd want me to laugh. What's in my heart is not irreverence but a full knowledge that God's laughing too.

So, this is a book wishin' you best dishes from my house to yours, but it's also a look into my home, my true life, my loves, and my Southern heart.

Chapter 1

TERROR WITH
NO NAME

What did I have, what was makin' me so scared that my heart about beat out of my chest? I just knew I was gonna die, knew my heart couldn't stand this kind of pressure, and it had happened too many times before. Almost every last time I had to go outside by myself, that panic would start in and drop me to my knees. Couldn't breathe, couldn't stop trembling. I felt weak and nauseated and dizzy, and I just knew I was gonna die in front of other people. If I dropped over in public, think how horribly humiliatin' it would be.

But, oh Lord, the magnolias smelled so damn good out my window, and all morning I'd been fixin' to take my eleven-year-old son, Jamie, to baseball practice. After, I figured I'd hang out at the mall store in the housewares section, then maybe go strollin' for a bit, just to breathe deep some of that sweet Georgia air. I wanted to walk through my door so bad and maybe today I could do it; maybe today I could go outside.

There would be no breathin' deep, no goin' *outside*. The thought of *outside* grabbed my gut like a 'coon grabs a chicken. I started to sweat and my arms lost all feeling, like they belonged on someone else. At the very least, I was likely to faint at any moment. Would there be someone to see me, someone who would catch me if one of those panicky attacks came back and I lost control and fainted *outside*? Oh, my stars, I was frightened silly.

It was 1978, and I was thirty-one years old. Was this the day I was finally going to die, the day I'd secretly been waiting for and dreading ever since my daddy passed almost thirteen years ago now?

Well, maybe not, if I stopped thinking of going outside.

You're safe, Paula, I told myself. *You're safe inside this house. No one's makin' you go out, you won't die today. Fact is—don't you remember—y'all canceled the boys' after-school stuff for the whole year.*

What sickness did I have? What had happened to me? My terror had no name—least none I'd ever heard. I was alone with it. So scared about goin' *outside*.

It wasn't always this way.

Chapter 2

SOMETHING SMELLS GOOD

You don't have to be Southern to admire the smell of grits cookin'—hang with me, and even if you're from New Jersey, you'll be lovin' grits.

If you had to pick out a delicious childhood, it would have been mine. I was born on January 19, 1947, and grew up with a passion for life and, for a long time, nothing ever frightened me—nothing. My earliest memories are from when my momma and daddy, Corrie and Earl Hiers; my brother, Earl Hiers Jr., otherwise known as Bubba; and I lived in Albany, Georgia, out at River Bend, which was my Grandmother and Granddaddy Paul's place. It was right at the Dougherty and Mitchell county line, about ten miles outside of downtown. River Bend was sort of a very mini resort sitting right on U.S. 19, and it was where all the snowbirds came—a little rest stop on their way to Florida and fancier pleasures. Our grandparents had a motel and cabins, a skating rink, a restaurant, and a big old swimming pool, and it was pure heaven, that River Bend. My handsome daddy worked at his car dealership and my momma helped her parents in the restaurant and I thought life was just grand: I lived in my swimsuit and my roller skates and you'd better believe I wore them both at the same time.

I had my own personal playmate, Momma's baby sister, Trina, who was just three years older than I. When Grandmomma told Trina that my twenty-year-old momma was gonna have a baby and that would make Trina an aunt, Trina immediately got underneath the table on her hands and knees and started crawlin' around, just a-cryin' something pitiful. Grandmomma said, "Trina, honey, why are you down there cryin'?" And Trina answered between sobs, "'Cause you told me I was gonna be an ant."

Well, maybe it was that first shock or maybe not, but Trina was usually so stinking mean to me; she was such a brat. Even though she was my buddy, maybe even my idol, she was a tremendous devil child. I remember her taking my arm and digging her long fingernails into it, and she didn't allow me to tell Momma on her. My earliest food memory is of Trina spoon-feeding me tablespoons of vanilla flavoring, and, believe me, that's a nasty memory. I remember we'd be playing in the family living area of the motel at River Bend and she would send me all the way back to the restaurant to get her a glass of water. When I'd get back, she'd pour out that whole dang thing into the sink and say, "I wanted cold water." And I'd have to go back and get her a big old glass of colder water. Once I asked her, "Why can't you get some water from the bathroom right here," and she said, "The faucets ain't working right here." She'd send me over to the restaurant for a Hershey's bar, a Snickers, and a Coke, and I'd gather up all the stuff, with my granddaddy yelling out the whole time, "Get that kid outta here. She's eatin' up all mah profit!"

That Trina. I had a Southern princess in my life, even at that young age.

I was seven when Bubba was born, and then it was *my* turn to be princess. I bossed him around something awful but I loved him so because I was like his momma when our own momma was busy. And, boy, Momma was pretty much always busy.

When I was about six, Momma and Daddy bought a gas station and souvenir shop right across the street from River Bend. It wasn't no River Bend. Paradise was done and finished for little Paula Hiers.

We lived in the back of that souvenir shop. We had no bathroom; our toilet was a big old slop jar inside a pink wicker chair. Of course we had a men's room and a ladies' room outside for the tourists; there was a shower in the men's room. I remember it being cold and dirty, and when we woke up on a cold morning, we would have to go outside in that nasty men's room to take a shower. I just hated it, *hated* it. So, even now, I don't associate bathing as being a good thing; I still remember that awful men's room. I could not stand it. And I remember my daddy saying, "This is terrible. I'm going to build us a bathroom, and I'm going to build one helluva bathroom."

Well, he finally did, but I don't know how many years we lived there using the public shower. When he finally built that bathroom, it was bigger than our whole living quarters, and I remember Momma's clothes washer being in there. Our dryer was a clothesline out back. And I remember my daddy going into the bathroom and just sitting forever on the toilet; what a luxury it was for all of us. That toilet was a throne.

We never thought about it then, but we were living in the midst of what was fixin' to be a huge social change. A small town of twenty-five thousand people before World War II, Albany, Georgia, had grown to a Deep South city of about fifty thousand and became the pecan capital of the world, as folks like to brag. Racial unrest was brewing, and in just four more years, five African-American college students who belonged to a civic organization called the Albany Movement would be arrested for a sit-in at our own Trailways bus station lunch counter. Shortly afterward, nine Freedom Riders would arrive to test the segregated train station, and Albany Movement president William Anderson would invite the Reverend Martin Luther King Jr. to Albany, Georgia, where he drew overflow crowds at Mt. Zion and Shiloh Baptist churches. The next day King and 264 demonstrators were arrested when they marched to City Hall. But that was all four years in the future and could have been a million years away as far as us kids were concerned.

Still, it was happening right under our noses: our local African-Americans were claimin' their right for fair and equal treatment and some white folks were inspired to rethink old ways. Slowly, things began to change. Culture evolved as the Motown sound brought African-American music onto the charts. Still, I hardly noticed, even when the Albany-born black singer Ray Charles recorded a wildly successful song in 1959. "Just an old sweet song keeps Georgia on my mind," sang Ray Charles, and "Georgia on My Mind" was eventually to become the state song.

Everybody would be so busy working over at River Bend and at the gas station that sometimes I would be told to stay with a real nice black woman who often babysat Trina and me. I remember this one day she had brought her little girl to work, and that child had many big, fat blisters on her hand, probably from helping out her momma. Something about those blisters just attracted me and I remember hitting those little hands with a bolo bat, and it busted her blisters good. It was pretty satisfying.

I don't know why I did it. I have a hard time thinking I did it out of meanness. But her mother—I can't remember if she slapped me across the face or she spanked me, or both—but either way, now I know I sure had it comin'.

Well, still, I was heartbroken, and I went running to find my

Grandmother Paul and Granddaddy and my momma. And my granddaddy had the woman arrested for hitting me. The little black girl's momma went to jail.

All this time it's bothered me.

It was me who deserved to be sittin' in that jail for breaking a little black girl's blisters in 1957.

Even if we all kind of knew something was happening, it didn't seem so grand or momentous. The civil rights movement belonged to the nightly radio news and it didn't have nothin' to do with us. Black folks had always been a big part of our lives in the South; I played with the kids of the black women who took care of me and they were my friends. None of us were strangers to the black community, although they seemed to live their lives, and we lived ours, separately for the most part. I would say we lived a pretty unexamined life in terms of politics or civil rights. When I look back now, I remember going to the Arctic Bear, one of the popular drive-in restaurants in town where you got your burgers and ate them in your car. On the side of the building were two water fountains: one was marked WHITE ONLY and the other was marked COLORED. The bathrooms were also marked WHITE ONLY and COLORED. That's just the way it was. Remembering now, it just shocks me. I'm plain horrified that things could have been that way and I was so blind I didn't get that it was wrong.

My senior class in Albany High School, 1965, was the first class in our neck of the woods to be integrated, by five black girls. They did not talk to anyone; they kept to themselves. To my knowledge no one harassed them, but no one was particularly tight with them either. There was no sense that we were in the middle of something historic. We knew having those five girls in school was some sort of a big step, but we never thought it would change anything for us.

They were so brave. Even then, I felt a little sorry for them, but you know why? For all the wrong reasons. I felt their families had to have been paid or somethin' to convince them to put their girls in such a hard position—the only black girls in our all-white school. My parents wouldn't have put me in an all-black school. I'm so embarrassed and ashamed to admit it to y'all that I thought that. Those families were pioneers. They were so effin' brave, all of them, the kids and the parents. The five girls had to be majorly lonely—five small black faces in a sea of unthinking teenaged white faces. Even if the black girls had a mouthful of words, they would have never said "Boo," let alone "How 'bout goin' for a Coke after school?" to any of the rest of us. I so wish I could take back my actions then. If I could do it all over, I'd have dragged them all into cheerleadin', I'd have shared my lunches with them, I'd have held them to my heart.

I didn't do one of those things, but I think I was polite to them. That was about it for any grand social consciousness on my part. I was slow to admit it, but I didn't pay no mind to any part of it. How could I not have made it easier for them? I get mortified playin' it over in my mind's eye.

My world was so small then and we kids were so full of ourselves. Bubba and Trina and I were blissfully unaware of Martin Luther King, Ray Charles, or even President Eisenhower, who hunted quail in our neck of the woods while he was president. I was thirteen in 1960. When we were sophomores in high school, we did notice that President Kennedy was pretty cute, but it was really Jackie's style that interested us. Times were simpler and there were fewer hidden messages; if you were at a *gay* party, you were having fun. A *Coke* party meant the drink of choice was Coca-Cola. For me, these were the good days because they revolved around family, which to this little Southern girl was the heart and the currency for everything solid and dependable and safe.

Speaking of cute—the future proprietor of Uncle Bubba's Oyster House was really cute, but, oh my, his room smelled so bad—

like rotten socks. He played baseball with all his brave heart. He was the best little player.

About the time we lived across from River Bend, our momma had an old black man who worked for her named Les. Daddy was working hard at his car dealership in town and Momma pumped gas and changed oil and worked at the souvenir shop where that creepy men's bathroom was. So, if Les didn't show up for work, she had nobody to watch her little boy and I would simply take the two-year-old Bubba to school with me. You just did what you had to do back then. I'd throw him on my hip, and off we would go to school. He would sit at that desk on my lap, quiet as a doll for a couple of hours, and then we would go out at recess, and I'd let him play. Then we'd come back in after lunch. I went to this little country school, and I remember in the second-grade classroom the teacher's name was Miss Bowles. She was old (probably about forty—that was *real* old then to me), and she had frizzy hair that stood out all over her head. She wore glasses and those black lace-up shoes that you would think old-fashioned schoolteachers would wear. She didn't seem real happy, but she taught the second and third grades and she had that classroom divided with the second grade in one half of the room and the third grade in the other half. She would go back and forth and teach each class.

School wasn't my favorite activity, specially with Bubba on my lap, but, oh, how I loved lunchtime. There was a cafeteria, and those country women could cook sooooo good. On Fridays, honey, I would step on your back to get to that cafeteria. It was vegetable soup, toast, and peanut butter balls every Friday. I still make those peanut butter balls, years later. How did I get the recipe? I'm fixin' to tell y'all this minute.

I was about thirty years old and already suffering from those panic attacks, but that wasn't the worst of it. During one of the short periods of time when I could manage to get out of my house, I'd met one of my best friends, Becky Geer, on the street. She worked for the Internal Revenue Service, and on the spur of the moment she said, "Paula, we need some help—would you come in and do some temporary work?"

I thought, *We sure need the money and, yeah, I could probably do that,* and I went down there, and I got to talking to this woman. Would you believe, I came to find out her mother was the cook in Baconton Elementary School—my old school? And I said, "Oh, my God, since I was ten years old I've been craving a peanut butter ball."

"Well, I've got the recipe," she told me.

Pure bliss.

Ever since I got to making those peanut butter balls, things seemed as though they were trying to pick up.

But back to the fourth grade. Oh, my gosh, Fridays were so good, and not just because of the peanut butter balls. The school was probably five miles from River Bend, and so we would ride the school bus home, and every Friday the driver would stop at the little country store, and we could get off the bus and go in and buy us some candy. Why was this so important to me? Goodness knows. In five minutes I could walk into my momma's souvenir shop after school and start eating the stuff for free. But I looked so forward to Friday and buying candy with the rest of the kids. My favorites were BB Bats. They were chocolate, chewy things on a stick, and they were hard. I loved those BB Bats.

I remember this one particular Friday in February. It was so cold. I had on an overcoat, and socks and shoes, of course, and I had to pee so bad. I went and asked the store clerk, "May I use your bathroom?" and he said, "No, we don't have one." And I said, "What am I gonna do?" I mean, I had to pee really bad.

So, I walked to the farthest aisle away from the cash register. I just spread my legs, and I peed on the floor. And it ran all down in my socks and my shoes, and I took them off. I was so humiliated but I walked back out barefoot and got on the bus. All age groups from first grade to high school rode the bus. When I got on, one girl said, "Paula, what are you doing walking around barefooted? It's cold outside." Here I was wearing this humongous heavy coat, but all I could think of saying was, "I just got hot."

There was this big old boy who always rode the bus and he was a senior. He was so tall, and he had big old dirty hands and he was on my bus every day and I just hated when I had to get on that bus and the only seat was next to him. He was disgusting.

It never failed: when I wasn't looking, and just before I took my seat, he'd reach over and ball up his hand except for his thumb which stuck right up. I would sit on his thumb. Nowadays, I guess they'd call that sexual abuse.

But, I'll never forget that day—it was probably thirty degrees out—when I peed in my pants and I told everybody I was hot.

That horrible senior got a surprise when I sat down.

It was at River Bend that I first fell in love with food. Not just the eating of it, but what it meant in life: food as comfort, food as friendship, food as sensual expression. If you go to a party, where does everyone end up? In the kitchen. The kitchen is the heart and the hearth of a home. The South is all about tradition, and most of those traditions have their origins in the cooking pots and the recipes we pass down from generation to generation. My momma was an excellent cook, but she didn't do a whole lot to develop my inner chef. I'd ask her if she would just let me into her kitchen so I could help her and maybe she'd teach me how to cook. She'd always say, "Well, come on in, honey."

Five minutes later, she'd be sayin', "I'm sorry, honey, but you have to go."

Actually, now I can kind of understand it because I also like to be in control of my pots. But I would just get on her nerves so bad.

Momma cooked three meals a day—she would get up and cook breakfast every morning for Bubba and me before we went to school, and she even cooked lunch for Daddy. She cooked him a hot meal in the middle of the day, because he would always come home for lunch. Listen: I knew it was more than lunch. I always thought that was when they had their boom-boom time. You know—we would be in school, and I never ever overheard any noises or anything like that at night, so I felt in my bones that they *really* looked forward to their lunches together. Sharing food is the most personal way to connect and it often leads to other good stuff.

But watching my Grandmother Irene Paul was another matter entirely. Something always smelled good in her kitchen. She taught me the traditions of Southern cooking, especially the way she seasoned food with herbs, fatback, peppers, and even hog jowls. She made a memorable turtle soup, fried chicken that caused you to salivate, and fried peach pies that made you think you died and went to heaven. She was a great, inspiring cook, pure in heart, and, best of all, I didn't get on her nerves. I spent days and days and days in her kitchen; I didn't realize it then but I was getting an education there in which I'd eventually get all A's. I sure couldn't say the same for any other school I attended. It was gradually coming to me that Southern cooking was a hand-me-down art. It came from within Grandmomma Paul and it was how she showed her love, her compassion, her godliness, her neighborliness. Her staples were butter—as much as you could get your hands on—sugar, salt, pepper, hot sauce, vinegar, ham hocks, and fat of all descriptions, including lard.

I didn't think of my grandmother as being pretty but I remember she had long gray hair. She parted it in the middle and made two pigtails, then she pinned the pigtails up like a crown. She was a *presence*. She'd been an incredible wife to her husband, John Paul, my granddaddy. Oh, he had dark, curly hair and he was a ladies' man, my Granddaddy Paul. I heard he had girl-friends during his whole marriage, the fact of which my grandmother hated, but she hardly ever mentioned it to the family, my momma told me. You didn't mention stuff like that in those days. But I do remember them fighting—today, I guess you'd call it verbal sparring—probably about all those ladies' man activities. My Grandmother Paul had balls. She got what she wanted, in the end.

He had the world by the tail, my granddaddy did. He had those lady friends. And he also had two daughters who were very efficient—my mother, Corrie, and her sister, my Aunt Peggy, who has saved my butt on more than one occasion. Last, but sure not least, he had his wife, who worked like a dog. Although Grand-daddy used to drive a dry-cleaning truck, it was his wife who made him his first serious dollars in a little hot dog stand he bought for her by the airport in Hapeville, Georgia, a suburb of Atlanta. She produced the product; he managed the finances. My granddaddy was a very shrewd businessman but he didn't believe in insurance. When he died, all of his money was in cash: a hundred thousand dollars, and back then, to accumulate a hundred thousand dollars in cash was major. But it was my Grandmomma Paul's cookin' in that little hot dog stand that did so well they were able to move on to country steak and creamed potatoes. Grandmomma told me that one day, a customer tried to get fresh with my momma, who slapped him silly across the face with one of those raw steaks. My granddaddy was also driving a laundry truck then, and Grandmomma would tell me that she would take the money bag and walk to the stand at four o'clock in the morning, and when she closed, she'd walk home with the money. Oh, my goodness, I wish I'd given a tape recorder to her because she had the good stories.

Finally, my grandparents sold the stand and moved to a little town in southwest Georgia called Albany, where my granddaddy bought a restaurant called The White House. That was the start of River Bend. And that's where I come in.

Thinkin' back, I remember my momma was so much a lady, you'd never know I came from her loins. She was a *proper* Southern lady, and you couldn't guess what she was thinking. She kept her feelings to herself, which, to me, wound up being her downfall. It seems to me now that if you keep a secret down deep in your guts because you think folks will think little of you if they knew the secret, it tends to fester and grow rank. Tell a secret, you get one back.

My mother was the disciplinarian in the family. It was she who'd whip my ass. We had a hedge, and she'd make me go out there and pick that damn switch for her to whip my ass with. I remember she would switch my legs, and I'd be just jumping up and down hollerin'. I remember one time she was switchin' me, and my girlfriend was over in the corner, with her legs crossed so she wouldn't pee because she was trying so hard not to laugh while I was getting my own legs tore up. Once I made the mistake of telling my mother that I hated her. Afterward, I was so mad at myself for hurtin' her so bad. I only told her the *hate* thing once, though, after she said, very quietly, "Don't you ever say those words to me again."

My momma meant business. Sometimes, I still said hateful things behind her back, but you know, I would never seriously get in my mother's face, and I would never say all these fresh-mouth things to her face that young girls do today, like:

"I most certainly am wearing that outfit. I don't care what you say!"

"I'm gonna do it! You step outta the way."

"I want some new shoes and they gotta be designer shoes like everyone else!"

On the other hand, no matter what, Daddy would walk in that house and he never once laid a finger on me. All he'd have to do was act like he was going to go for his belt and then it was "Yes, suh, Daddy. Yes, *suh*." It's funny how Momma would spank me at the drop of a hat if I deserved it, and Daddy wouldn't. That's the way it was. You spent most of the time you weren't in school with your mother, especially in the fifties and sixties. Daddies were just not a real important part of a young girl's life. The dad worked, and then he did what he wanted to do. My daddy was so kind. I'd bring home these horrible report cards and look at Daddy and say, "I failed algebra again," and he'd say, "Honey, it's all right—I stunk at algebra, also." He'd tolerate my weaknesses, but let me tell you what he would not tolerate and that was being unkind or rude to people. If my parents had company and I'd walk in the back door and go straight to my room, he'd be sure to call me back down and say, "The Fletchers are here. Speak to them." And I did.

Our daddy was in the car business at this time. I worshipped and adored him, and I think I'm just like him now. He loved life and he always was laughing. That's really my legacy from my daddy.

Finally, when I was nine or ten, our grandparents sold River Bend and moved to Florida, where they bought another motel. It didn't feel the same without them, and a year later, we moved back to Albany.

Times were tough. Money was hard to come by. But I didn't realize we weren't rich because it seemed my folks gave me everything important I ever wanted. I was turning into a young woman. Funny—I remember the day when that was made clear to me like it was yesterday. I was eleven years old, so it would have been 1958.

Bernice and Hugh Crum, Momma and Daddy's best friends, had moved to Little Rock, Arkansas, and we decided to drive out to see them. So, along with Shirley and Dale Dingler, we loaded up the car, and back then cars were huge. The Dinglers had a pudgy little son we called Fudgie. So, it was Momma, Daddy, Bubba, and me, and the Dinglers—all seven of us piled into the car. I remember lying under the back windshield. It felt like it took a million hours, and all that time Shirley Dingler was curled up on the passenger floorboard asleep, and she wasn't a small woman. I'm sure all four of the adults were also smoking. Not a comfortable million hours. So, we went to Little Rock, then we got back in the car and drove home. I remember on the way back I rode on the floorboard. The next day, I woke up with blood all over my pajamas. I went and found Momma, and I started crying in terror. "I'm bleeding, Momma!"

My momma made it all better and made me feel good about getting to be a woman. "Oh, honey, it's just your period coming on. Congratulations," she said, like I did something good.

"Do you think it was all the jigglin' in the car?" I asked. She said no, of course, but I secretly always felt like lying on that floorboard and having all those bumps maybe brought it on.

Then, sure as a rainbow follows a rain, I discovered the male gender. When I turned into a teenager, all those hormones were flowing like crazy. I was fueled with nuclear energy, a high-octane mix of curiosity and passion, and I found out I was pretty good at flirting. I liked to flirt. Still do, I might add. Men are damn cute. And, I found out I had this woman power—it felt *good*.

I remember we had a little baseball park right between my best friend's house and my house, and I walked on by it every day and all the boys were doing those cat whistles, callin' out, "Oh, I wish I had that swing in my backyard."

I started realizing my power. I liked it plenty.

Comin' to the end of high school, life turned for me; it turned in many directions, and mostly down. I was seventeen years old and soon to make a bad decision. I didn't know it then, but I was about to meet the most gorgeous boy on the planet. I wonder how my life would have been had I never set eyes on his beauty.

One day, in my junior year, I was walking down the hall alone and happened to glance over at a couple, also strollin' down the high school hallway. Well, there was the most startlingly beautiful young man I had ever seen and he had his arm around a girl named Betty Sue, and she had the most tremendous boobs you've ever seen. I knew for a fact she had to have her bras special-made.

I didn't think a thing about it. I just remember seeing that couple and watching this beautiful boy laughing and looking down at Betty Sue. And then I didn't see him again for almost a year. Forgot plain about him. I thought.

Around this time, I'd settled comfortably into going steady with Bill, a nice young man who had graduated from Albany High School. He was attending Auburn University, and he came home weekends to see me and he drove this darling little burgundy Volkswagen. Oh, I was crazy about Bill—he was hardworking and smart, he'd played football for Albany High, and he was just so sweet and everyone loved him. In his time, he'd been a Senior Superlative. Senior Superlatives were big-time at Albany High School; the ten girls and ten guys who were the most popular and talented as voted by the senior class. I was going to be a Senior Superlative too when I graduated—but I didn't know it yet. I wasn't much for the academics (I failed algebra three times), but I was a big social butterfly, excelling at dating, beauty pageants, and cheerleading. Actually, I did not give a rat's ass about the books; it was *rah rah rah* I loved. If I could have made a livin' cheerleading, that would have been my chosen life path.

We girls all pretty much wore the same things: penny loafers without socks, pleated skirts, shirtwaist dresses with cinched-in waists, pedal pushers, and, best of all, dyed-to-match alpaca sweater sets and skirts. Peter Pan collars were everywhere. We'd have slumber parties with seventeen girls all in baby-doll pajamas with fat curlers in our hair and big daisy-flowered bonnets to go over them. In the middle of the night, if we got hungry, we'd sneak out of the house, put the car in neutral, and push it to the corner so Momma and Daddy wouldn't hear us going; then we'd hop in the car and drive down to the local fast-food joint, the Krystal, right in our curlers and pj's, to get us a sack of burgers.

The boys wore blue jeans, button-down oxford shirts, and crew-neck sweaters. The guys who sported greasy, longish hair were playin' like they were Elvis, but we considered them hoods. My own hair was very bouffant. We did the twist, danced to the Stones' "(I Can't Get No) Satisfaction," and I thought Bill and I were a perfect couple—you know, eventually to marry. And, listen . . .

. . . Bill and I were doin' *it*. Back then, you did *it* but you didn't talk about *it*. Once in a while, a poor girl would get caught and get pregnant. Many of us were lucky, because we sure weren't all that careful. But there were a lot of us doing *it*, especially if we had a steady boyfriend.

Anyway, here it was, my senior year, and Bill was home and something was wrong with his little car and we took it to this service station that sat on the corner of Sixth Avenue and Slatton. And we had to get out of the car for the garage guy to take a look at it, and suddenly, *there was that beautiful boy.*

Betty Sue and her mega boobs was nowhere to be seen.

He must have been a mechanic or something at this service station, I thought. And then I said to myself, *Oh my stars! I can't stand it; he is* so *handsome!*

Tall, dark eyes, dark hair, dazzling. I wasn't exactly mashed potatoes myself then. Some said I looked like Elizabeth Taylor. I'm not so sure about that, but I had an eyebrow pencil and a tube of lipstick, and that was all I needed. I think maybe it was my reaction to the good-looking boy that made me start thinking maybe I wasn't ready to make a commitment to Bill. Maybe I needed to experience more than cheerleading and cooking with Grandmomma Paul, to get out in the world now and then?

We never said a word to each other, the boy and I. We just looked, this long, *fatal* look. Then Bill and I left.

I broke up with Bill soon after. It was hard and I didn't want to hurt him, but I thought maybe I should go slower. I sure didn't want to get married yet, and I couldn't stop obsessing about it: what did that beautiful boy mean to me?

His name, I found out, was Jimmy Deen.

Aside from Bill, I hadn't dated a lot. I was the type of girl who had one guy and stayed with that guy. After I broke up with Bill, I had two dates with two other guys in the senior class—one at a time, naturally. That was it for my social life.

And then, one evening, I went to Gary's Super Sub, a big teen hangout. In the back, there was a game room and pinball machines; I adored pinball machines, still do. I remember it was one night after a game. I still had my cheerleading outfit on: the sweater and the little skirt. My waist was like twenty-two or twenty-three inches, believe it or not. So, I was in there playing the pinball machine, and in walked the beautiful guy. It turned out he'd asked out Marilyn Milson, one of my best friends, for a date Saturday night. Well, don't you think Jimmy walked up to a mutual pal also playing the pinball machines—a boy named Johnny Halliburton—and said, "Johnny, ask Paula for a date tomorrow night, and we'll double date."

Turning to me, Jimmy whispered, "Go over there and stand by Johnny and just wait till he asks you out."

Like a dummy, I did it. I was besotted with Jimmy Deen. And Johnny finally said, "Well, Paula, you want to go out tomorrow night?" And I said, "Yeah."

Well, Saturday night came. I slept over at Marilyn's house, and the guys came to pick us up. I remember I wore a blue alpaca cardigan, a dyed-to-match blue skirt, and a little white shirt with a Peter Pan collar. I also had on black diamond-patterned hose, which I thought were fabulous.

Well, I walked out of the house with Johnny, and Jimmy sidled up to me and said, "Those are the ugliest hose I've ever seen."

And I answered, "Well, I'm not ya date, and it's none of my business whether ya like my hose."

After that it was like Johnny and Marilyn didn't exist. Jimmy and I just talked and talked and talked to each other.

The evening passed, the guys brought us home and said good night, and ten minutes later, Jimmy Deen called me up for a date on Sunday night.

I said yes.

My mother answered the door and she let him in and then she turned and went to her bedroom and cried because she knew that he was so beautiful, I was gone from her. I was eighteen years old, and she knew I couldn't resist that Jimmy Deen.

My momma knew.

Chocolate-Dippy or Sugarcoated Doughnuts

I sure loved those peanut butter balls when I was little, but coming in a close second were Momma's quick doughnuts dipped in chocolate or sugar. They were so damn easy to make.

Momma would just buy a can of big, fat biscuits in the dairy section of the market. She would remove the biscuits from the can and then poke a hole in each one with her thumb and form them into doughnuts. Then she'd drop them into hot grease and brown them on both sides until they were done—about two minutes on each side. The best part came next: she'd dip each doughnut into a pot of hot fudge sauce and they were ready for the devourin'.

Sometimes she'd coat the doughnuts with confectioners' sugar. I can see her right now with her paper sack full of sugar, because just as those doughnuts came out of the grease, she would drop them into the bag, shake, and pull out these mouthwatering sugar-coated doughnuts. I can see Bubba and me in there watching TV and her walking in with a big old plate of chocolate- or sugar-coated doughnuts, and maybe both, if we were real lucky.

Let me tell you, these are different from and better than Krispy Kremes or Dunkin' Donuts. They're mah momma's doughnuts!

CHOCOLATE-DIPPY DOUGHNUT SAUCE

One 4-ounce bar Baker's German's sweet chocolate
½ ounce (½ square) unsweetened chocolate
1 stick unsalted butter
3 cups confectioners' sugar
1½ cups evaporated milk
1¼ teaspoons vanilla extract

Melt the chocolate and butter in a saucepan over very low heat. Stir in the sugar, alternating with the evaporated milk, blending well. Raise the heat to medium and bring to a boil, stirring occasionally. Lower the heat and cook, stirring, until the mixture becomes thick and creamy, about 8 minutes. Stir in the vanilla, then remove the pan from the heat. Stick a fork through the doughnut holes and dip the doughnuts immediately into the chocolate mixture before the chocolate starts to cool. Place the doughnuts on a plate and serve when the chocolate on the doughnuts sets, about 5 minutes.

Chapter 3

ON NOT LISTENING
TO YO' MOMMA

"Contrary to what you may believe about yourself, Paula," my momma said, "you don't have the ability to change people."

M omma was right, naturally.

Our courtship was rocky. I was a popular little girl and I had a lot of girlfriends and boyfriends—just friends, but it didn't matter to Jimmy, who was always big-time jealous. He didn't even want me talkin' to anyone else. And controlling? *Whoa!* Jimmy had something to say about the way everyone should do.

He even wanted to monitor what I wore: the comment about the black diamond hose should have been my first clue. If it was too sexy, I'd hear, "No, you can't wear that, you look like a tramp." It was like datin' the Proper Police. If I came in late on an afternoon when he was waiting for me, he wanted to know exactly where I was and with whom. If it was Saturday night and I was feeling real happy, I'd ask him if we could go hang out at the burger joint where all my friends always went. No, Jimmy would say, it may be Saturday night but why didn't we just go to the drive-in by ourselves?

What was Jimmy Deen studying at school? Try nothin'. What were his plans for the future? Had none. He was a good basketball player in high school but his family didn't have money to send him to college, so he'd just hang out till something good came along. It wasn't that he was lazy—he was always working at some job or other and I always thought he could whip the world if he wanted. He never did seem to have the big dreams, though.

Me? I wasn't worried about any of it. He had those intoxicatin' eyes. Furthermore, I knew, even then, you didn't need an education to be successful. My own dreams for myself were actually pretty limited as well. I just wanted to be a good wife and momma, like I saw my own momma doing. That's what I planned. I wanted children so badly, I could already smell their little baby-powder selves.

But, let me tell you, girl, if his prospects weren't so impressive, Jimmy was sexually hypnotic. He was a very good lover. A very, very good lover. The sex was always the best part of us—during our courtship, and during our marriage.

I'd started dating Jimmy in January of my senior year, and for graduation in June, Momma and Daddy gave me a two-week trip to New York to see my Uncle Bob, who was having a ball being a model in the big city. Arriving in the city, in about a New York minute I was weak with excitement and I wanted to be a model also. I got to go on shoots and all that with him and he wanted me to stay in New York so I could break into the business. I loved the fancy restaurants, especially the one where they put these little white britches on the lamb chops, but every day I got letters and phone calls from Jimmy saying, "When are you coming home? I want you to come home."

I couldn't wait to see him. When I got back, he had me an engagement ring.

My Momma and Daddy weren't one little bit happy. They knew, for one thing, that Jimmy's mother was an alcoholic. It was true that I'd been learning there were different levels of drinking. I'd noticed that Mrs. Deen wouldn't drink at all for a while. Then, she'd only drink beer. Then, she'd settle into a steady binge of harder stuff. It scared my mother so badly. I'd never been around an alcoholic, didn't know what one was. Momma knew I didn't have a clue as to what I could be in for.

I told them flat-out, "I'm not marrying his family. I'm marrying him."

A know-it-all at eighteen, I was.

But they were devastated. Their baby at eighteen—getting married? And then, beautiful as he was, this young man didn't really appear to have a future, and that was so upsetting for them. One night, my momma came to snuggle in my bed with me but she wasn't wearing her usual sweet smile. Now her face was full of concern and even sadness. She wanted me to be absolutely certain I loved Jimmy, and if there was anything that bothered me about my sweetheart, it had better be something I could live with because I couldn't change him later.

Change him? Why would I want to do that? There was nothing, nothing at all, that wasn't perfect about Jimmy Deen. Oh, maybe there was that teeny, bitty controlling thing, but he'd stop that stuff soon enough after I was his legal wife. I was going to be the perfect wife and momma, and I knew for sure he would be the perfect husband and daddy. Surely she was wrong and I was right: wasn't I a whole lot smarter than my momma?

My momma and daddy didn't give up so fast. We talked a lot

about what else I could do. Daddy thought I would be a great dental hygienist and he would send me to a Florida school to learn how. Wasn't goin' to happen. He must have been bitten by a rabid coon to even have suggested it.

"Ain't no way I'm smellin' stinky breath all my life!" I told him. "No, I'm not doing that, Daddy. How about I go to Atlanta to be a model?"

Daddy said, "Over my dead body. No daughter of mine is going to Atlanta by herself." Little did he know that I had already applied and was accepted to the Patricia Stevens Modeling School in Atlanta. I told him. Went over like a lead balloon.

"Oh, no, you're not," said my daddy, my hero. Not an option. Period.

I should have realized his answer would be no. I'd never really been away from home except for those two weeks with Uncle Bob, and we'd always called Atlanta "little New York," so it probably was a bad and dangerous place, Daddy was very sure of that.

I'd *had* it with my blessed momma and my hero daddy.

"Okay, you two, if you won't let me do anything else, I'm getting married right now," I decided. Sounded good as soon as I said it. Solved every problem. I wasn't scared. Everything had always been rosy, and it would continue to be.

My parents gave in. We married five months later, on November 28, 1965. It was a very small wedding because Daddy had said to us, "Paula, honey, we can give you a stove and a refrigerator, or a big wedding."

"I'll take the stove and the refrigerator," something made me say. Little did I know how my choice was gonna set my destiny. Turns out, the stove and the refrigerator were really ugly: the fridge was used and the stove was coppertone, but oh, how I loved them anyway. I was all grown up, playing house, and couldn't have been more thrilled.

It took only three more months to realize I would have been a perfect dental hygienist.

The trouble started early. First of all, the good stuff. Jimmy Deen was the hardest-working man I ever knew—there was not a lazy bone in his body. Later on—I know I'm skipping ahead, but this has to be said, he adored his children—I think he was a good father in many ways. And even later on, he did something so wonderful for me, I will never, ever forget it, and I'll always owe him. But that was later.

In the beginning of our marriage, I was soon to taste the really bad part. He drank, and he drank way too much to suit me. Even one or two beers was too much as far as I was concerned, because that's all it would take to drive him away from me. The drinking changed him. When he drank, he became dumb as a rock and I couldn't depend on him. He wasn't physically abusive to me, but we sure had our shovin' matches. I don't even think he wanted to be verbally abusive, and I'll tell you the truth—it was me who forced him to say some awful mean things. I wasn't so lily-pure and innocent.

This is why: When he drank, I could be talking to the drapes; he simply couldn't hear me. I was always trying to get him to listen to me, but even one can of beer changed Jimmy Deen so he wasn't my Jimmy Deen, my husband. I don't understand it—maybe some people have a lower tolerance than others for alcohol. All I know is the one or two beers I'd *see* him drink made me know I'd soon feel abandoned and insecure. I could compete against another woman, but I could not compete against that can of beer. Most of the time, I felt the man I married wasn't even there—even when he was standing in front of me. Oh, listen—I was far from perfect and I probably handled it terribly: I'd get in his face, I'd cuss and I'd spit at him just to get a reaction when he was staring at me, bleary-eyed. The only reaction I ever got was a shove. But, I was only eighteen and just wanting us to survive and I saw our lives going down the tube because of a zombie-good-looking hus-band. Inside, I was scared out of my wits.

To this day, I don't know exactly how much he drank, because he wouldn't tell me and he sure couldn't show me because I didn't let him drink at home. I was such a bitch—I forced him to do his drinking away from home because if he had just that one beer at home, it was like he'd instantly become dumb and one eye would almost cross over to the other one. It about drove me insane. I just adored this man, I worshipped him, but I wanted to hit him so bad: he wasn't dense when he wasn't drinking, but drunk he had the brains of a chicken.

One day it kind of came to a head. We'd been married about three months when I truly understood that our marriage was in for hard times. I'd gotten a job at the Albany First Federal Savings bank and I had to go to a meeting in a nearby town. I told Jimmy, "You're gonna be home when I get home, baby, right? Won't you please be home when I get home because I don't have a house key." After our meeting, at about ten at night, a group of friends dropped me by my house. I just hopped out of the car, and they took right on off, something that you'd never do today. You would make sure the dropped-off person got safely into her house.

Well, you know it: I was locked out. Jimmy was out drinking with his buddies. It was raw and raining out. And so I walked down to Slappy Drive—a main street in Albany—walked down to a service station to a pay phone, and called my momma and daddy. Turns out, they both answered the phone at the same time.

"I hate his guts," I said. "I have come home from this meeting, and he is not home. He's got me locked out of my own home. Come get me, Momma. I am not staying here." And I remember Momma saying, "Now, honey, you have to kiss and make up." Well, my daddy piped in on the other extension. He said, "You tell him to kiss your ass! That's what you tell him to kiss!"

My momma came and got me and it was clear to both of us

that my marriage was going south. I had thought it was so romantic, he was my high school sweetheart and all, we were such a
pretty couple, we were *family,* and already trouble was rearing its
ugly head.

I didn't know what trouble was. In just a few months more,
my life was to shatter, my mind would be stricken, my heart was
to tear, and it would be more than twenty more years before I
could get it all back together again.

Courage Chili

When I'm under stress and I sense that trouble's coming, I need to eat something hot, something substantial, and something that gives me what feels like strength and courage. There's nothin' like dippin' into a bowlful of chili in such moments. Chili's a nourishing rib-sticker; you don't need no fancy food dishes when you need your strength. Y'all need chili.

Note: Some Texans don't like beans with their chili. I do.

2 pounds lean ground beef
2 large onions, finely minced (about 2 cups)
1 teaspoon garlic powder
1½ teaspoons salt
3 tablespoons chili powder
1½ teaspoons dried oregano
1 teaspoon sugar
One 10¾-ounce can condensed French onion soup
1 tablespoon all-purpose flour
½ teaspoon Tabasco sauce
One 28-ounce can chopped tomatoes, with juice
Two 16-ounce cans kidney beans, drained
1 large bag Fritos corn chips
1 cup sour cream
1 cup shredded sharp Cheddar cheese

Brown the beef and 1½ cups of the onions in a large skillet. Drain off the pan drippings. Add the garlic powder, salt, chili powder, oregano, sugar, soup, flour, and Tabasco. Mix well. Simmer for 1 hour, covered, stirring occasionally. Add the tomatoes and beans, stir, and simmer, covered, for 20 minutes longer. When the chili is done, empty the bag of Fritos into a large serving bowl, scoop the chili on top of the Fritos, and top it all with dollops of sour cream, remaining ½ cup onions, and the Cheddar cheese, which will melt all by itself on the chili. Serve immediately.

Serves 4 to 6

Chapter 4

HOW DO YOU GET TO BE A WOMAN OF SUBSTANCE WHEN YOUR WORLD'S FALLIN' APART?

Funny, when you're young the world seems to revolve around you, but maybe you have some little, teeny, bitty problems—you just think things have got to get better, you think it just can't get any worse in your life. It can.

The tragedies began. And with them, I began to die.

My daddy was sick. Two months after we were married, he just wasn't feelin' all that good but he never worried anything about it. We all thought it was gas, and he'd been taking baking soda every night, so he could burp and relieve the pain in his hurting chest, but after a while the baking soda didn't seem to do much good.

So, he went to our local Dr. McCall, who listened to Daddy's chest and finally said, "Earl, I think you must have had rheumatic fever as a child and, as a result, you've got a bad heart valve."

We didn't know what to do and finally we went to the famous Emory University in Atlanta where we'd heard they were just starting to practice this new procedure, valve replacement. They told Daddy he needed to go home to prepare himself for surgery now, while he was fairly young: only forty, and in good health except for his missing part. That would be his leg. Daddy only had one leg. When he was sixteen years old, he worked for a telegraph place, and once when he was delivering a telegram, a truck hit him, gangrene set in, and they wound up removing his left leg right then.

Well, now, Emory University kept pushing him to have the heart-valve surgery, and Dr. McCall kept saying, "Earl, I don't like it, please don't have this. Wait five more years. Bubba's only twelve years old. Wait until he's seventeen to have the surgery."

Momma and Daddy thought Emory University knew more than Dr. McCall, so Daddy arranged for the surgery in February 1966. Well, he had that valve fixed, but my daddy had a light stroke on the table. Still, he finally was able to leave intensive care and come home. It was so sad to see him like he was. He could still walk, but I remember him keeping his thumb in his pocket to try and support his right arm, which just hung there after the stroke. Still, we thought all was well and that he was recuperating. He'd even gone back to work.

Funny the things you remember: when daddy was recuperating, he and my momma rode over one Sunday afternoon. "Oh, Daddy, Daddy, Daddy," I remember saying, "I made you some sweet tea that's as good as Momma's," and I gave him a glass. "Isn't it as good as Momma's?" I asked.

"No, honey, I'm sorry, it's not. It's very good but no one makes sweet tea as good as Momma," he said with a grin. He was right.

We both knew I'd be trying my whole life to make sweet tea as good as Momma's.

Well, on June 15, 1966, Daddy was on his way back to work after his lunch at home and he had a car wreck on North Davis Street. A policeman who knew Daddy was the first one on the scene, and would you believe he thought Daddy was drunk and that's why he crashed the car? Daddy was not drunk. Later they found out that he'd had a blood clot form around the new valve in his heart and it broke off and hit his brain. My daddy was brain-dead. He lived two more days.

The day my daddy died, I remember getting a call about five-thirty that morning, and they said, "Come to the hospital." I didn't know it but Daddy was already dead. I would no longer have the living love of my father.

After they told us, I remember walking down the hospital hall with my momma and I saw this man whom Daddy knew, and I started screaming and crying to Momma, "He's coming to see Daddy, and it's too late." The guy looked at me like as if I was crazy because he was only delivering bread to the hospital. See, my thinking when Daddy died was as screwed up as a Chinese checkbook right off the bat, and it didn't get much better for a long time. That night, I was so scared, I had to sleep with my momma *and* my husband. Momma slept on one side, Jimmy slept on the other, which made me feel safer, but not for years would I ever feel really safe again.

Friday morning before Father's Day on June 17, 1966. I'd already had his Father's Day gift bought, and it was a white shirt, and it was that kind of soft silklike material. Daddy just loved those shirts, and he was buried in it. He was just forty years old.

I simply tore apart. I remember after my daddy died, I'd sit in this rocking chair, and I'd just rock. And eat. That was my comfort. Tears would just be rolling down my cheeks, and I'd be eating everything soft and easy. How would I ever live with this devastation, how would I ever fill the hole in my heart that Daddy's death dug? I started by practicing his favorite dish. I was driven to making chicken and dumplings just like he craved them. I wanted to make them as perfect as I could, just in case some crazy something was going on and my daddy came back. Perhaps that gives you some idea of my state of mind.

That's the exact time my panic attacks really started. When something snatches away that rug that you call security, you land on your ass. My daddy was my security. I'll tell you, I was raised Baptist and was taught that everything happened for a reason. So, what was the reason for Daddy's dying so soon? I was so frightened because I had no idea why death would affect my life so early.

I started trying to figure it out. Why did God take my beautiful daddy? He had the surgery, he was getting well. Why would you do that, God? What was the reason?

I finally figured it out.

The reason Daddy had died was because *I* was gonna die soon, and God did not want my daddy to see that happen, so that's why God took Daddy first. And so at age nineteen, after that terrible time, I started waking up many mornings and wondering if this was the day I'd die. I'd get up and check my pulse, feel my heart, cough as I tried to spit up the blood that would finally tell me for sure that it was all over for me.

I never told anybody. I just got up waiting to die by myself. And these thoughts just went on and on and on for twenty years, more or less.

But life went on too.

I worked to try to save our marriage. Jimmy Deen was a sweet man but that drinking was a problem that neither of us could solve. In 1967, when Daddy had been gone a year, our first son, Jamie, was born. During my pregnancy, Jimmy still drank every night, but he tried to be as good as he could be to me. There was an Rh-negative problem but we were fortunate to have no problems with the new baby.

Jamie was born with Bubba's coloring, which is kind of dirty-blond hair, fair skin, and blue eyes, and he had deep beautiful dimples from his father's side of the family. From the moment he arrived, though, he had a snotty nose and bags under his eyes, and to this day he's still got the bags. The snotty nose kind of disappeared after a couple of years, thank God. When they brought him to me for his bottle on the second day after he was born, I unfolded the blanket and checked that baby, starting at his toes and working my way up to the top. Would you believe that covering one side of his head there was this huge soft knot that I could move? It scared me so bad and I thought, *Oh my God! My child's brains are coming out!*

I got out of bed, and I ran down the hall to the nursery as best a new mother can run anywhere, and I screamed, "Something's wrong with my baby!"

They got in touch with the doctor and took the baby from me to put him back in the nursery; finally the doctor arrived to tell me, "It's like a blood sack and it will dry up and go away. There's nothing to be concerned about." He was right about the drying up, but underneath that blood sack was a whopper of a knot that made the shape of Jamie's head not one of perfection. So, after about a year, there's my little boy with snot running down his lips, bags under his eyes, and a knot on the side of his head sticking up unattractively, but we loved that kid to death. My Aunt Peggy didn't tell me that until he was ten years old she was afraid that knot meant he was retarded. But he was so cute and outgoing; he'd get so excited and just go nuts over everything he liked.

Two years after Jamie's birth, Bobby was born. I had already started with my panic attacks and Bobby's birth didn't do nothing to help them. Seems when I was eight months pregnant with him, they had to induce labor because they said the baby was in trouble with that same Rh factor, and he'd live only till Tuesday lunchtime if he wasn't delivered immediately. This baby was so sick they put him in critical care and started changing out his blood and I was weak with fear for him.

Shortly before Bobby's birth, Momma had gone to JCPenney and got her a job as the head of the linen department. She was on her feet all day. It was then she started complaining that her knee was hurting a lot.

Bobby was the most beautiful baby I have ever seen. Even though he was a month early, he still weighed six pounds ten ounces, bigger than most of the babies in the well nursery, and he was beautifully developed. Birth had not played havoc with Bobby. Unlike Jamie, he had this perfectly shaped head, dark hair, dark eyes, and olive skin. Of course, he was jaundiced because of all of the complications, which gave him a shine like a little gold brick.

Soon after he was born, I remember Momma coming to the hospital and limping. All that standing around in the linen department, she said.

Then, suddenly, things just turned to ashes for a while. Bobby was really sick and we didn't know if he'd make it. No wonder we all pretty much ignored Momma's limping. Bobby was the person on our radar.

I was released from the hospital but had to leave the baby there and I cried like a bellowing cat all the way home. Finally, after nine days, the doctor told us that they'd just completed the final blood transfusion. Bobby had undergone four complete blood changes—the first baby in the hospital ever to survive that—and the doctor said, "Paula, it's taking. We're home free."

On the eleventh day I brought my child home. But we were not home free.

It was Momma. Our family doctor could find nothing wrong with her knee, but it wasn't feeling any better, and one day she said to me, "My knee hurts so bad. I've got a lump right here that's hot." And I remember putting my hand over it, and I could feel the heat. She finally went to the chiropractor, who saw a tumor in her leg, and he made an appointment with a bone specialist. She was diagnosed with bone cancer.

I remember going over to Momma's, and her holding Bobby and rocking him, tears rolling down her face, which was so sad because I knew she was thinking maybe she wouldn't be here to watch him grow. I couldn't believe it. Inside, I felt she'd get better with the cobalt treatments and all.

One day, I took her to the hospital for her cobalt, and I was standing waiting right outside the door when I heard this bloodcurdling scream; she'd turned over on the table to take cobalt on the back, and her leg had broke because the tumor had got so big. They wheeled her out into the hall, and she said, "I want them to amputate my leg." That was my momma. So brave.

"Okay, Momma," I said, "whatever you want. You lived with a man for twenty years who only had one leg, and you saw him survive beautifully. And you can too. You were taught by the best."

She had that leg amputated—the same leg taken off in the same identical spot as my daddy's.

Well, still, we thought it was wonderful that the pain was removed from her. We took her home, and Grandmomma Paul moved in to take care of her child, and they slept in the same bed. Grandmomma had to do it because I had the two little babies under three years old, but she would have done it no matter what.

Then there was Bubba. He was sixteen at the time and no one was taking care of him—such a young boy and just eaten up by all the pain and fear around him. He wouldn't talk about anything to anyone, just ran wild.

Then, one day, Grandmomma Paul called me and said I needed to get over to the house because now Momma had found a knot on her chest. I started sweatin' like Mike Tyson at a spelling bee.

"Grandmomma, I can't go into her room," I moaned when I got there. "I'm gonna need a nerve pill." Grandmomma gave me a nerve pill, and I took it and went into another bedroom trying to calm myself down, and finally I got the courage to go in to see my momma. She showed me this lump right there on her chest. It was like a goose egg, and it had popped up just like that. We called her chiropractor, Dr. McDaniel, who came to the house immediately to check it out; he thought it was nothin'.

I remember crawlin' up in the bed right next to Momma, and all of a sudden I just burst into tears; that's how relieved I felt that it was nothin'. Momma put her arms around me and asked, "What's the matter, honey?"

"I just was scared so bad, Momma," I told her, and she held me in her arms and said everything was gonna be all right. She was always comforting me like that.

Everything was not all right. The cancer had spread. We were in big trouble.

Egg knots had started popping up all over Momma. She hadn't been home long after her leg was amputated when she began to have constant, unrelenting pain. At the end of August, I called the ambulance to come pick her up and take her back to the hospital. She never again left that hospital. I remember that Momma was screaming so bad when the nurses came in to change her sheets, I had to walk away. I'll never ever forget those screams.

Her leg surgery was in August, her birthday in the hospital was October 9, and she died exactly one month after her forty-fourth birthday, on November 9, 1970.

I was twenty-three years old, I had two babies under three, a sour marriage, a sixteen-year-old brother, and our momma and poppa were both dead. My spirit was broken. My mind wasn't doing too good either. I felt increasingly fearful when I had to leave my house. So mostly, I stayed in.

And then my husband gave me the perfect gift, one for which

I'll always be grateful. As much as he didn't hear me when I tried to talk to him, Jimmy was so good about certain other things. I felt overwhelming sorrow at the death of my parents, but the pain I felt for my little brother's grief was unbearable. Jimmy took my orphaned, heartbroken sixteen-year-old brother into our home and loved him just as though Bubba was his child. Afterward, even when our marriage was so shaky, he never once came to me to say, "This ain't fair; we can't afford to keep Bubba." He did nothing but love my brother and Bubba loved him back. They'd go hunting and fishing together and Jimmy was the best stand-in father. Jimmy had many good qualities, and kindness was one of them. I will always be thankful that he passed that kind of sweetness on to our children.

But I was in pretty poor shape. I felt my mental growth had been frozen when I was only nineteen from the pure shock of everything. Now, at about twenty-three, an impending sense of doom really hung over me, as if I'd be living in a dark valley forever. Every day I thought I'd die, or, even worse, someone I loved would die. The blackness still didn't have a name. The days dragged by. I hated to leave my home, my comfort zone, but my kids were so small, they were totally dependent on my shopping for them and getting them some fresh air. I got out a little, a very little—and then hurried back home as though something was chasing me.

Jamie was like a Mexican jumping bean. He would get so excited if company came over. He'd just run and make crazy dances and all these wild faces and go bananas. Once when he was about three, he tripped over a rock and yelled out with all the ferocity he had in him, "Damn wock!" He was such an animated kid, but Bobby just sat there, smiling. Once in a while, Jamie could get his baby brother cranked up, but Bobby was always so low-key. I remember him at eighteen months sitting way up in a high chair and if someone came in and said, "Hey, Bobby," he'd look at them and, like a good Southern boy, answer, *"Suh?"* That would be it for the communication.

Those two boys were so close, they always kissed each other good night before they fell asleep. They're still the most lovin' brothers on the face of the earth. I remember their daddy had gotten them a big old white pit bull with one black and one sky-blue eye. We adored that dog despite the breed's reputation for meanness. I remember one particular day when they were a little older, my two lazy kids were lying in bed with this dog named Blue between them, and I walked into the room, put my hands on my hips, and said sternly, *"Y'all get your tails out of this bed right now and go help your daddy in the yard."* Well, they didn't move an inch, but that pit bull slowly got himself out from between them, stepped over one boy's body to face me, and then just growled—you know that kind of low, deep growl that shows their fangs, that growl that means business?

"Screw it," I said. *"Y'all just stay where you are. You too, Blue."*

Things were going to get a lot worse with my illness that had no name. When my babies were small, I became so overprotective. I was frightened of everything and so terrified something was going to happen to my boys. I watched them like a hawk and we lived in the doctor's office; I was a true hypochondriac both for me and for my sons. Fear of death was beginning to take over my life, and worry about a panic attack coming was always in my mind, even though they were not yet coming on a regular basis. When they did happen, I learned to inhale and exhale into a paper bag; that would somehow make it better. I never went anywhere without a paper bag in my purse to blow into if the bad thing happened. Without that paper bag, I'd start to hyperventilate for sure, and just thinking about that would cause me to have a panic attack. I never told anyone about that paper bag, but one day Bobby saw me blowin' in it, and he was terrified. He just didn't know what was happening and he was too little for an explanation. Jamie remembers me havin' an attack once in a store and me duckin' down and drawing them both close so I could kind of hide behind them. Jamie tells me he doesn't remember much about that time, thank God, because he thinks they were both pretty resilient kids and in his case it was, "Oh, my gosh, what is *this*?" and the next minute he was sayin', "Hey, buy me a football!"

When I was twenty-five, I read a book called *A Woman of Substance* by a lady named Barbara Taylor Bradford. Oh, I just loved that book. I whispered to myself that when I *really* grew up, I would also be a woman of substance. I would have grandchildren and they would call me Grandlady—that's what they called the grandmother in the book.

But so far I felt very insubstantial. I felt weak, flimsy, almost falling apart with fear.

Substance would have to wait.

Mississippi Mud Cake

Mississippi Mud Cake is serious comfort food, my friends. You can sink into that deep, chocolate-y mud, and those sweet and mushy marshmallows, and feel safe. I could eat a whole cake when I was hidin' under my bed.

2 cups sugar
½ teaspoon salt
2 cups all-purpose flour
1 stick unsalted butter
½ cup vegetable oil
½ cup cocoa
2 eggs
1 teaspoon baking soda
½ cup buttermilk
2 teaspoons vanilla extract
1 bag miniature marshmallows

ICING

1 stick unsalted butter, softened
3 tablespoons cocoa
6 tablespoons milk
One 1-pound box confectioners' sugar
1 cup chopped pecans or walnuts
1 teaspoon vanilla extract

1. Preheat the oven to 350°F. Grease and flour a 13 by 9-inch baking pan.
2. Combine the sugar, salt, and flour in a large mixing bowl. Bring the butter, oil, cocoa, and ¼ cup water to a boil in a sauce pan. Add to the flour mixture.

3. Beat together the eggs, baking soda, buttermilk, and vanilla. Add to the chocolate mixture, mix well, and pour into the prepared pan. Bake for 25 minutes.

4. While the cake is baking, make the icing by melting the butter in the cocoa and milk over low heat. Bring the mixture to a boil, then remove from the heat. Stir in the confectioners' sugar. Slowly mix in the nuts and the vanilla. Take the cake from the oven, and when it cools a bit cover it with miniature marshmallows. Pour the warm icing over the cake and the marshmallows. Cool the cake before serving.

Chapter 5

THE TERROR *DID*
HAVE A NAME

Okay—I wasn't a woman of substance,
but I was still foggin' the mirror, not all
fallen apart, yet.

*L*ook—when you wake up in the morning on the right side of the dirt, it's a good day. I knew I had to try to remember that. If you're on the right side of the dirt, you still have another chance to make bad things better.

After Momma and Daddy died, I was trying to keep my panic attacks a secret. Some days, though, it was so bad I wasn't sure that I was still on the right side of the dirt. If I told anyone what was going on inside of me, I thought I'd sound like a loony; who would want to be my friend if they knew how crazy I was? I'd always been pretty, an all-together, popular girl, and I didn't want to admit to anyone I might have a serious problem. If I didn't go outside, I figured, if I didn't really live my life, it would reduce my risk of being hurt.

But there were my boys. I felt so guilty. They didn't have a whole, healthy momma; they'd been shortchanged.

In the late seventies, the panic progressed even deeper. Of course, we had no insurance to pay a real, live, licensed, grown-up psychiatrist, but I felt I was so depressed, I had to make myself save some money so I could go at least once. Well, I went once, but the one time sure didn't help. The doctor charged like sixty dollars an hour, and we couldn't come up with sixty dollars a *year* for anything that wasn't food. That's how close to starving we were.

I decided to go see a church leader, hoping he would know what in tarnation was wrong with me. I'd heard that my church, the First Baptist Church, had started a health service and hired a Southern minister who had a degree in psychology. Now, man, you turn one of them ministers who think they're Freud loose, your ass is through. But I was having a real, real hard time. If I wanted to shop for groceries, Jimmy had to take me. If the boys had to go anywhere farther than they could walk, a neighbor or Jimmy had to take them. I was so embarrassed and I really wanted to get better, so I decided I'd try this minister with the degree. Jimmy had to come home from work and pick me up to go to the session because I couldn't drive anywhere by myself.

Once we got to the church, I just walked in and started pouring my heart out to this man. Jimmy was just sittin' there so quiet, and it came out that we were having problems about Jimmy's drinking and him turning to stone and not hearing me as soon as he finished even one beer. I knew our marriage problems didn't help my own problem, but here I was like a babbling idiot telling everything. I was that desperate.

Well, the minister man looked hard at me and, when I finished crying, when I finished talking, he stared into my eyes and said, "Your husband having a beer every day does not make him an alcoholic. And you are a spoiled brat."

Jimmy only smiled. I was flabbergasted and so hurt, but Paula Deen was never so hurt she didn't have words. I said to that powerfully mean man, "Well, you know what you can do? And that man over there—that *husband*? Y'all can kiss my ass and call me *Shorty* and go to hell." And I never went back.

In a way, he was right; if being protected and cherished by my parents was being spoiled, then I guess I was. If being loved too much by my parents was giving me panic attacks when I wasn't being loved at all by my husband, then I guess I was spoiled rotten.

My husband said nothing more than "This guy just told you I have no problem, so get off my ass because our troubles are not me, they're you."

Jimmy had gone to work for his brother, who was a very successful car dealer in Albany, but they had a disagreement, and his brother fired him. We were desperate, and our financial troubles were startin' to smother us.

Then began a terrible period—I guess it was between 1977 and 1983—when I was really crippled by this fright I had. I couldn't leave my house, no way, no how.

The one thing I could rely on was my stove. Backed against the wall, I cooked everything my granny taught me and then some. Fried chicken, collard greens, country fried steak—my family ate *good*.

For a while, we were hopeful. When they died, my parents didn't have much money to leave me—it was maybe fifteen thousand dollars—but whatever little it was, early in 1977 I'd given it all to Jimmy to invest in a Chrysler Dodge dealership franchise. Jimmy had made my twenty-three-year-old brother, Bubba, a partner in this dealership because we wanted Bubba to have something too. They opened it in a little suburb of Albany called Dawson, a farm town that depended on its agriculture. But, oh God, late in 1977, there was the worst drought ever and all the farmers were dead broke and the Chrysler dealerships were dropping like flies. Ours was one of them. In a while, Lee Iacocca was to come in and turn Chrysler around, but it wasn't soon enough for us. Plus, I'm thinking that maybe Jimmy made a bunch of bad business decisions. That was when they repossessed our little house. Of course, Bubba also lost everything he'd been left.

It was awful. Bubba and Jimmy and the kids and I took a cheap apartment in Albany, but we didn't even have a car to move our stuff from the repossessed house to the new apartment. One of the peanut farmers, a cute guy named Billy Martin, had become friends with Jimmy, and Billy offered to move us. He loaded our furniture in his peanut wagon and I was so scared on the way that I totally wrapped myself up in a blanket so I couldn't see I wasn't near home. There was a full-blown panic attack happening: I was just praying no one would notice I was wrapped in this blanket so I couldn't see. We moved into this low-rent apartment complex called the Terra Villa. I never trusted the folks who lived there. I called it the Terrible Villa and I couldn't stand it. Jimmy eventually was to move us about twenty times before I was forty. It was at the Terrible Villa that I stopped doing anything that required me to leave my four walls. Creditors would knock on the door, and I'd hide. The years to come would be the worst in my whole life.

Fear of death ruled me. Panic was the king of the road.

When you're close to paralyzed, there isn't that much you can do. I listened to the news on the radio—1977 was the year Legionnaires' disease was brought to our attention. Now I could also worry about dying from the bad air that came from the radiator. Elvis Presley died that year and I felt bad about that: Elvis was the Mississippi Southerner who sang blues laced with country and gospel, and he was my secret idol—a real sexy, cool rebel. I wanted to do something big, and I also wanted to be a sexy, cool rebel, but it was going to be hard if I couldn't leave my house. Later, I heard on the radio that Jimmy Carter was elected president and I felt happy that a Southerner would be running our country. Little did I dream that Mr. Jimmy and I were to become friends . . . but that would be in my next life, the one I didn't even dare to dream about. And I didn't know it then, but a little baby named Orlando Bloom was born on January 13, 1977—the year my home was grabbed away by the bank, the year I carried a brown paper bag in my purse in case, God forbid, I'd suffer a panic attack and couldn't breathe. Little did I know, one day little Orlando Bloom and I would be in a movie together. People would ask for my autograph.

There was one thing I could do while I was prisoner in my home, and that was to cook. I got real good at it. I particularly loved baking—and I baked every possible combination of pies, cookies, and cakes. Sometimes, my Grandmother Paul's lessons were able to come tearing through my depression. I also made maybe thousands of pots of chicken and dumplings, the best soups on the planet, and tons of candy. The cooking didn't give me wings to soar, but it gave me a grounding, a feeling of safety just in smellin' the good aromas of my childhood. I was in my own home, I was cooking, I was feeding my family; I was almost like a real wife, I told myself.

And, I was definitely still a real sister. Living two doors down from me was a cute, cute woman with the most precious little six-year-old boy from a past marriage. I talked with Jill occasionally, and decided she'd be terrific for Bubba. Being Paula Deen, I couldn't resist matchmaking even during the depths of my fear. Bubba listened to his big sister especially when she was playin' Cupid, and on St. Patrick's Day, 1980, Jill and Bubba were married. I remember my brother telling me that he fell as much in love with Jay as he did with Jill, and soon after the marriage, he adopted that adorable boy with the big dark eyes and the curly black hair as his very own child. On March 6, 1981, Jill and Bubba had a little girl whom they named Corrie who was to become the beloved daughter of my own heart.

Then Jimmy went to work for Zep, a company that sold cleaning supplies, and we damn near really starved to death. By then we'd left Terrible Villa and moved into Nottingham Way, another set of apartments not far away, but one that seemed to have nicer people. Money was so short, I don't even know how we paid the rent, but somehow we managed.

We became real good friends with our next-door neighbors. Their door was just half a minute away from ours. They had two little children and we did also, so our doors became revolving doors. They had a son about Bobby's age and a little girl who was about three.

We got real close to this couple. Loved them to pieces. We talked and played cards and I was in heaven because I was either in my own home or right next door to home. When we went over to their place, six steps there and six steps back—not that I was counting—and I could be in my own house. I was starting to get real crazy by then.

I tried to talk to Jimmy about this ever-growing terror, but being afraid of anything was completely foreign to him: he just could not understand because he was scared of nothing, not even a two-headed snake.

"For God's sake, get over it, Paula," he'd say. Of course, I thought I was the weak one and he the strong one. I thought I didn't have a whole lot of value. But what was really necessary to being a good wife was being cute, I thought, and that was still pretty easy. I was fun to be around. I faked cute every day of my life back then.

I tried not to complain about being scared all the time. And, I got cuter and cuter. That I could do.

Occasionally, I was put on the spot. If the nice next-door couple would say "Let's go to a movie" or "Let's go out to eat," I had to make up a lie. However, when someone is living right next door to you, how many times can you say you're busy when they see you there—very unbusy. I was never free of the thoughts about death, but sometimes I could live my life pretty normally, and I was such a good actress, people would have said *"You're shittin' me"* if I'd ever told them who I really was. But, I never told.

The husband—his name was Dale—was slowly catching on to my tricks. One day, I will never forget, he said, "Paula, pardon me for interferin', and you won't believe this, but I had what I think you're sufferin' from—like when your heart runs away with you? It's terrifying! I had panic attacks for a long, long time, but you know what, I've gotten over it."

What a thing that was to hear! What a gift to me even though I was a zillion miles from getting better—if that could ever happen.

But something did happen soon afterward that was a pure miracle for me. It didn't make me better, but it gentled my heart. I finally had to "fess up" about my problem to these sweet people living next door. We'd become very good friends with them and I couldn't lie one more time about being too busy for a movie. It felt good to tell about my panic: I resolved then to try and share my secrets with everyone for whom I cared. Tell a secret, get one back. Telling secrets is a great gift you give to others. And I simply felt so good about having gotten it off my shoulders with these darlin' neighbors.

I was particularly close to Dale, who'd become like a brother to me. One day, the phone rang after Jimmy and the kids had left the house, and Dale said, barely able to contain his excitement, "Paula, turn on Phil Donahue. You're going to find out what's wrong with you." I turned on the TV, and I sat on the end of that bed and I cried. Bless that Phil Donahue.

Finally—it finally had a name. Agoraphobia. I thought nobody else could be this crazy, and here was Phil Donahue devoting a whole program to it. It turned out that about two million Americans had agoraphobia—almost 1 percent of the population.

He said that agoraphobics had horrible anxiety about being in places or embarrassing situations from which they might not be able to escape. *That was me.*

He said that symptoms included being chilled to the bone yet clammy with sweat, shaking, rapid heartbeat, numbness in the arms and hands, feelings of choking and not being able to breathe, fear of dying, vomiting, fear of losing control. *That was me!*

He said agoraphobics only felt safe in their own homes. *That was me!*

He said they had a fear of crowds and public places. *That was definitely me!*

He said it was first diagnosed before the twentieth century and most of the people who had it then were men. But he also said that most people who had it today were women. *That was me!*

And most of them were homemakers. *Oh, that was me!*

I sat speechless while I watched Donahue's guests, all former agoraphobics, tell about how they'd been unable to leave their homes and now they could go on elevators and even fly in an airplane. They could go up escalators.

Around that time, knowing my problem had a name, I became what you'd call a "functioning agoraphobic." If what I had was shared by others, I would learn to deal with it also. I was not real happy when I wasn't home, but I could finally leave the house for short periods of time, particularly if I was with someone. There was a store in the Albany mall, and if I was with Jimmy, I could go to the ground floor but I could never go up that escalator to the second floor. I was afraid I was going to have a panic attack in front of folks. How horrible would that be? I just loved the housewares on the second floor. I loved anything that had to do with the kitchen and the home and decorating, but I couldn't get up to those damn housewares.

Still, it was a blessed relief to be able to put a name to my problem and know that I wasn't the only one. But knowing about it didn't cure it. I longed to understand why it happened to me; I felt I could shake it if I only understood.

Listen—we were *so* poor. My illness got on all our nerves. I didn't have any way I could even help to support us. And Jimmy was so frustrated: he was getting angrier and angrier, which meant he was drinking more and more. It also meant that verbal violence seeped more regularly into our lives.

I remember Christmas of 1981. Every single Christmas Eve, Jimmy would have too much to drink, and I'd get so mad that we couldn't have a peaceful and loving Christmas. Could he not put down that damn drink and let us enjoy ourselves as a family? Apparently not. This Christmas Eve, I couldn't stand it any longer and I really got in his face.

"I hate your guts," I told him, "and the children and I are leaving as soon as Christmas is over." He grabbed me, threw me over his lap, and he spanked me so hard, like I was a really bad child. I wanted to kill him. I had a gun I kept without any bullets, and I just grabbed it and, I'm ashamed to say, I pointed it in his direction—that's how desperate I'd become. I wanted to get his attention. But he just laughed—he knew the gun wasn't loaded, and anyway, he never, ever listened to me. He never heard what I said about the kids and me leaving. That won't do wonders for a woman's self-esteem.

Little by little, I crept out of the house. Always feeling frightened, always worried about dying, I still knew I had to find work because we were desperate for money. Food and rent money was getting tighter and tighter. Whatever Jimmy touched in the work world soon fell apart. Although I'd had many different kinds of starter jobs, I was then very limited in what I could do. Finally, in the mid-eighties, I got a job at the Albany bank, which seemed like a relatively safe place to be. The boss put me up in the front lines as a teller because I loved people and was good with them. Although I was not having my attacks on a regular basis then, I still carried my brown paper bag in my purse in case I hyperventilated. I still worried about having a panic attack in public, but at least I was out in the world, and I wasn't dead yet.

Seems as though Jimmy Deen couldn't stay at a job for any longish period of time. He wasn't lazy and he was very hard-workin', but he was like a rolling-stone man where the grass always looked greener somewhere else. He had these pipe dreams of glory days and he got uninterested in his present work when he was dreamin' of glory. More than just *havin'* pipe dreams, he'd follow them, and drag us all along. One day in 1986, Jimmy came home and said we were moving to Savannah. I was devastated and sick with fear. I didn't know a soul there, and we'd all have to move so far from home and everything we knew. Impossible. But we had to go, said my husband. He'd heard of a car dealership that needed help. Later, he said it was the worst thing he ever did, but you know what? For me, Savannah was the best thing Jimmy ever did. But before we moved, I had to go through the fire in yet another way.

Jamie was away and Bobby was a high school senior. I'd given my notice at the bank in Albany, and was at home, packing boxes. The bank called and said, "Paula, we hate to ask you, but we need a favor. Would you come out to the East Albany branch and work Friday?"

I was nothing if I wasn't cute and agreeable. "I'd be happy to help y'all out," I said.

I had never worked at this branch. When I pulled up, got out of my car, and walked into the bank, I said to myself, "Holy crap!"

This young woman who had been there just two months asked, "What's the matter?" And I remember saying, "This is a perfect setup for a robbery."

I've got pretty good gut feelings. There were no officers in that branch—just me and this girl. It was in a pretty iffy neighborhood. And Friday was a busy day, being payday. We went about getting ready to open. I had not emptied the vault, but I had finished filling the drawers with cash. There was plenty of money because by five we would be cashing some big payroll checks: probably ten thousand in the other teller's bank drawer and ten or fifteen thousand in mine.

I heard somebody coming in the door, and I looked up to see a guy in a green mask that completely covered his face. Did I mention he had a gun in his hand? I had to figure that this one had bullets. My heart just about came out of my chest, but I was so frightened, I didn't have enough time to think about a panic attack. That green-masked guy did not pay attention to that other girl. He came straight to me and put that gun to my head. That gun was *dancing* around my head because the robber guy was so scared, his hands were shaking.

To myself I said, *It's over. It's finally gotten here. I'm dead, today. My worst fear is happening. He's going to shoot me by accident simply out of his own fright.*

What would you have done? Well, I didn't do that. Instead, I started scooping out the money. I started with the ones and was working my way over when he hissed, "Only large bills." So I got the large bills. And that other little teller next to me, she finally saw what was happening and started gathering up her money. He took it all and walked out, simple as that.

I told the young woman to call the police but I went straight to the phone and called Jimmy, who was already in Savannah and working at his new job. I told him what had happened.

Jimmy said he'd be with me the next day. He told me to hang on. I prayed that I could. I prayed that it would be one of the times that I could get in my car and just leave; I knew it was very important that this robbery didn't set me back to the worst years when I couldn't leave my home. I had to be very careful that I didn't relapse. This robbery could have turned me back into a limp dishrag.

But it didn't. Something in me, some inner strength, some Paula stubbornness that maybe my folks had instilled, took over. I went home after the robbery, got Bobby from the high school, and I went to Bubba's and said, "I'm so sorry. I just can't stay at home. I would be too frightened." Bubba, Jill, and Jay took us in. When it's family, they gotta take you in.

Every time I closed my eyes for the next month, this robber man would jump in my face with the gun. I was never free of the thoughts.

After Jimmy moved us all to Savannah I went into my bed for two full months. I was relapsing—I just felt it. Back to square one.

Again, I couldn't tell if I was on the right side of the dirt.

Baked Savannah-Alaska

When you feel relief, when you want to celebrate a getting-well—even if you're not *all* well yet—you need a celebration recipe, and there's nothing more celebratory than a traditional baked Alaska with all its peaks and snowy sweetness. There's not much snow in Savannah and I ain't never been to Alaska, but the South sure knows about that state's most famous dessert. My personal baked Alaska gets to be called Baked Savannah-Alaska because I garnish my serving plate with edible southern magnolia or hibiscus petals. If you can't find those, try crystallized violet or rose petals.

For starters, we're going to take a yummy piece of cake—any kind of cake, actually. It can be a chunk of your Mississippi Mud Cake—before you add the marshmallows and the icing. It can be a piece of your own sour cream pound cake, your carrot cake—whatever kind of cake you want, even store-bought cake. You could even use a blueberry muffin. Place the cake in an ovenproof dish.

Next we're going to make the meringue. You need 3 egg whites at room temperature, ¼ teaspoon cream of tartar, and ¼ cup sugar. We're going to beat those egg whites together with the cream of tartar with a handheld electric mixer until they form soft peaks. Then we're going to gradually beat in the sugar until the meringue is really stiff.

Then we're going to ladle into the center of the cake a big old scoop of ice cream—probably vanilla, because that would go with any kind of cake. We're going to frost the whole thing, every drop, no cake or ice cream exposed, with a thick layer of meringue and press some ripples in the meringue with a spoon, a knife, or a spatula. Then put what will become the Baked Savannah-Alaska in a 425°F preheated oven and just brown it quickly so that the ice cream won't melt. You need to watch the baking process closely, because you don't want your meringue to burn.

Taking the cake from the oven, I'd garnish the dish with those organic or pesticide-free southern flower petals and perhaps put a little candle or flag on the very top of the meringue for a real celebratory sensation.

Bring this fabulous dessert to the table with a spoon (or two spoons, one for you and one for whoever is celebrating your victory with you). Then, all dig in together with cries of *"Delicious!"* or *"Congratulations!"* or *"Well done!"*

Chapter 6

THE BAG LADY

*Rednecks know how to eat like kings 'cause they
figured out how to cook food that don't throw
them in a new tax bracket.*

When I was transplanted to Savannah, it was
1987, Georgia was starting to celebrate the
two hundredth anniversary of its statehood, and I could not have
cared less. Televangelists Jim and Tammy Faye Bakker were in big
trouble when he was caught in the middle of a sex scandal. Didn't
care. Sonny Bono started his campaign to be elected mayor of
Palm Springs, California. News left me cold, honey. The world
population hit five billion and little Jessica McClure fell down a
well. Ditto about not caring. Danny Kaye, Jackie Gleason, and
Ray Bolger died. I didn't mourn them.

I was mourning my own losses. I mourned everything I'd left
behind in Albany. First of all, I had to leave Corrie, Bubba's daughter, who was only six years old. I was Corrie's main nurturer and I
just adored her. She needed me. When Corrie's own momma told

me she thought I was far more maternal than she was, it was the living truth.

Jamie had already left for Valdosta State University, but Bobby—oh, Bobby. When I moved to Savannah, I left my younger son as well. I'll carry the guilt forever for leavin' Bobby. Even though it's what he wanted, I should not have left him for a minute. Bobby was a senior in high school and we up and told him in the middle of his senior year that we were moving and he couldn't graduate with his friends. Well, he was devastated. In a way, I understood. I would have laid down and died if my momma and daddy took me away from my friends at that age. I didn't want to do that to my child. Well, I guess it was about that time that Bubba remembered a certain sixteen-year-old kid who'd gone to live with his sister and her family when he was left an orphan; he said Bobby could stay in Albany with him. Okay, okay. I told Bobby that he could stay with his uncle as long as he was passing his courses, but if he started failing school, he'd have to come to Savannah to live with us.

Not that things were great in Savannah. Actually, they were the pits. I had been living in terror of leaving my home for almost twenty years and now I was in a whole new town. My new home, a little house on Sixtieth Street, felt strange and unfamiliar, but I was more terrified than ever that I'd die if I went outside. I'd been on a roller-coaster ride for so long: sometimes I was functioning, but if something bad happened, I was totally stripped emotionally. Lately, I'd seemed to be making some progress, but now I felt as though I'd really relapsed. I'd been in Savannah more than two months, and I was just lying in bed, not getting up except to eat and go to the bathroom. I'd never been worse.

Then I met my guardian angel. Her name was Denise, her husband worked in the same dealership as Jimmy, and she looked more like a swift pain in the ass than a guardian angel to me. Relentlessly, Denise tried her hardest to befriend ungrateful me. She called me every day, two or three times a day, and she would get on my nerves so bad.

"You've got to get out of bed," she'd say. "You've got to go outside. You can't just stay in that bed forever. Let's go shopping, let's go have a coffee, let's play cards, let's let's let's . . ."

I wanted to tell her to go freak herself and leave me alone. I wanted to ask her why she didn't recognize a basket case when she saw one.

Well, Denise saved my life. Got rid of my basket. She was a secret godsend. Maybe it was because I was finally ready to bloom, maybe it was because I sensed I was at the end of my rope and I had to save all our lives by climbing back up, but whatever the reason, Denise was the unwitting instrument of my salvation.

I feel like I need a drum roll here. One day, I was lying in bed, and, well—you know what? All of a sudden Denise's words made sense to me. Simple as that. "Get out of bed," she'd said. So, this particular morning, I got out of my bed, stood up, and looked in the mirror. I was only forty but I was stuck in my bedroom and dying inside. Out loud, I whispered to my mirror image, "I can't do this anymore, I just can't."

Like a thunderclap, the words to the Serenity Prayer—the ones that alcoholics use at Alcoholics Anonymous—went through my mind: *God grant me the serenity to accept the things I cannot change; courage to change the things I can; and wisdom to know the difference.* I'd heard it for years, never paid it much attention, but on this Savannah morning, this sweet, sunny day, I understood the prayer and what I should be praying for. I was free, free at last.

At last, I *got* it. Sure, I'm gonna die, I said to myself. My children are gonna die. Everyone I love is gonna die. But God has given me today and I'm gonna go out and live today. I won't die today.

Maybe it was because I was ready, maybe because I'd come to

the bottom of my rope and there was no way to go but climb back up, maybe the annoying Denise bugged me so much I had to do something: for whatever reason, at last I understood that I had mentally struggled against accepting my momma's and daddy's deaths for too long. Inside, I'd thought if I fought their dying, they might come back. I'd thought if I fought their dying, maybe I'd find out I was adopted and my real parents would come find me. I'd thought—oh, I don't know what all I thought. You just think crazy like that from the pain. Finally, I knew I would be able to start living. And breathing. *And going outside.*

It didn't all get better right away, of course, but now I had that prayer to fall back on when I felt I was going to panic. It was a maddeningly slow process but now I had a handle on it. I devised a gradual cure for myself—walk one block, go home; drive two blocks, drive home; walk two blocks, walk home . . . Finally, I was able to separate from my safe place. I wanted desperately to improve my life and, most of all, to give my boys wings through either education or a business. Prospects for a college education didn't look that rosy because money was so tight, so it was going to have to be business, I figured. Together, just maybe, we could figure out what we did best.

I got better and better, and the next thing you knew, I could get in my car and drive all the way to Albany, which was a good thing because too much was going on in Bobby's life and he failed all his courses in his senior year. I had to go get him and bring him back to me, that was the right thing to do, the thing I should have done right from the start. Bobby finished up his senior year at Windsor High School in Savannah, and by the end of the school year he wouldn't have gone back to Albany for all the tea in China, but at the time when I retrieved my child, it was traumatic to the bone for him. I was forty-one years old. I'd lived for twenty years in anguish, waiting every day to die. Death fear didn't paralyze me anymore. I felt as though I had two birthdays; the first was January 19, 1947, the day I was born to my momma and daddy; and the second was June 19, 1989. That was the day I was born to myself, the day I came back to living my days, the day I took control of life. Slowly, I left my house, all by myself. Step by step, I began to make my way in the world.

My husband, in contrast, was losing his way in the world, working less and less and making almost no money. He still held a certain amount of security for me, though, even if his credit in the outside world was pretty horrible. He couldn't have borrowed a plug nickel if we needed it, and the time was fast comin' when we'd need that nickel, plug or not. I had to get a job. I decided that I wasn't putting myself on any front line of a bank again, so once I got out of my bed, I thought I'd be best off registering at a temporary-employment agency and just work around at a couple of places so I could learn my new city. It was only a day or two later that the agency called me to say there was a two-month position available with a Savannah hospital, Memorial Medical Center. Was I interested? Was I! I never will forget the day that call came. Bobby was in his bedroom, and I went in and said, "Son, you will not believe this, I just got a job."

"Where, Momma?" he asked.

"At Memorial Medical Center," I answered. "They have hired me to do only light surgeries like tonsillectomies and appendectomies and things like that."

And he looked at me and he said, "Momma, that is wonderful."

I had to tell him I was kidding but it felt good to know he thought I could do anything once I got out of the damn bed. Why shouldn't his momma be able to go over there to do simple tonsillectomies and appendectomies? I kind of thought, after that, if my son had that kind of faith in me, I really could do anything, maybe even a simple hernia repair.

Sometimes when I meet people today, they just assume I was a cook all my life, but it isn't so. I wasn't born with a silver spoon in any of my orifices and I also wasn't born with any great desire to cook. I didn't know *what* I was born to do but I knew as a young woman that my greatest desire was to be a wife and mother, as I had seen my mother do. It was my dream that my husband would earn the living and take care of us, and that making money would never be my responsibility. I was there for the home and for the children and that's just the way it was, especially in the South.

It turned out that many times came when I had to rethink my Southern upbringing and assumptions, because I needed to bring in that second income to give Jimmy some relief. At different times in my married life, depending on how well I could function, these are some of the occupations that I pursued: Would you believe I got a real estate license? Would you believe I got an insurance license? I was a banker. I've hung wallpaper for a living. Would you believe I took a job at Kroger's Market hoping one day to be promoted up to a checker? That job was particularly horrifying to me because when you first go to work for Kroger, you start by cleaning. So, there I was in that big old Kroger store on Slappy Drive in my uniform out mopping that floor, cleaning those bathrooms. I was so frightened that an old boyfriend might come into Kroger and see me mopping floors and think that's how far I had come in my life. I was married. I had children. It was an honest living, but in all honesty, I felt like I was too good for that kind of job and I was just so embarrassed that people would come in and see Paula, the captain of the cheerleaders, carrying a Kroger mop. Is this what I had come to?

One time, I even got this harebrained idea that I was going to sell a grease absorber to garages. Jimmy built me a wagon and painted it the color of my car. I went to the animal-supply wholesalers and bought fifty-pound bags of kitty litter. Then I went around to different garages selling those bags as grease absorbent that could be sprinkled on garage floors. I made sixty dollars a week selling kitty litter.

Not one of those jobs had anything to do with Southern cooking, as you might have noticed. And when I got the job at Memorial Medical Center, I thought that job was just so perfect—even though I wasn't hired to do no simple tonsillectomies. I was only one block from my house so I could walk to work. I was a biller in Medicaid/Medicare, maybe the easiest position on the planet, but I made some good friends, really enjoyed my work, and I loved being able to breathe again in the outside world. I probably brought home about two hundred dollars a week, which certainly helped out our situation. That two-month temp job turned into two years.

So, we rocked along for a couple of years. Then it had to happen: in 1988, Jimmy began to get dissatisfied with the Savannah job, as he did with every other job. He decided to take another position, in Warner Robbins, which is right outside Macon, Georgia. He moved there, leaving me and the boys in Savannah, and he'd come home and maybe spend Sunday with us. It was lonely; I still wanted to be with him. I still wanted us to be a family.

There was nothing for it but for all of us to move to Warner Robbins. I emptied out the old house that we'd worked hard to fix up, and put it on the market. The realtor called me one night with a lousy offer. As badly as I needed the money, I said, "No, that offer is pretty insulting. I don't think I'll take it." I would not give my house away, even though we were desperate for money. Maybe that should have been my first sign that I could be a businesswoman: I knew instinctively that you don't jump at the first offer. But we had to move and we had zilch in our pockets. Until now, I had never asked anybody for money. I would eat shit and bark at the moon before I would ask anybody for money. But now I had to break down and go to my Aunt Peggy, my momma's sister, and ask her if she would cosign at the bank with me for a twenty-five-hundred-dollar loan. It was humiliating, but Aunt Peggy came through—she did then and she always does.

So, Jimmy was working at this new dealership, and I was staying at home in Warner Robbins, but I knew I'd have to find a job in this town soon. I was wrong. We were there three months when Jimmy came home and said, "Well, this guy can't pay me a salary anymore. He doesn't have the money. I'm going to have to go on straight commission. We're dead."

I could not believe it. We'd never survive without a salary.

"The house in Savannah hasn't sold," I told him. "We're going home." And we did. We moved back into our old Sixtieth Street house and I went right back to work in the hospital. Now I was plotting and planning how to better take care of myself and the boys, figuring out how we could gain our independence. It had finally become crystal clear: I couldn't rely on my husband. I had to take charge of my own life, and that of the boys.

My friend Ann Hanson told me about a lady in Atlanta who would come into beauty shops with a basket of little snacks and things for women who were having their hair done on their lunch hour and didn't have the chance to actually eat lunch. Then came my zillion-dollar inspiration: "Well, if she can do snacks, I can do lunches," I thought. I planned and planned, and decided to call the business The Bag Lady. I talked to my Aunt Peggy and Uncle George every day about my ideas; they were so smart and supportive and wanted nothing more than for me to succeed big. I would lie in bed at night and dream about this little business. I went home to Albany for a weekend, and my Aunt Peggy's friend drew the most adorable little logo of a bag lady you've ever seen.

She wore a flowered cape and a flannel skirt, and socks and a hat with a flower in it. She had those long false eyelashes that I love to wear, and wore gloves with the fingers cut out of 'em. And she had this *big* smile. It was a pretty fair caricature of me, and I was thrilled. My idea was that I would pack an entire lunch, tie it up in a brown bag with a ribbon, and try to sell it in office buildings, where people often didn't have the opportunity or time to take lunch. I was gonna go into banks, law offices, doctor's offices, beauty shops—everywhere—and just sell those bag lunches.

I called my Grandmomma Paul to tell her that I'd finally decided to follow in her footsteps. After I rattled on till I was out of breath telling her what I had in mind, I realized there was just silence on the other end. I thought we were disconnected, and was about to hang up, when all of a sudden the silence was broken by my grandmother's booming voice.

"Paula, have you lost your damn mind?" she bellowed. "Food is the hardest business in the world to be in and you're telling me you're jumpin' into the food business?"

"This is what you have to know, Granny," I laughed. "The apple don't fall far from the tree."

I'd talk with my friends every day about my new idea. I was so excited and everyone cheered me on. Except Jimmy. He just said I was an idiot. It was his favorite word for me. He called me that a lot. Still, he helped me in two big ways. The first was when I told him I wanted to start The Bag Lady, and I also told him I needed some money. That's when he gave me two hundred dollars from my income tax return check, and that's what I was allotted to spend on my business. When he gave me the money, he said, "Knock yourself out, bitch."

Years later, I asked him if he remembered saying "bitch," and he answered no. But when I asked him if he remembered calling me an idiot so many times, Jimmy looked at me sadly and answered, "I'm the idiot, Paula."

It was a bittersweet victory.

So, in 1989, when I was about forty-two years old, I jumped into the world of being an entrepreneur. At the time, if you had asked me what that word meant, I could not have told you. All I knew was I needed to become that woman of substance; a responsible, strong person to save my own life and the lives of my boys. Our salvation had to lie in food and cooking because that was all I knew—with the possible exception of cheerleading and being cute.

First off, I wanted our little business to be legal, not some two-bit operation I had to hide from tax collectors. It wasn't an easy thing to do because the Health Department had certain strict rules about who could prepare food to sell to the public and where the food had to be prepared. I kept calling the Health Department and asking, "Can you come out and look at my house and let me fix sandwiches there?"

"No, Mrs. Deen. That's against the law; it has to be a place sanctioned and licensed by the city as a proper food-preparation place."

I'd call back and say, "Well, I've got a garage. How about if I go out and clean it up and make sandwiches there?"

"Mrs. Deen," they said, "it will take a lot of money for you to put a professional kitchen in your garage. Then it'll have to be inspected and approved. And after you go to the expense, it still may well not be approved."

Who was I kidding? Putting a professional kitchen in my garage was about as financially possible for us as buying the Supreme Court Building. But then Jimmy did the grandest thing for me—next to taking in Bubba. He had a friend who owned a downtown pool hall that was licensed to prepare and sell sandwiches.

"Any way my wife could get licensed through you?" Jimmy asked his friend. "Sure," said his buddy. Well, that was wonderful, I thought. I'd work during the night down in their kitchen when it was closed, make my lunches, and then my boys could go out in the morning and sell them. Well, it turned out that pool hall had the *nastiest* kitchen you've ever seen. I wouldn't want to fix my dog a sandwich in that kitchen. It may have been clean enough for the city of Savannah, but it wasn't clean enough for me, licensed or not. There were things in that kitchen I wouldn't want in my sandwich, and they weren't no pool cues. Hell, I wouldn't even want those things in my pool hall. No sunshine ever entered those four walls either, so the room was always cold; cold as a well digger's ass.

Still, if city hall was going to be stubborn, and I had to do it that way rather than in my own shining, clean kitchen, I'd have to figure out a way around the bureaucracy.

Look, sometimes you have to take matters in your own hands, and sometimes there is more than one truth in a telling. I wanted to use the pool hall's license, but not its kitchen. A gentleman I'll call Mr. Burrows, this sweet man who used to work as a Health Department inspector, met me at the pool hall one day, and together we were going to fill out the paperwork. You know, I always had the feeling that Mr. Burrows knew what I was up to, but he was so kind, and if I had to lie a little to be legal, he was going to help me. He'd seen that pool hall kitchen.

He pulled out his papers.

Answering the very first question, I knew I was going to have to lie seriously. Thing is, I don't lie well. Even little white lies show up in my face. But I had to say I was going to make the sandwiches in the pool hall kitchen and get my sandwich-making license through this pool hall. The pool hall was legal. Chez Deen was not. The truth was that I had absolutely no intention of making sandwiches in their hellhole. I would have killed off half the population of Savannah.

I tried to figure out how to truthfully answer the first question, which needed a lie worse than I needed mayonnaise, but the effort stopped me dead in my tracks. I looked hard at Mr. Burrows. As I stared hopefully at him, Mr. Burrows quietly said, "Paula, say yes." I felt as though I had a stamp on my head saying, *Liar. This woman is a liar.* But I wrote *yes.* He asked me the next question, and again I just looked at him. I know that he saw a desperate woman. Again, he said, "Say yes, Paula. And the answer to the next one is no." We went through the whole trial application like that.

Oh, that Mr. Burrows. I hope he's readin' this. I hope he knows how deeply I love him. I filled out the real papers as he taught me, got the license, I was legal, and I made my sandwiches in my own shining clean kitchen. No one got hurt.

Now, had my husband not laid the groundwork for me there's a very good chance that I wouldn't be sitting here writing this book today. I owe him for that. I took the two hundred dollars he gave me, spent about fifty on groceries, forty on a cooler, and the rest on the license and incidentals. I was legal. The Bag Lady was born.

The Bag Lady. It had a nice ring to it.

I could not get myself going quick enough to make those sandwiches. Frankly, it was a good thing I didn't know how long and hard I'd be running, because I might not have started if I knew. Sixteen-hour, even twenty-four-hour days were not unusual. The worst thing was, in the beginning, it was all a pig in a poke. I couldn't take orders before I started making the lunches. I didn't have one customer yet. Instead, I had to make all the lunches first, then try to sell them—not exactly a road map to success.

From the get-go, I operated with another kind of fear—a real one this time. There were always a few people who were calling in to the Health Department and reporting The Bag Lady for "being out and peddling illegal meals that the Paula lady cooks in her house." Of course, the Health Department would always answer, "Oh, no, she's licensed. She's legal." It petrified me that one day an inspector would follow my children home and find out I was indeed preparing the Bag Lady lunches out of my kitchen.

I've got to tell you that making sandwiches was not the mashed potatoes I thought it would be. I knew how to cook, but I didn't have any lessons on picnicking, and, no question about it, I was making picnic lunches. I started with tuna fish salad sandwiches. The first morning, I got up at five AM and made like thirty-seven tuna fish sandwiches. I wrapped them in Saran wrap and put them in the cooler. In an hour they were totally squished. But our first route was the Medical Arts Building in which I worked, and my friends bought all those smushed-up, ugly, but delicious sandwiches. I developed a routine: when I finally made a few customer pals, I'd take orders for the next day, sometimes in person, sometimes over the phone, which I much preferred, because I wasn't completely over my fear of leaving the house. Jamie would deliver them reluctantly. He didn't love the sandwich business. He never wanted to be part of it.

My Best Ham Salad Sandwich

The tuna salad, egg salad, and chicken salad sandwiches seemed to fly from The Bag Lady's basket, but one of the most popular was always the ham salad sandwich. The trick is to use the best ham you can find; my momma's favorite, and mine, was a traditional Smithfield ham.

I adore, in particular, a Smithfield spiral-sliced ham because you don't even have to slice it. It's already done for you. When I get to the end of that ham, I love cutting the leftover meat off the bone—and there's always plenty. Trimming any fat off, I make a ham salad by putting the ham in the food processor to gently chop it all up, stopping before it becomes mushy or pasty.

2 cups leftover ham, chopped in a food processor
1 cup finely diced celery
¼ cup finely minced sweet onion
1 teaspoon Dijon mustard
2 hard-boiled eggs, diced
¼ cup hot pickle relish, drained
½ cup mayonnaise

Mix all the ingredients until well blended and spread on white bread—crust and all—to make a generous, fat sandwich that does justice to The Bag Lady.

Chapter 7

THE BOTTOMING OUT AND THE NEW BEGINNING

People will step on your back to get in ahead of y'all.
That's why you gotta be tough even when you feel so
stinkin' bad, you need yo' momma's comfort.

In the beginning, it was just Jamie and me. Bobby had a job working at Circuit City.

Before The Bag Lady was born, Jamie had gone off to school at Valdosta State. Fact is, I didn't have any money for college. He didn't have any money for college. His daddy didn't have any money for college. But off he went to Valdosta anyway on a partial scholarship. At that age, like many kids, Jamie's biggest ambition was to enjoy some serious college partying, and he figured he'd eventually get a job that would pay his way through school. Jamie, who's the smartest, most talented guy in the world (and have you ever checked out those dimples?), is just not cut out for studying and academics. Sorry I said it, but this is his momma speaking, you'd better believe it. Oh, he might have taken one class while he was there, but mostly he wanted to be part of the whole social scene. His dream was good times and my dream was making a livin'. The truth? Even if I could have scraped up the money, I wouldn't have given it to him for college—I'd have definitely thought that'd be pure pissin' it away.

But Jamie's his own man, and when he went to Valdosta he moved in with his best friend and went to work in a restaurant. Then he got himself a job digging swimming pools. The poor things lived in a house that I don't think had any electricity or runnin' drinking water, and I *know* it didn't have any water to flush the toilet. It was a serious challenge when nature called. Lord have mercy!

"We didn't have anything," Jamie remembers. "Just like there's not a tooth fairy, there's not a toothpaste fairy, and there's sure not a toilet paper fairy. Our water was cut off many times before we figured out how to turn it back on. The house was either freezing cold or burning hot, and at times very dry."

Well, my heart really about broke when one day Jamie, who is so law-abiding, had to tell me on the phone, "Momma, I stole candy bars to have something to eat." Soon after, he called again to tell me he'd gotten a job at the Dairy Queen. I was pretty happy about that because I knew that at least he could eat at the Dairy Queen.

"Yup," he said, "you know, Momma, this job's gonna be good, but they wear double-knit uniforms, and those ugly little crown caps."

I guessed right then that there was going to be big trouble. There was no way my Jamie would wear a little crown cap. For a week he was in luck because he was so big they had to special-order a uniform that would fit. When the week was up, Saturday rolled around and I called him at the Dairy Queen. "May I speak with Jamie Deen, please?" I asked. The man on the phone told me he was certainly sorry but Jamie wasn't there because his grandfather died, and he had to go home.

I said, "His grandfather's been dead now for almost twenty-five years."

Jamie's uniform had come in. He would have eaten shit before he'd wear that uniform. So, he just told them his granddaddy died and walked out.

I had been making some noise about starting some sort of business, but Jamie would have done about anything to avoid workin' with me, so he got a job at Yellowstone Park, and, wouldn't you know it, he'd call collect every week and tell me how homesick he was. I'd say, "Oh, son, I'm so sorry," but I wasn't sorry. Well, finally he got over his homesickness, started enjoying the park and making some friends, but very little money. He was twenty-two and I worried so about his future.

This was in 1989, and I'd been batting around the idea for The Bag Lady for a while. I knew Jamie was just marking time till he found a way to seriously support himself; it was my personal opinion he just shouldn't play around anymore. I wanted him home. I needed him home. It was time to tell him about my plan.

"Son, I'm really starting a business," I said on the phone one day. "I've got this idea, and I think we can do it, but I can't do it without you. I need you so badly to help me with this, and I need you right now."

My Jamie didn't have an option, to tell the truth. Neither did his brother. I needed them.

Looking back, I think that maybe one reason my sons and I have such a great relationship today is that we went through some pretty rough times together. Jamie and Bobby didn't have the same opportunities as kids whose parents have the money for educating them. Those rich kids leave home at eighteen for college and then fall into the lawyering, the banking—the cushy office jobs. My sons had only one choice—if you call it a choice. The choice's name was Momma.

So, grudgingly, Jamie said okay, but he wanted to make a little detour before coming home. His girlfriend at the time lived in Atlanta, and he wanted to go see her for a week before he came back to Savannah.

"Okay, son," I remember telling him, "but you've got to be home by Friday at the latest because we're gonna start The Bag Lady Monday, and I desperately need you to help me think all this stuff out and make serious plans."

You may be thinkin' I sound pretty mean, and maybe I was, but it's not like I was just dying inside because I had to deny my academically driven son a college education. A love for books was not driving that child. Jamie was doing himself no good at Yellowstone at all, he'd be the first to tell you that. It was a temporary position, it could never last, and he knew it. Jamie was ready to get his feet on the ground, and it wasn't going to be in no advanced philosophy or tree-hugging course.

Well, he went to Atlanta to see his girl, and he got home Sunday afternoon. I was so devastated that he didn't come home Friday like he said he would that when he ambled in the door, I walked past him like he wasn't there and didn't bother speaking to him.

Thinking of it, it about kills me that I acted that way. I think he holds that against me, even today, and I still feel guilty about it. Truth is, I had missed him so bad and now I needed him so desperately. I felt I was literally fighting for our lives and he disappointed me, but I know now that I should not have reacted the way I did. No one ever said I was no angel. But my biggest fear in the whole world was that I was going to die and leave my children with no security, in the very same financial boat I'd been left in. No way. I was going to do whatever it took to make them safe.

◀◀
I'm sure Momma's tellin' Aunt Peggy, "Take care of my Paula." And Aunt Peggy turned out to be my champion.

▶▶
Momma and Daddy on their weddin' day: Daddy was always laughing, just like me.

◀◀
Me and my beloved childhood companion, Auntie Trina.

Momma and Granddaddy Paul at River Bend

Grandmomma and Granddaddy Paul
at their last motel, the Casbah,
just before Granddaddy died.

River Bend pool in the early fifties, the waters of my childhood.

▲ Grandmomma Hiers holding
the future Bag Lady.

▲ My inspirations: Grandmomma Nellie Hiers
and Grandmomma Irene Paul, and boy, did
they make a mean fried chicken!

◀◀
Jamie (six), Bobby (three),
and wide-eyed friend.

⬆ At a modeling shoot.

⬆ Bobby Deen, who would grow up to be one of *People* magazine's "most gorgeous and eligible bachelors in the country."
Got it all from yo' momma, son, and don't you forget it!

⬆ Jamie Deen. I gave him that haircut. I think he's forgiven me, but I wouldn't swear to it.

↟ Jimmy and Paula Deen and their sons in 1978: behind
my smile are the crippling fears of agoraphobia, full-blown.

↟ Bobby in the hospital
after his tonsillectomy.

↟ Jamie, Bobby, and me: tough
times ahead, but wonders in store for us.

⩧ The original Bag Lady team: me, the boys, and their girls, and who slept where in our shared house, I do not want to think about.

⩦ Here she is—The Bag Lady herself.

⬆ Aunt Peggy and Uncle George Ort, who helped make it all happen.

▶▶
We did it!
The proudest day of my life . . .

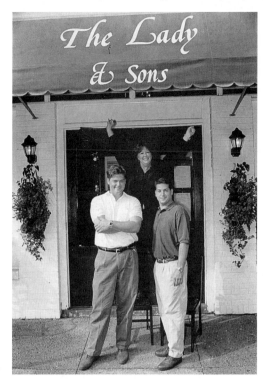

⬆ The staff of The Lady & Sons: Aunt Peggy is in the second row on the right, always along for the ride.

▲ Me and my niece, Corrie, on our first trip to Six Flags amusement park: we haven't stopped laughing yet.

▲ Dora Charles, me, and Aunt Peggy—three tough dames.

▲ Ineata Jones, better known as "Jellyroll,"
making her famous hoecakes.

▲ The lady just loves to give hugs to her guests
at The Lady & Sons in Savannah.

◀◀
Jamie and Bobby with Sam, Otis, and Dixie at the house on Turners Cove. I was indoors prayin' for a neighbor.

▶▶
Michael hasn't even had his sandwich yet and he's already thinkin' about dessert.

Captain Michael and friend Otis doin' their best to relax.
▼

Me and my beautiful "bridesmaids" at my weddin' shower. (Jamie–forget your presidential aspirations.)

Michael and me on our weddin' day with our children, Anthony and Michelle.

The famous "titty twister" photo of me aggravating Bubba big-time, but with big-time love. ▶▶

Bubba and family:
Ian, Trevor, and Bubba's fiancée, their momma, Dawn Woodside; Bubba's in the chair, and his kids, Jay and Corrie, are at right.
▼

⤒ My brilliant, loony, and lovable producer, Gordon Elliott,
giving me direction from the last available seat in my bathroom.

⤒ Jamie and his exquisite bride, Brooke, on their weddin' day.

⚜ Getting a foot rub from a spiffy harbor pilot at our daughter Michelle's weddin'.

⚜ At the Georgia State Senate on Paula Deen Day. Do you believe it?

◀◀
Paula the movie star being interviewed on the red carpet at the Toronto Film Festival showing of *Elizabethtown:* life don't get much more glamorous than this.

⬇ Cameron Crowe, the producer of *Elizabethtown*, gave me this signed poster after we finished shooting the movie: the little Albany cheerleader travels in classy company!

Me and my precious grandbaby, Jack Deen: *You don't know grits about how good it gets, child.*

I just love this picture of Michael and me: I must have just fed him some oxtails.

Cooking was my first, last, and only hope. I had nowhere to turn, nobody to turn to. It was all up to my sons and me: family was all we had.

To be fair, Jamie had a different take on it.

"I never really believed it was going to be a real business, I thought it was just a crazy idea of Mom's," he says today. "So, how early did I have to get there to fix ham sandwiches, put 'em in a cooler, and knock on a few doors?

"Why didn't I just walk away from her crazy scheme? Well, it's only in hindsight that now I know we were all going to have grand, beautiful homes on the water and a business we'd all love. It's only in hindsight that I know the tougher the vine, the sweeter the grape. It's only in hindsight that I know that Bobby and I would have our own television show, our own cookbook, and even be able to buy a wonderful house for our dad, who is the hardest-working man I know. The truth is that our momma was the headlight on the locomotive that Bobby and I didn't believe in at first. But my brother and I were blessed from the start to have a relationship so close with our momma that today we three, Bobby, Mom, and I, are blooming together. Sure, a lot of times I wanted my mom and not Paula Deen, my boss. She can be very, very tough, even mean; she can turn on a dime, and can use enough angry guilt to make anyone do anything for her—and not happily! But today, we're blessed. And we did it together."

There's a lot of things none of us knew would happen then, but all I knew was that the next morning was Monday and we had to start. I was to make the sandwiches and Jamie was to sell them. I had to run the route with him the first day. His job was to go into the Medical Arts Building with his basket of lunches, and say, "Hey, I'm Jamie Deen with The Bag Lady, just stopping in." Now, this was the kid who would give up a steady job rather than wear a little crown hat, so you just know that carrying that big old lunch basket wasn't easy for him. So here we're going around with all these smushed tuna fish sandwiches. Jamie was so embarrassed he liketa died and he was feeling hopeful about at least dropping into a black hole to disappear.

We probably knocked on sixty doors. Only two turned us down, and that's because they'd closed their offices for the lunch hour. Even I was a bit mortified at the knocking and pleading we had to do, but we sold those damn sandwiches. Jamie says people bought the sandwiches out of pity. So what? I'd take pity at that moment in our lives. It was a great beginning, and I was so encouraged.

It didn't take me but a minute to realize that my packaging sucked; why were all those sandwiches smushed? When I started trying to sell them in banks and offices and places where I didn't know anyone, we would surely fail. Nothing for it but that I had to go out and find a sturdy container. I went down to the paper-supply houses, and they had these beautiful transparent plastic containers so people could check out the food, and it was clear that nobody would ever have touched that food except me. And nothing would smush. I sprung what little money I didn't have for the containers.

Well, I fixed the most beautiful meals in these little boxes. I'd wake up at five every morning and make about 250 lunches—everything from sandwiches to beautiful fruit salads with French custard and a French crème. I made grilled chicken and lasagna, custards and banana pudding. And on Thursday nights, I would put a Boston pork butt on the grill and let it barbecue slowly all night, get up on Friday morning, chop it into bite-sized pieces, and put it on a hamburger roll and serve it with a small container of barbecue sauce. Banana pudding was dessert.

How'd I get the money to buy all the stuff? Once we got going, Jamie would bring back each day's revenues for me. Then I'd go to

Polk's fresh produce market and buy some big old bananas or whatever I could find that was half-price (not half-price because it was bad, but because it was day-old. Don't worry; even then I knew the difference between bad and just a little bit dated!). Bargain never did mean bad to me. What looks pretty isn't necessarily good and what looks wrinkled may be the juiciest, most delicious peach in the universe. I bought the soft day-old fruit everyone else thought was rotten but I knew was actually sweeter than the fruit that just arrived at the market. I'd take a portion of money for the grocery and container stores, and buy whatever we needed there for the next day; we operated out of the house like that for about a year and a half. It had to work. I was liketa become a true bag lady if it didn't. I was *real* motivated.

Jamie remembers feeling so frustrated as soon as he had to leave the Medical Arts Building, where I had some friends, and go into the banks and offices, where we knew no one.

"It was all so rag-tied and homemade looking," he recalls. "Even me; with no uniform, no experience, nothing—I was just a guy with food. I'd go into an office wheeling my cart and say, 'I'm from The Bag Lady, would you like some lunch?' and I'd get mostly polite *no*s. When I told Momma, she said I was to pay that no mind and continue going to the same places at the same time every day, until they counted on me to be there. Then the sandwiches would start to sell."

I was right. Gradually we began to see a real profit. I knew I was onto something. I called Bubba one day and yelled into the phone, ecstatic, "Bubba, this week I made a thousand dollars! I've never made so much in my entire life!"

Pretty soon, Bobby had quit his job at Circuit City, which he'd taken when he graduated from high school, and joined his momma and brother in the business. Was life wonderful because a momma and her sons were working together? Nooooo, darling. We fought something terrible.

• • •

I remember that first Halloween, Jamie dressed up like a Bag Lady, in a dress and makeup, and went out to sell the sandwiches. It was funny, but I knew he was hiding behind the costume so no one would recognize him.

I think the kids believed they were in this only temporarily, but I finally told them, "I need permanent help. Y'all are gonna have to stay here. But maybe we can hire someone to run these Bag Lady routes and find something else for you."

Well, we did hire, but it didn't work. I'd get someone who'd come back after a couple of hours and say, "Didn't have any luck. Couldn't sell any sandwiches."

As soon as I hired people off the street, sales just never were the same. For all I knew, they were goin' out to sit in the park with the lunches, then come back and say, "No luck again."

I needed family. From my point of view, there was just nothing sweeter than these big old boys walking up to potential customers and saying, "My momma's cooked meat loaf today. Would you like some for lunch?" But that was my point of view, not theirs. Still, they had to do it.

Other family pitched in as well. When things were real tight, my Aunt Peggy would regularly come over for a week or so to help us out. She'd stand with me, and sometimes cry with me, and cook with me, and always cheer me on in her unique Aunt Peggy way. I'll never forget the first time she came after I started The Bag Lady. In the morning, I was stirring away in my kitchen, and down comes Aunt Peggy with a pair of white cotton underpants on her head. "I'm so afraid," she said, "that I'm goin' to get hair in your precious food and since we don't have no hairnets, I'm usin' my underwear."

I laughed so long and so hard and told her I sure hoped they were clean and could she rustle up another pair for me? And, I want to tell you, we didn't waste no money on hairnets for a long time after that. We continued to use those underpants because my motto is *Make do with what yo' got,* the whole thing was pretty ingenious, and, anyway, we kinda liked the look.

My sons and I lived in our two-bedroom, one-bathroom house, and the boys then both had new girlfriends who also wanted to live with us. I'd said, "Y'all, come on in." That there started an endless round of fighting between all of us about who slept where. I insisted the girls sleep together in a small morning room where I'd bought a pull-out trundle bed for them. The boys had twin beds that they pushed together in one of the bedrooms. I'm sorry to say the sleeping arrangements didn't always end up as I planned, and that's all I'm gonna say about *that.* I learned you gotta choose your battles. I'd have done anything to keep my family happy and with me. So I had these four children in my house, and all four of them now were running Bag Lady routes.

It was very, very hard and I realize now that was so because I was annoyingly gung ho and interested in nothing else. My boys, on the other hand, were interested in *everything* else *but* The Bag Lady. Jamie didn't hesitate to tell me on a regular basis, "Momma, this is your dream, not mine."

"Well, you don't know how freakin' hard it is to make a living!" I'd hurl back. "That's real and no dream. You go ahead and be a writer and see how poor you are. Now, get your ass out there and sell those sandwiches." Every morning, I felt like I was pullin' this wagon by this big old thick rope, and I'd pick that rope up and put it on my shoulder and say, "Okay, boys, climb on the wagon. I'll tell you how we'll manage to live, if y'all would just get on."

In the end, they climbed aboard. Good boys.

You ask Jamie why they climbed aboard and he'd tell you, "I'm a Southern boy and Southern boys can't turn their back on their mommas. We take care of our mommas; there's no negotiation there."

The only bright spot was my little eight-year-old Shih Tzu, Magnolia. I just adored her tiny, solid white body with just a perky spot of tan on her back. She was such company but scared to death of loud noises. One Fourth of July, I had friends over, and Magnolia was so terrified by the fireworks, she up and ran away. I looked for her for four days but she was gone and I was devastated. Eventually, the dog pound people found my baby, none the worse for wear, and we were reunited.

Besides The Bag Lady lunches, I'd been doing more and more private catering; small parties mostly, but my darlin' high school friend Jeannie Sims opened me up to the world of serious catering. She's a tough woman, Jeannie, and you'd better believe she wanted her parties just right. It was summer and it turned out she was planning two dinner parties, for a total of three hundred people, and she threw those parties my way because she knew how bad I needed the business. They were my first big catering jobs. I figured out they would bring in a profit of ten thousand dollars. Three hundred eaters! Maybe ten thousand dollars! I *really* wanted that business.

Jeannie left the menus up to me, and I chose beef stroganoff for the main course because it seemed like that would be an easy dish to make for so many folks. I didn't figure on the heat in Savannah in July.

It was horrible. I had this little bitty kitchen in our house, with no dishwasher and about two feet of counter space. It was so hot, there was no way I could cool the blasted house down. Jimmy Deen went and rented us a big old fan that just about blew the food off the stove, and my Aunt Peggy came over to Savannah to help me. I moaned to her, "I'm never gonna make it. How am I gonna get that ten thousand dollars? I've got to produce." The entire family—the boys, their girlfriends, Jimmy, me, my Aunt

Peggy—we worked and we sweated and we worked and we sweated and we finally got that damn beef stroganoff made. It was divine. But I'll tell you what, by the time I got those meals served at the parties, I muttered to Aunt Peggy, "You couldn't pay me to eat beef stroganoff, never, never, ever again."

And Aunt Peggy said, "Me neither."

One day, my friend Kenny Edwards called me and said, "The restaurant space is available in the Best Western hotel. You need to get down there, girl, and if you're going to be in this business, get in it." Boy, was he right.

I went down and, sure enough, the restaurant in the Best Western on Eisenhower and Albercorn, the south end of town, near the mall, was for rent. The neighborhood wasn't great; it sure wasn't the best of Savannah's historic pride, but it was a chance for me to grow a little bit, anyway. I talked with Robert Anderson, the owner, a really good-looking man, but with a reputation of being very, very tough. He looked me up and down and finally said, "I'll tell you what: I see that you don't have any experience, but something tells me that you have what it takes. I'm gonna give you a chance." He rented that space to me for a thousand dollars a month, plus utilities. It was a tremendous amount of money for me, but I took the biggest risk of my life and signed a lease for five years to serve three meals a day, seven days a week.

Well, I couldn't make a move without my family. I talked with my Aunt Peggy for weeks, told her what I wanted to do, and together we decided that I'd start a double-purpose food place in that Best Western space. The Bag Lady had done well so I'd continue to operate the deliveries out the back door of the Best Western, and, honey, I could relax because now we were as legal as the Constitution. Jamie started putting all the Bag Lady routes together by himself. I made the hot meals for him, and all he had to do was package them. Then he would make all the cold meals and salads; he would work all night long. Then he'd do his routes, come back home and sleep a little, and the next day it would start all over again. He was getting terrific at the business. I *knew* I needed family in there.

I planned that we'd have this cute little sit-down restaurant in the front of the space. Because I wanted people to associate the new restaurant with the good food that came with The Bag Lady, I decided to call the little restaurant simply The Lady.

The Lady was a charmer of a restaurant, a dream fulfilled. I could probably seat thirty to forty people. I'd been rat-packing money from the week I started The Bag Lady, and I'd managed to save four thousand dollars. I had to come up with the first and the last month's rent for the owner of the Best Western before we could open the doors to The Lady; that was two thousand dollars. The other two thousand would have to go for food supplies for The Lady. The beauty of this tiny restaurant was that it was a turnkey deal; because a restaurant had been in the space before I got there, pots, pans, dishes, and silverware were part of the package. I had to buy nothing except the groceries.

There wasn't a dime to pay for employees. When we moved into the new place, I said to my sons' girlfriends, "You girls are gonna have to wait the tables," and they did. In the beginning, I'd take the orders, run back to the kitchen to make the food, come back to deliver the order, go to the next table, take their orders, bring the coffee to the first table, with the girls filling in when I was busy doing something else. In some ways, it was pure hell. I was working sixteen-hour days, providing three meals a day, seven days a week. I wasn't sure I could stick it out, but it was my last shot at making something of myself: I was forty-four years old and almost out of time. But listen: Aunt Peggy told me I could do it. Aunt Peggy's never wrong.

Let me say a word about the kitchen in the Best Western: you had to be dedicated to stay in there for even twenty minutes. The focal point was a beautiful Vent-A-Hood range; it was so popular back then because it would draw out the heat and smoke and beautifully ventilate the kitchen—when it worked right. I would cut on the range every day, but I was so inexperienced—this was the first professional kitchen I'd ever been in besides my grandmother's when I was small—and I didn't know the Vent-A-Hood wasn't working. So the kitchen was unbearably hot and smoky and awful. One day I was back there working and my heart was beating so fast and hard, not because I was agoraphobic this time, but because I was so damn hot. I thought I was gonna die, and I said to Jamie, "I'm gonna have to call an ambulance here in a few minutes."

The spell passed and I never had to call for that ambulance. I was still being pretty tough to my boys; tough to everyone except my customers. Personally, though, I couldn't even look at anyone having a real good time because I couldn't afford to want that, couldn't afford any diversions because it might break my stride, and once that stride was broken—that was it for the Albany High School cheerleader. There wouldn't ever be a road to success, only streets of doom and gloom to walk.

I wasn't a whole lot of fun.

With all the work pressures and emotional strains, I certainly didn't have time for my husband's bad habits. The Lady was an exciting turning point for my business life, but it was also the beginning of the end of my marriage. For about twenty-five years I'd endured not only my own awful agoraphobia but also Jimmy's drinking, his insults, and both of us tearing each other down in a thousand different ways. But I'm here to report that there's nothin' like a little business success to lend a lady some personal courage. I'd about had it up to *here* with my husband. He'd lost yet another job while I was trying to build up The Bag Lady, so he started running a route for me. One morning, Bobby told me that he had to stop by the local store, and his daddy was up at the counter with a beer in his hand getting himself a hit before he started The Bag Lady route. I was furious and terribly worried that Jimmy would ruin my reputation before I could even get started. Still, I didn't do much about it. I didn't want to hurt him or embarrass my children by asking for a divorce.

Then it came: that famous straw that breaks the camel's back.

Bobby had bought himself the neatest old white pickup truck. It was in mint condition. It had been completely restored, and he loved this truck something fierce. He was making the loan payments from his salary by giving the money to his daddy so that Jimmy could put the money in the checking account and then write a check to the bank for Bobby's loan payment. The checks were always bouncing and Jimmy always had a tough time explaining why. One day, when I was at The Lady, a distraught Bobby called me and he said, "Momma, somebody just came and took my truck. They hauled my truck away."

I exploded. "What are you talkin' about, son? Let's find out what happened."

It didn't take a brain surgeon to figure out that although Bobby had faithfully given his car payments to Jimmy, his daddy now had really stopped sendin' the checks. The bank had repossessed the truck. I knew Jimmy loved his boys and would not intentionally hurt or steal from them, but times were tough for him, and he'd forgotten to make those payments one time too many now.

Whoaaaaa. I was madder than a wet hen. "Son, don't you worry about it, we'll get your truck back," I promised.

I went down to the First Union, where I had my own checking account; I had saved up four thousand dollars and bought a certificate of deposit with that money and I told the bank manager I wanted to make a loan against my CD.

Do you know the bank turned me down? It was my own money, and they turned me down. I went back there, and I said, "Listen here. *I want my money. Now.*"

They finally gave it to me, but they made me dance through every beat there was. This bank had previously made me some small-business loans, but I hadn't been in business very long and they didn't really trust me. Their mistake.

When I finally got my money, Bobby and I took it to the sheriff who had repossessed the truck, and we paid off the debt and Bobby got his truck back.

But that was the final blow. I told Jimmy I wanted out. Frankly, I wanted to tear my husband limb from limb. You don't screw with my children. You can screw with me, but not them. All my feelings for Jimmy Deen died at that moment; anything that had been left was gone. I was finished. For years I'd begged him, "Please address our problems while I still care, while I still love you, 'cause one day I'm gonna get up, and I'm gonna flatline. And once I flatline, there's no turning back."

The day I found out he'd not been sending Bobby's truck payments, I flatlined. It had been twenty-seven years, and now he was dragging us all down. But even when I filed for divorce, he never left the house. I was the one who had to leave. Jamie moved in with his college girlfriend and Bobby remained with his daddy.

Well, it only took about three or four months for Jimmy to default on making the house payments, and I got a notice that the house was being repossessed. He was finally leaving.

It was the end for the cute cheerleader from Albany High School and the handsomest guy on the planet. I had to go to the bank, catch up on all the payments, and I eventually moved back into the house. But, oh, there were lonely times to come.

. . .

My life was grim. I was working such long hours at the Best Western and I only came home to sleep for a short time. I'd lost my little Shih Tzu, Magnolia, to cancer, and her death was so devastating to me that I told myself I'd never have another dog because it hurt too much to lose her.

Still, I yearned for some company that would be around as long as I was.

I chose birds. They live a long time. I got in my car and drove to the store and bought this three-week-old blue and gold macaw. I called her Ladybird, and still have her. I brought her home in a shoe box and the bird went everywhere with me. Wherever I was in the house, if I moved from one room to the next, I had her shoe box with me. She was like my baby. Baby birds at birth have to be mouth-fed by their mommas, so I became Ladybird's momma. I fed her with this special bird pump that had a long rubber tube attached so you could put it down the bird's throat. She wouldn't eat at first, but gradually she took food from her new momma. I would pump this cereal into her and you'd immediately see her crop fill up. I didn't know anything about birds, and later I found out this was very dangerous. Even people who know birds well have killed their pets during feeding by putting the tube down the wrong pipe.

I was so alone and yearnin' for company that I let Ladybird sleep with me on my pillow after she had feathered out. One day, I went into a pet shop to get her some food, and there was this precious little yellow-tipped umbrella cockatoo named Dixie. I fell in love with her, too. One of the salesgirls said she thought she had been abused, and when I heard that I said, "Load her up. I'm taking her home with me and Ladybird."

What a nutty sight we three were! Dixie would sleep between my legs, totally covered by the comforter, and Ladybird would sleep on my pillow. I slept on my back, and I wouldn't move so that my birds would not be disturbed.

Paula, this is a sad existence, I said to myself one morning, but, never mind, those birds gave me something to come home to at the end of the day. Of course I saw the boys at work, but when the day was over, it was just the birds and me. I would bring chicken legs home to Ladybird; she just adored chicken legs. She ate everything that I ate: grilled cheese sandwiches, macaroni and cheese, grits—she was a real Southern beauty. It takes a while to marry birds together because they'll fight and seriously hurt each other, so when I went to work, I'd leave Dixie inside the cage, and I'd let Ladybird sit on top of the cage. She thought she was a free bird, an in-the-wild creature, and she let loose some pretty wild amounts of droppings. I never knew what I'd find when I came home. First, she ate the entire front of my chest of drawers. Then she would open the drawers, pull out all my pictures, and rip them up. She was a challenge, but she called me "Momma." I was a sucker for "Momma." I was the first thing she saw when she opened her little eyes and the last when we both closed down for the night.

Then the most disgusting thing I'd ever heard of, dreamed of, or guessed at happened to me. When I think of it today, I still shudder.

I didn't do anything to tend to my house; in those days, I was just walkin' around in a nervous daze and ignoring the fact that my house was now more repulsive than the old pool-hall kitchen in which I refused to cook. I put newspapers under the bottom of the birdcage, trying to catch the chewed chicken legs, the macaroni-and-cheese leftovers, the butter beans, and the impressive droppings of those two birds, but they didn't aim so good. Crap was everywhere. Half the time, I didn't bother to clean it up. I would come home and get more and more depressed about my living conditions at that house because I knew they were bad, but I couldn't help it.

One night, I arrived home very, very late from the restaurant. It was dark, and I came in and flipped on the bedroom light.

I saw a huge, black mass slowly move under my bed.

"Oh, my God," I said out loud, and lifted up the dust ruffle to see better.

What I saw was a mass of black, wiggling, shiny cockroaches, like a single lump of stuff with a million legs, all now running to-gether—now fast, now scurrying even faster. I'm not proud to be telling y'all this.

They were there under my bed feeding, and when I'd flipped on the light, they'd started to run for cover, a clump the size of a dinner plate, like a horrible science fiction creature. Listen, it took so much courage to lift that dust ruffle, and now I watched those breeding roaches disappear again in the dark underbelly of the dust ruffle and, I knew, into the bed springs. I didn't have any-where else to go, so I crawled into my bed in this roach-infested bedroom and I cried and I couldn't stop until I fell asleep.

That was my bottoming out.

I got up the next day, and I said to my mirror, "Momma and Daddy would be so hurt to know that I've sunk to this."

I went and rented me a big old truck from Budget Rental, and I had some men come in and take every bit of my furniture out and put it in that Ryder truck. I threw that mattress and box spring in the outside trash myself. I didn't want to spend the money be-cause I was trying so hard to save, but I had to go ahead and have the whole place fumigated. Then I had everything painted, the wood floors redone, and new carpet put down. That Ryder truck set out on my front yard holding all my furniture, which I sprayed, scrubbed, and scrubbed again. I bought myself a new bed. And I made a vow and said to God:

As You are my witness, I will never live like that again.

Beef Stroganoff

My family may be sick of this recipe, but you might feel differently because it's so damn good.

Unlike all the new recipes in this book, my recipe for a perfect beef stroganoff has been published before, in *Paula Deen's Kitchen Classics* (Random House, 2005). Still, this chapter called out for the exact stroganoff that my Aunty Peggy and I can no longer eat but which you will find extraordinarily yummy.

1½ pounds cubed round steak, cut into thin strips
House Seasoning (see page 96)
All-purpose flour
2 tablespoons olive oil
2 tablespoons butter
1 medium onion, sliced
8 ounces fresh mushrooms, sliced
One 10¾-ounce can condensed cream of mushroom
    soup
One 11-ounce can beef broth
1 cup sour cream
Salt and black pepper to taste
Cooked flat noodles

Season the steak strips with House Seasoning, then dust the strips with flour. In a large skillet, quickly brown them on both sides in the olive oil and butter. Remove the steak from the pan. Add the onion slices and mushrooms to the pan drippings. Cook for a few minutes, until the onion is tender, then sprinkle with 1 teaspoon flour. Put the steak back into the pan with the onion and mushrooms. Add the mushroom soup and beef broth. Cook over low heat for about 30 minutes, covered. Stir in the sour cream. Adjust seasoning to taste, adding salt and pepper as needed. Serve over cooked hot buttered flat noodles.

Serves 4

House Seasoning

> 1 cup salt
> ¼ cup black pepper
> ¼ cup garlic powder

Mix the ingredients together and store in an airtight container for up to 6 months.

Makes 1½ cups

Chapter 8

WHAT I DID FOR LOVE

I was a hardworkin' woman, looks gone, but was I truly finished? I didn't want to be by myself the rest of my life, didn't want the boys havin' to feel responsible for my happiness.

I was exhausted from The Lady, lonely and hungry for affection, disgusted from the roach attack, and, boy, was I ready to fall—either down or in love. I had been working like crazy for a year, spending but also saving money as fast as I could make it, giving orders to everyone, and in the meantime, more than once in a while, I noticed I didn't have a life.

My marriage was over and I was starved for conversation with a guy. Just to be able to sit with a nice man, talk and laugh and flirt and kind of unburden myself—that's all I wanted. Nothing serious. Wait: I'm a toucher, and I love to be held, cuddled, snuggled. It had been a long time—try twenty years. Maybe talking was not all I wanted. I was growing dry and sad and stale even as my business thrived. I was looking for love in all the wrong places.

I'd had the restaurant for almost a year when one night this man walked in just as we were getting ready to close. He was tall, with gorgeous blond hair, and he had a hearty laugh and an infectious grin. Somehow, he reminded me of my daddy—his personality, and something about his nose and forehead.

Well, we had a part-time waiter at The Lady that weekend. He knew the guy; he told me he was an engineer, and that sounded respectable. I asked the waiter to introduce us. I didn't think anything of it but, oh, I just immediately liked him. Naturally, I fed him, then sat down at the table with him as he ate, and we talked and talked, and we laughed and laughed, and it was about three in the morning when we finally got up out of that booth. It was the first intimate interaction I'd had with a man since I was divorced, and I was starved for this kind of attention. Unlike Jimmy, he listened to me. I fell head over heels in love. I didn't mention that to the guy, of course.

That first evening, he told me he was married—unhappily. He never lied and he never hid it, I'll say that for him. In fact, in the weeks to come, he would sometimes bring in his wife. I was always glad to see them; I didn't think anything about it, and after I got their meals ready, I'd go out and speak to them. Mostly I'd speak to him. She didn't seem to be interested in anything but her food. That was pretty okay with me. I don't even remember what she looked like—that's how much attention I paid to her.

One night, he came in late, by himself. I think it was a sign— at least I took it as a sign. The juices started flowing for both of us. Oh, honey, we couldn't resist each other. We arranged to meet at a local park the next day.

The first time we met away from the restaurant, we sat in the park, and again just talked for hours. The Savannah sun is heady and passionate—but maybe that was my own heat speakin'. I was feeling enormous guilt because he was married, but he convinced me the marriage had long been over in everything but name. I wanted to believe him so much. I was so needy it was pathetic. Any man who didn't call me an idiot or a bitch looked like a knight in shining armor.

It wasn't long before our relationship turned sexual and we slept together. The second time we met away from The Lady, he rented a motel room and that made me feel adventuresome, risky, so carefree and young. I was also petrified. He'd brought wine; I got drunk and became sobby. He took what he came for, got dressed without a word, walked out, and said, "Sober up."

It was my first clue that he was not an awfully nice guy.

I am ashamed to tell you I didn't write him off like a bad debt, and instead went back for more, but I promised I'd tell secrets, and this is my true story. I want it down on paper, even more than I hate for anyone to know I was ever that bad off.

You just wouldn't believe how prideless I got. Just totally prideless. I would call him and he would say he would meet me, then stand me up. I remember one night, I rented a room at the motel, and he was gonna come spend the night with me. I sat up all night in that bed, and he never showed up.

I would cook for him. I have always felt that food and cooking have a lot in common with desire. I mean the texture of certain foods, the shape of them, the way some foods melt in your mouth, or make you salivate just thinking about their texture, the fullness you feel after a good meal or good sex—well, it's not unrelated. I would cook the dishes I loved for him and get pleasure watching him eat with pleasure. He was an electrical engineer but I never thought of him in terms of his work. I never even asked him what an electrical engineer does; I only knew what he did for me and that was to give me the identity of a woman who was hungered for. The thrill of secrecy and longing didn't hurt either. So I cooked, and we made love, and I basked in my newfound feeling of being sexually attractive and my newfound shame of being with a married man.

As I write, I know that this does not sound like a lovely, sensual love affair, a mutually pleasing thing that I'm describing, and it wasn't. Instead, this is Paula atoning, Paula abasing herself, Paula apologizing to herself for all those years of allowing herself to be humiliated. But I couldn't help it. I wanted so much to be wanted.

Here's the worst part, the most embarrassing part: it went on for ten years. I sat on the sidelines of his life for that long and waited for crumbs that he'd throw me, any crumbs at all. How could I have thought so little of myself? I didn't feel like I deserved any better.

Sometimes he'd go months without calling. I called him. I debased myself deeply. Sometimes in order to get him to answer his pager, I'd have to go to a phone whose number he wouldn't recognize; he wouldn't call me back if I called him from my number. He was an accomplished torturer; I was a willing slave. Boy, he had it good. He had two women, but the wife always won out on the holidays. I spent many Christmases alone.

Thinking about it now, I understand that it wasn't the Paula I've become who lived out this humiliation. Should I write down about the money I gave him? Do I have to go into details?

Okay. I'll tell you one thing.

One night, he was waiting for me at my apartment. I'd been working particularly hard that night at the restaurant, so I ran my bathwater almost as soon as I got home and stepped into the tub. In about five minutes the door opened, he looked in, said something, and stepped out. It felt peculiar. Later that evening, I checked my wallet. Four hundred dollars was missing. I can't be sure, but I think he opened that bathroom door for one reason only—to see if I'd started my bath so he could rifle through my purse. I thought this when it happened, but I didn't say anything. Over the years, in one way or another, I gave him—or he took—thousands of dollars.

Don't judge. It could have been you. It could be you. Why not? Don't you cook like me, eat like me, talk like me (even if you're not from Savannah), think like me, love your family passionately like me? It could have been you.

Why am I telling you all this? I'm telling you because I promised you the truth. I don't want y'all to make the same mistakes. Don't ever, ever, ever get intimately involved with a married person.

I'm too embarrassed now to write more about this.

It was time to think about moving The Lady. The nonrenewable contract at the Best Western was up anyway, and I was just staying on with a month-to-month deal. The space was now too tiny for us to grow, and I had so much glorious cookin' still to do.

I had very little money but I had a huge, huge dream. I was pretty good at dreamin'.

Sexy Oxtails

What I did for love? Oh, far too much. But one thing I never did was make his-favorite-in-all-the-world dish for the man I *thought* I loved. I cooked my favorites—not his. That should have been my first clue that something was wrong: you definitely want to cook his own sensual preferences for the man you really love, and if it never came up, true love wasn't inspirin' me.

That's why it wasn't long after I met Michael (and you'll hear all about that on page 137) that I made a point of asking what his most special dish was. Oxtails, he said. They're real sexy.

Sexy oxtails? You bet. Michael's favorite dish in the whole world is my oxtails, because they're so damn good, juicy, and sexy to boot. If I tell Michael I can fix him any recipe in America, he will choose oxtails every time. He calls them swingin' sirloins. You pick them up with your hands, you gnaw the bones, lick 'em, and suck out the marrow. I got so good at gettin' that marrow out, I could suck the chrome off a trailer hitch. It is a loving dish; a hearty, lip-smacking dish; and those tails are better than a passionate kiss. Boy, you are ready for some serious lovemakin' when you're finished. All over the world people eat oxtails, but few realize it is a dish to feed a lover.

Now you can buy packages of presliced oxtails at most markets, but I carefully pick the particular grocer that carries the best fresh ones. In Savannah, there's a shop down on Martin Luther King Boulevard that carries the whole tails, and I'll have the butcher slice them on a meat slicer with a sharp blade, for me, special. I have them cut about 1½ to 2 inches thick, and the reason I like to get the whole tail is because up close to the rump, the tail is big and round before it narrows. My favorite part of the oxtail is that narrow piece. I just love the texture, which is like a very soft gristle. Love to gnaw it apart.

I trim as much of the fat off the tails as I can, season them with House Seasoning (see page 96), and lay them out in a big casserole dish. Then I sprinkle them with soy sauce—not drown them, just toss them. I cover them with sliced onions and bay leaves and just a cup of water, cover the dish with foil, and put them in a 325°F oven for about 3 hours. The hardest part is waiting the 3 hours.

When it's ready, the aroma of that wonderful, rich stock fills the house and we pile the whole dish of oxtails on top of buttered rice.

Then Michael and I are in hog heaven. We start eating them with a fork and a knife like most civilized people do, but we wind up just dipping into them, pickin' them up and chompin' into them with our teeth.

Sexiest dish in the world.

By the way, you can substitute beef short ribs for the oxtails. But I wouldn't.

Chapter 9

THE LADY & SONS

Build it and they will come.

—ADAPTED FROM THE MOVIE *FIELD OF DREAMS*

I knew I had to move on because I'd never get to be a woman of substance in that teeny, tiny Best Western space.

I had my secret heart set on a larger restaurant in downtown Savannah. Originally a port city born from the coastal wilderness in 1733, there's a story sayin' General Sherman gave Savannah to President Lincoln as a Christmas present in 1864. True or not, the city was growing, and the area I loved best to wander was the historic downtown. Even though it was still pretty much undeveloped, the architectural splendor of the fine old buildings, the magnificent parklike squares, and my own sense of "I'm home" always made me feel serene and strong at the same time.

I knew this wonderful woman, Miss Wilkes, and she owned a great boardinghouse right there downtown on Jones Street, which she opened in the early 1940s. The boardinghouse and its tiny restaurant had prospered enough to take care of four generations.

She was the same age as my grandmother, and although they never knew each other, they both made their marks in the food business when it wasn't fashionable for women to work outside the home. I just admired Miss Wilkes so much and wanted to be the next Miss Wilkes of downtown Savannah.

There was only one tiny problem: money. I had a little saved but not nearly enough to fix up a place to my satisfaction. Still, I kept my fingers crossed: money, or the lack of it, hadn't yet stopped me. Something would turn up; it always did.

Because I have a big mouth, I'd always told customers about things going on in my life and I'd become friends with many of those customers. I gabbed about my downtown fantasy, and over and over I heard that I'd better not go to the downtown area—a single woman could be stomped on, held up by robbers—anything could happen. Still, I knew I belonged in a restaurant among the historic buildings of what had become my beloved city.

In 1991, when I started The Lady in the Best Western, there was a new movie in the theaters that everyone just adored. It was called *Field of Dreams* and it starred Kevin Costner as an Iowa corn farmer in love with the memory of a long-dead baseball team and his hero, "Shoeless" Joe Jackson; the farmer was searching for his dreams—and one day his dream came looking for him. He heard an otherworldly voice that told him to build a baseball diamond in his cornfields and Joe and the dear departed Chicago Black Sox team would come back to play.

"Build it and he will come," said the voice, and they did.

Well, *build it and they will come* was my theory also, in my case, *it* being a fabulous restaurant, and *they* being a million hungry tourists.

One day, my dream came looking for me—just like in the movie—and he walked into my restaurant.

Mike Brown was a building developer. He hadn't been in town very long, but he used to come into The Lady and we always enjoyed a good gossip as I fed him. He strongly believed that down-town Savannah, then pretty run-down, was a potential gold mine. It was in part from our talks that I started yearning to be there in a business of my own. Mike had started to buy up properties in the area, and he'd recently rented a building at 311 West Congress Street. That afternoon, Mike had his lunch and told me to meet him downtown the next morning at the corner of Congress and Montgomery streets. When I arrived, I found him leaning on the building on the corner. He crossed his arms and just nodded to-ward the building across the street.

"I'll take it," I said, and consummated the deal with a hand-shake.

Now, you have to know that all my life a lot of people have worried about me because they say I make rash decisions. Fact is, I rely on my intuition and my gut feelings, and I've rarely been wrong. But this one even I knew was a stretch.

The empty building he indicated had been Barnett's Educa-tional Supply House, built in 1910, and it was located between two of Savannah's best restaurants, which were well established in the area. Well, Barnett's had closed down and I immediately saw that it was only purely logical that Mike's leased building should house another of Savannah's marvelous restaurants. It took me less than a minute to visualize a new Restaurant Row. I was certainly aware that many local people still didn't want to venture down-town to dine: those empty streets were pretty desolate, and besides the two restaurants, there wasn't much else. But three restaurants? That could change the equation. The place looked perfect—just big enough for me—but it sure was in desperate need of TLC, and maybe the most expensive tender loving care the area had ever seen. I walked around it, checking out the area and the building. It needed serious work: appliances, furniture, *everything*.

Mike again stressed that he didn't own the building; he just leased it and was looking for a twelve-year sublease. Any alterations or improvements I would make to the space had to be on my dime.

Twelve years! Could I afford it? Of course not.

I signed the contract.

God, was I naïve! I had no idea how I'd get the cash. I knew my expenses for rent would increase substantially, and Mike figured that the building would cost a lot of money in renovations before we could open as a restaurant. How much exactly, he didn't know, but a lot, he thought. *A lot* was an understatement.

Paula, I said to myself, *you're an insane optimist. Where the hell do you think you're going to get that kind of money?* Well, I'd saved about $20,000. It took me five years. I would have had more if I hadn't given money to that crumb bun man I mentioned awhile back. What I did for what I thought was love . . . but never mind about that.

First stop, the bank, where I was informed that $20,000 was definitely, positively, not enough even to put down as collateral for the rest I'd have to borrow. Nothing had been done to the building in about a hundred years; it was in horrible condition. During the next week, I sent out for some professional renovation estimates and finally they came in: $150,000 was the most conservative guess. That was about a zillion dollars to me. Had to think, had to think.

Then I did about the stupidest thing you can imagine. I went ahead and told my landlord at the Best Western that I'd found another place and I would be moving in a few months.

"Wrong, Paula," he said. "You're moving *now*. And you owe me for the rest of last month, plus this month." He kicked me out that minute. Couldn't do a thing; I was on a month-to-month lease.

I was a mess. All I could do was pack up my things and move them all back to the East Sixtieth Street house. I'd try catering again like I did when I was just The Bag Lady.

"You can't do this," Bobby told me. "You're paying rent at the Best Western and also rent for the new building now. We're in way over our heads. Try to get out of the new lease; maybe Mike will be kind."

Tell me I can't do something, and I can usually juggle chain saws, but this one was stumping me. Still, I had a stubbornness rooted in anger—anger that I was poor and alone with two kids, anger that it was all up to me. I simply had to figure out where I could get the money to fix up the new building so I could have a restaurant. In the meantime, I was back to where The Bag Lady had started.

When I first started at the Best Western, a wonderful woman named Dora Charles had fallen into my life. I was doing so much catering out the back door then, and was literally about to drop. Dora came in and interviewed for a job as a cook, and I remember asking her the very first question, "How long have you lived where you are?" And when she said, "All my life," I said, "You're hired." I knew that the woman had character and she had roots. Anybody who had lived in the same house all that time was not a quitter. I was right. So during this awful time when I was catering jobs after I'd left the Best Western and while I was waiting to hear if any bank would lend me the money for the new restaurant, Dora would come over and help me. If I lost Dora, I would have been devastated. If I had a big catering job that I couldn't handle alone, Dora came in and I'd pay her so she could keep a little money in her pockets till opening day of the restaurant.

I remember I had a catering job for a Christmas party at a private club. It gave me the opportunity to make things pretty—not just good-tasting—and I was so glad to be able to get creative. I had made all these wonderful hors d'oeuvres—like little new potatoes, hollowed out and stuffed with a salmon cream cheese. The best thing was that I'd bought a Styrofoam Christmas tree and had just so carefully wrapped it in lettuces and all these vegetables that I'd cut just perfectly in little Christmasy shapes. When it came time to deliver the food, I put this precious tree right up in the front seat of my car. My soul sister, Dora, was following in her car because we had so much food and it all didn't fit in my car. Dora always took such pride in what she did and I remember we were running late, and I said, "Dora, we gotta go! We gotta go!"

We set this big old silver tray of potatoes up in the back of my Lincoln Continental that had no paint on the hood. It was drizzling rain, and we were in a hurry. I was going down Eisenhower Drive, and all of a sudden the car in front of me stopped short. I had to get that Continental under control, which I did, but when I looked up into my rearview mirror, there was Dora. *Bam!* She hit me, the potatoes came flying over my head and hit the windshield. My beautiful tree snapped in two, vegetables flew everywhere. I ran back to Dora's car and said, "Dora, we ain't got time to file no accident report, it's just you and me, so let's try to repair this damage, fast." We had to try to somehow bend the tree back together, and we sure lost a lot of potatoes. We were crying so hard, we sounded like cows that had been cut.

We got to the party and managed to patch up most of the food, so no one noticed any problem. Then we snuck out to the club's kitchen and collapsed into each other's arms. Dora's very emotional, even more than I am. I mean, she can cry something awful, and we cried through the whole party. I remember saying, "Well, we'll never get this business ever again," but, you know what? When The Lady & Sons finally opened, many of the people at that Christmas party became our best customers. That day I learned the art of putting the best face on trouble, and it works. Most of the time.

But now I was trying to raise money for collateral so I could open the restaurant of my dreams, The Lady & Sons. Every which way

I turned with the first bank I went to was a dead end. They wouldn't help me out of my predicament. I remember going to Coastal Bank and they played me along for weeks saying they thought they could help me, until they called and said, "Sorry, we can't take the risk with you." Then I went to First Union Bank and was told I had to talk to a man named Doug McCoy. Doug gave me a tiny glimmer of hope. There was a chance, he thought. I was desperate and clung to that chance.

I felt so hopeless because I knew that if the bank didn't come through, there was only one option left—and I hated the idea of it like poison. There were a couple of tough businessmen in Savannah who'd often told me they'd like to be partners with me. Each time I heard that, warning bells went off in my head. I knew it wouldn't work; I was concerned that they would just use my growing good reputation, have me work myself to death, and then take most of the profit. Now, having heard I'd signed an expensive lease, they were circling me like sharks in the water. I knew I would be no good with a partner I didn't trust with my life. Still, I was almost to the point where I had to consider it when Doug Mc-Coy called to say maybe I could go through the Small Business Administration and put together a package with a loan from his bank. Problem was that his bank needed twenty-five thousand dollars in addition to the twenty thousand I had already saved as collateral in order for the bank to lend me money for the renovation. It was twenty-five thousand I sure didn't have.

So it seemed the Small Business Administration wouldn't hop aboard. The businessmen circled closer.

During all this time, I'd been talking and moaning and groaning to my Aunt Peggy and Uncle George Ort every day. I knew they felt so bad for me. They offered the most loving sympathy.

One day, I got very tired. I could feel a depression setting in; it was a terribly familiar feeling. I got up, did a catering job, and then went back to my bed. For a week, I dragged myself around but spent most of my time in bed. There just seemed no use to my fighting for this location because there was only one bit of bad news after another.

I recognized that particular kind of exhaustion, that particular kind of dread.

It didn't help that Jamie had moved to Atlanta to start a new life for himself. He was just so ready, so eager, to get away from me and the business. He could not run fast enough. He would have rather starved to death in Atlanta—which is what he was doing at a job paying less than sixty bucks a week.

Bobby was unemployed because I'd taken him away from his job in sales to work for The Bag Lady. I needed him to deliver the corporate lunch catering jobs, which he despised. He was renting a room from a couple of his friends; he'd come pick up the catered lunches when I was done making them, deliver them, and I'd give him a portion of the money when I got paid.

We were living hand to mouth once again. And agoraphobia was creeping back into my life, slowly, slowly.

One day, when I was close to the end of my endurance, Uncle George called with more than sympathy.

"Paula," he quietly said, "your Aunt Peggy is fixin' to loan you the money you need."

That's Southern roots. I was not her biological child but I was hers, anyway. Aunt Peggy knew I was being pushed into a terrible corner and I'd have to give up everything I worked for in the last seven years. She believed in me and was willing to put her money where her mouth was. She and Uncle George came over that night and brought with them a certificate of deposit for twenty-five thousand dollars—exactly how much I was short for collateral for the bank loan that would let me start renovating the building. They put up that CD and saved my life; they saved all our lives. My Aunt Peggy gave me more than money—she gave me a choice. I didn't have to kowtow to any businessman and just take what some stranger would be willing to throw my way because it was a good deal for him. I could be self-sufficient and stand on my own two feet.

I will never forget: here I was, scared and powerless, and that was the exact moment when my Aunt Peggy told me she was so proud of me. "I know a winner when I see one," she said.

Oh, I will never forget. The depression flew out the window and I was back in business!

It crushed me so bad that I had to be helped that way, but I vowed it would be the last time I was ever in that position. Well, don't you know that not only did Aunt Peggy's CD money earn her the regular interest because it was still in the bank (only in my name), but I also paid her double that interest. She was making three times as much as she made before she lent me the CD. Aside from having the greatest heart on the planet, my Aunt Peggy is a shrewd businesswoman. It was a good deal for her, she said, and she trusted me to make her whole again, financially. We were family, weren't we?

I would have eaten dog poop and barked at the moon before I didn't get that CD back to her, plus the double interest while the bank held it as collateral for me. I'd do whatever it took to make it work. In only one year, actually, I built up our account so much that the bank felt comfortable in releasing that CD back to me, and Aunt Peggy.

But money was still so tight, so tight. Bobby and I couldn't even bear to watch the renovations as they started; it was too painful and too scary. Finally, I saw the light at the end of a great darkness—we were really going to get it done.

After that, every single day I didn't have a private catering job I came downtown to watch my restaurant grow during the year it took to get the job done. I'd take bologna and bread so Bobby and I could have sandwiches at lunchtime.

In those days—now we're talking 1995—it was like I was

wearing blinders. I was a one-vision gal—a single woman with two children trying to survive—and I didn't allow myself to mentally move out of my own little world. I'm ashamed to tell you this, but I still didn't know, nor did I care about, anything else that was happening in the United States, Europe, or Africa. It was my way: if I didn't concentrate on what I needed to do I'd be distracted from my way.

It happened to be the year O. J. Simpson was on trial for murder, 168 people were killed when a federal building in Oklahoma City was destroyed, and everyone was talking about the Unabomber. I hardly noticed. Closer to home that year, the Carolina Panthers beat the New York Jets, and in Virginia, Christopher Reeve was paralyzed in a riding accident, ending his career as Superman.

I wasn't really connected to any of it. I was working too hard on being Superwoman, or, at the very least, Miss Wilkes.

Even watching the new restaurant get rebuilt was stressful—and expensive. I was driving a used-up old Lincoln Continental that I'd bought from my ex-husband, who was back selling cars in Albany. At first I was so proud of that car, but I didn't have it long before the darned engine burned off all the paint on the hood. *Not* a good look. I would park downtown to oversee the renovations as best as I could, but some days I literally did not have parking-meter money. To add a little more misery, I had an expired registration on the car and couldn't afford to buy a new tag. Every time I got a parking ticket (and I got plenty!), I also got an extra fifty-dollar ticket for the expired tag. Before that restaurant was finished, I owed the city well over a thousand dollars in tickets that I simply didn't have the money to pay off.

It was a year of downtime with literally no income but what my catering business brought in. As the construction dragged on, I became poorer with each passing day. One day Bobby came to me and said, "Momma, I'm real hungry but we have zip money."

It was true. We had none, none at all. It was then I thought of a little change box I'd stowed away and, with Bobby following close behind, we went to check it out. Sifting through the coins, my heart stopped: there at the bottom of the box was a fifty-dollar bill I'd hidden for a rainy day. The rain was coming down but the sun was shining! Bobby and I laughed our heads off, then quickly headed to McDonald's and ordered two number-three Value Meals.

As for Jamie, Atlanta had not turned out to be everything that he had thought. I said, "Well, son, we've got the building, and Bobby and I are going to open this fabulous restaurant downtown and we're going to call it The Lady & Son." My heart about stopped when, one day, my older boy told me he'd thought about it and realized he had to be with his mother and his brother. Jamie came back, and Bobby and I were ecstatic. Now the restaurant would become The Lady & Sons, in honor of my boys.

Before we opened I had to deal with hiring a staff. I was the main cook, of course, but now we also needed some trusted professional help.

When we finally got The Lady & Sons open, there was Dora, of course, Jamie, Bobby, me, and a young man whom I will love forever like he was my third son—Rance Jackson. I'll never forget the day he came into our lives. We had a cardboard table set up in the restaurant, and Rance, who had been a cook in the army, came in to apply for a job as a cook. I was on the phone but I was watching this young man talk to my sons, who told him we didn't need any more cooks—and I watched him walk out. Just as soon as I could get away from what I was doing, I asked Jamie, "Who was that young man and what job did he apply for?" Jamie said, "Don't know who he is but he wants to be a restaurant cook."

"Chase him down. Go get that young man," I said.

I'd seen pure goodness in his eyes. I can always tell about people. So my two boys hauled ass running down that street to catch Rance and they brought him back and we hired him on the spot.

Our projected opening date kept getting moved back, and moved back, and moved back. My dream was to open by St. Patrick's Day, 1995; then I said if we can open in September 1995, it will be all right. When that didn't happen, I remember saying if we can open in November and get some Christmas business, we'll still be all right. Well, everything just drug out, and drug out, and drug out. We were still living on my catering jobs out of the house—I had one almost every day. But it was like God was trying to tell me it was time to move on: the day after Christmas, all the calls for catering just stopped. It was like someone turned off a faucet. How would we have lived if we didn't have the new restaurant opening? I don't know. I only know that God was on my side.

Nobody called me for another catering job, and we opened the restaurant on January 8, 1996.

My children didn't want me to open for dinner. They wanted us to come in, serve lunch, and get out. Well, disaster almost struck that very first day. It wouldn't be a Paula Deen melodrama if everything went off smooth as butter. So here's a memory that sticks in my craw like a chicken bone; I don't ever open the doors to my restaurant today without thinking of it.

Early on January 8, the place was a madhouse, with us getting ready to meet and greet the world in the brand-new Lady & Sons. The telephone rang about ten in the morning, around forty-five minutes before opening time. It was my dear friend and accountant, Karl Schumacher. Karl's the most moral man you could ever hope to meet; I know his momma must be so proud of him. You know, I'm not the brightest bulb in the bunch, but I've had enough sense to hire people who are smarter than me.

"Paula, we have got to talk. We are in terrible trouble here," said Karl.

I was running around like a wild woman trying to get this restaurant open at eleven, trying to think of everything. I mean, I was *insane* running around, no makeup. I just looked like hell, and was trying so hard to get everything done, and trying to teach this little staff how serious it all was, no less than life or death, and if they were going to help me, they had no choice but to do it right. But Karl quietly said, "Paula, both your bank accounts are overdrawn."

He was talking about my business and my construction accounts—I didn't even *have* a personal account to be overdrawn. I said, "Karl, we're like forty-five minutes away from opening. Please just give me an opportunity to get this restaurant open."

When I hung up the phone with Karl, my heart in my mouth, I happened to look in the cash register.

"Well, just kick me running naked," I groaned, because I saw that I had no money at all to make change. I couldn't have made change for five dollars.

Lovely. Real professional.

I turned around and picked up the phone, and I called my banker friend Doug. Since I was only a little fish in the bank's big pond of big-shot customers, Doug had turned me over to a junior associate, the most precious young black man named Eric. Doug got Eric on the phone for me.

"I know my accounts are overdrawn, Eric," I said, "but I've got a terrible, terrible, problem. I'm opening in about thirty minutes, and I don't have a plug nickel. Would you and the bank please let me cash a really bad check for two hundred dollars?"

And, without missing a beat, Eric said, "Paula, we have not come with you this far to stop you now. Come get your two-hundred-dollar start-up change."

We finally opened at eleven AM and I could make change for people.

If any people came. I had no money for advertising. We hadn't served anyone in a restaurant in almost a year and there was no way I could have let my former patrons know that we were opening up in the new location.

We built it—and they came. Somehow, seventy-six of my old customers showed up—most of them people I had served at the Best Western. The boys and I spent the whole entire lunch on the floor out there with the guests, hugging them and crying and thanking them for not forgetting us and for supporting our efforts. I'd run back and forth from the kitchen to the dining room to try to make sure everything was just perfect for those perfect jewels, those old friends and customers.

I'm proud to say that I've never been overdrawn since. It took me only a few weeks to get enough money to get those accounts back up and running. I learned a lesson: you have to have faith in people. What would I have done had no one had faith in me?

And the food was glorious and good. And Southern. I would work the buffet with Dora. Bobby was great with people and so he worked the front of the house, greeting the customers he knew and especially the ones he didn't know. Rance turned out to be everything that I saw in his eyes; he, Dora, and Jamie were doin' most of the actual cooking, with my direction. Jamie was a line cook, and to watch him on the line was a beautiful thing. A line cook is up there on the cook line of stoves, griddles, and deep fryers, doing the frying, grilling, and baking—just as you'd think. It's a dance, an orchestration, a ballet. Jamie and Rance would station themselves back there, laughing and flipping the hoe cakes, and they became dear friends. I just loved watching those two cook together. They could turn and burn like no one else.

Well, word of mouth brought local people in. Then the tourists found us. On the south side, we didn't know what a tourist was. We would have the most fabulous time out there on that restaurant floor with everybody laughing and enjoying the food. I felt so blessed and fortunate. I was given the opportunity to become victorious.

That's the good news.

I'm here to tell you what excruciatingly hard work it all was. If I thought working at The Lady was tough, I had no idea what was in store for me here in my very own place. There was, by the way, no Food Network television crew back there making everything come out smooth and in duplicates. The hours were impossibly long, and frankly, I was the control freak of the world. My method of teaching somebody was, "Give it to me, let me do it. *Give it to me now, damn it.*" Deep inside, I felt like if I ever allowed anybody else to touch my menus, my pots and pans, my sauces, my refrigerator, my stove, it could never possibly be right because I was the only one capable of achieving perfection—and I wouldn't settle for anything less in my dream come true—a real restaurant of my own. Of course, Jamie and Rance and Dora and Bobby were terrific—but still, I was in everybody's pots. I was at everybody's station. I was taking orders and delivering plates to tables. I had my eye on every speck of food that was produced. I criticized everything.

Would you have liked to work with me? No? That's what I thought. Neither did my sons. But whatever was necessary to complete the mission is what I wanted to do. Some people call Southern women steel magnolias to show our unfailing survival instinct. Well, if we got dimples of steel, so what. Things have to be right.

A long time ago, I'd decided we'd only serve Southern cooking. My roots were Southern, and I had to be true to myself. I always believed the old saying "Do what you know." I couldn't have pretended I was some European chef. I would have made an ass of myself. But I knew I was a Southern cook, with Southern plantation cuisine my specialty, and couldn't nobody trick me there. So, that's what I had to do.

Fried chicken, for example, was always on the buffet, and we always had a second meat that would change daily. The other meat choice could be meat loaf, it could be country fried steak and gravy, it could be pot roast, it could be fried or baked pork chops. There were a few menu items written in stone: fried chicken, macaroni and cheese, and collard greens. Those three things would never change. Why? We listened to our customers, and we found that they wanted to know every time they came in that those three were going to be on the buffet menu. They also wanted rice and gravy. They would have killed you for my pan-fried corn. They loved the squash casserole and the broccoli casserole. And then we started putting sweet potatoes on the buffet. Well, Lord have mercy!

Our menu now almost never changes because we still know what our customers want, even though we may get tired of looking at it and cooking it. There's not an Italian in the whole damn kitchen, but we absolutely make the best baked spaghetti you ever put in your mouth. Our lasagna will make ya tongue want to slap ya brains out. It's got chunks of cream cheese all in it, and people are just not expecting that. So delicious! And don't forget the biscuits and the hoe cakes.

Probably one of the biggest questions asked by non-Southerners is what's a hoe cake? The answer is pan-fried corn bread. We use cornmeal, flour, eggs, and oil. It looks like a regular pancake, and it tastes like a corn pancake. Once, I did some research and traced the origins back to the Native Americans because corn was a big part of their diet. But folktales have it that when the field hands would come in from the fields, they would cook this corn bread over an open fire on a hoe. Not a "ho." We ain't talkin' about that girl on the corner!

Of course, we added baked chicken to the fried chicken because there are always those tourists who want to watch their intake of fried goods. We can always make concessions for the health-conscious by doing things like using smoked turkey wings to add flavor to our beans and greens instead of ham hocks, and we do. But you know what? Turkey wings aren't the same as ham hocks. Baked chicken can't hold a candle to the fried. Seems to me a better approach for weight watchers would be to look at Southern food as a treat.

You know, sometimes I get kidded about my love for the ingredient that strikes terror into the heart of so many—butter. To paraphrase *Saturday Night Live*, which maintains that Barbra Streisand is so delicious *she's like buttah,* I always have known that *buttah is bettah.* Because so many people are afraid of butter (and sour cream and cream cheese), I have to have a sense of humor about it or end up defending my choices every day. One day I 'bout fell off my chair laughing when I read New York comedienne Sara Schaefer's idea of a "Paula Deen recipe" on an Internet blog. I thought it was so funny, I want to share it with you.

Sara said, "I have made many successful Paula Deen recipes. I love her personality as well. I love that she is an independent, strong woman who maintains her grace, humility and kindness. She knows what life is all about—and she knows how to make it taste good. So it pains me to say this, but sometimes she crosses the line. Her recipes often look like this:

"Butter, for greasing pan
2 cups butter
1½ cups butter oil
¼ cup butter juice
3 cups all-purpose butter
1 teaspoon baking butter
3 cups peeled and finely chopped butter
1 cup shredded butter
1 pinch butter, for taste

"Preheat the oven to 325 degrees F. Generously grease a tube pan.

"For the cake: In a large bowl, combine the butter, butter oil, butter juice, and baking butter; and mix well. Fold butter, butter, and butter into batter. Pour the batter into the prepared pan and bathe in it until you go into cardiac arrest."

So, despite the butter, probably because of the butter, we prospered mightily at The Lady & Sons, and we didn't even have one case of cardiac arrest. Also, it didn't hurt when on a pretty day in 1999, Jerry Shriver, a food and travel writer for *USA TODAY,* came in with a bunch of guests. At the time, I had no idea who he was, but he and his friends were so adorable, so smiley, so appreciative of everything we brought them, that the whole staff fell in love with this group. They gobbled down lunch like it was the last one they'd ever have.

And then whoa, what good news! In the December 19 issue of *USA TODAY,* Jerry honored our restaurant as the one in which he enjoyed the "Most Memorable Meal" of the year, putting us at number one over restaurants in Paris, Chicago, Rome, and New York City. Me—the Albany cheerleader!

The lines grew to three times around the block.

I was given an honor by the Georgia Senate for bringing so much economic health into the state, and when I gave them my thank-you speech, the only thing I really wanted to say was, "I know my momma and daddy are watching today, and somewhere they're spinning, 'cause you don't know how many bad report cards they had to sign for me."

In many ways, *I* was spinning, still the little girl with the crummy report card. Here's a confession: with all the glamour of my life, in my heart I still feel a little like The Bag Lady. No, I ain't poor no more. But remember that first two hundred dollars I started with? Often, even today, it seems like that's really all the money I have. My brain knows it's not true, but in my heart, I worry that nothing real good ever lasted for long in my life. Now, that's stinkin' thinkin'. Often I have a sense of danger that follows me everywhere. I don't trust good fortune all that much.

And at the time The Lady & Sons was just peaking, my heart was so empty, it sure didn't feel like good fortune lived there.

Grandmomma's Fried and Steamed Chicken

At The Lady & Sons, our signature dish is, of course, the mouthwaterin' fried chicken. Here's a secret, though: I learned to make fried chicken from my grandmomma, who made it a little different because she both steamed *and* fried the chicken. I had to modify the recipe for the restaurant because it was impossible to both steam and fry each piece for hundreds of people every day.

Here is Grandmomma Paul's original recipe (with my own House Seasoning added), which I think she learned from her one and only mentor, Mrs. Henrietta Dull.

> *3 eggs*
> *House Seasoning (see page 96)*
> *2 cups all-purpose flour*
> *1½- to 2-pound chicken, cleaned and cut up*
> *Crisco or vegetable oil for frying (deep enough to cover*
> *the chicken)*

In a shallow bowl, beat the eggs with ⅓ cup water. In another bowl, add a pinch of House Seasoning to the flour. Roll each piece of chicken in the egg, then roll in the seasoned flour. My Grandmomma Paul used to always return the seasoned chicken to the refrigerator and let it sit there for about 2 hours before actually cooking it. Remove the chicken from the refrigerator, heat the shortening to 375°F in a frying pan—or, even better, in a Dutch oven—and put the largest pieces and dark meat in first followed immediately by the smaller pieces of white meat chicken. Cook, covered, for 5 minutes. Remove the cover and turn the chicken when the undersides are well browned. Cook, covered, for another 5 minutes. Remove the cover and cook until the chicken is well browned. The entire chicken will take about 20 to 25 minutes to cook. Don't turn the chicken more than once or else some of the extraordinarily fine flavor will be lost.

Chapter 10

SHARING RECIPES

I refuse to believe that sharing recipes from a
good cookbook or yo' momma's kitchen is silly.
The best butter beans do just as much good in
the world as peace talks.

As our business at The Lady & Sons grew, I had what
some told me was a crazy idea. I wanted to write a
cookbook. To cook good, you need a recipe. People kept asking
for my recipes and I'd kid around and say, "I'd love to share them
with you, but I'm goin' to keep them for my own book when I
write it."

Stay in the kitchen, do what you do best, don't be writing no
books; that's what I heard when I mentioned my idea. To be honest, I kind of agreed. Who would be interested in my dishes except
for the folks that ate at my restaurant? I could sell maybe ten to
twenty copies of a cookbook in a good month, I figured. Then I
refigured.

It could put us on the local map. If it worked—a big *if*—it could lead to other stuff. Maybe I could get a couple of Philadel-phians or Chicagoans into my restaurant, and maybe even a few more New York tourists. Good deal, and what fun. I really would write a cookbook.

I remembered the first cookbook I ever had; as a matter of fact, I've still got it, lovingly stained by a thousand different meals. *Better Homes and Gardens* put it out, and it was a red-and-white-checked number bound like my school notebook. When I was eighteen, Toni Nix, one of my mother's best friends, gave it to me at my wedding shower. You always remember the first boy you kiss and you always remember the person who gave you your first cookbook.

Since we were doing so well on Congress Street, and I'd gotten those bank accounts out of the red, I set my next goal and it was to be a Lady & Sons cookbook.

I would publish it myself, I decided. How else did books get published? In hindsight, I can tell you that it never dawned on me that there were giant publishing companies whose business was making books and distributing and selling them all over the world. I only knew that whatever I had, I'd gotten it by hard work, and I'd done it pretty much by myself. That's how I would publish a cookbook for the people who'd enjoyed the meals I served up in my restaurant. I knew it would take some money to get it done so I started saving toward this next goal—and luckily, for the first time in my life, the money was coming in pretty fast.

Someone told me about a lady who had her own desktop pub-lishing business. I was definitely computer-illiterate; I wasn't even close to buying one, let alone learning how to work one of those darn things. This nice lady and I connected and she sent out re-quests for bids to print the book. Well, wouldn't you just know it, I was thrilled to pieces when the bids came back and a little print-ing company on the next block down the street came in at the low-est bid. We could keep my money right here at home in Savannah.

The lowest bid wasn't so low—about twenty thousand dollars—but I was determined to go through with it, and I'd saved the money.

Was it hard to write? Let me tell you, that first cookbook was so stinkin' easy to write, it was unbelievable. I just went to my mother's brown paper sack and got all the recipes out that had been handwritten by the women in my family down the generations. Then I sent it to my new friend, who typed it out all nice and pretty. I called it *Favorite Recipes from The Lady and Her Friends*.

I decided that I wanted my cookbook to be fun. Cartoons were fun. Someone told me about Geri, this girl at the *Savannah News Press* who drew cartoons, and I asked her to do a cartoon of me and Aunt Peggy making gingerbread men who were six feet two with eyes of blue. I contacted friends and asked for their best recipes, and after each one I wrote a little story about that friend's connection to me. I just had a blast with that little book.

Finally, it came time to take the disk to the printer, and I asked how many we should print, and the answer was that a thousand would be more than enough.

"Well," I asked, "how much would one thousand cost and how much for five thousand?" Turned out five thousand was much cheaper per copy.

"I want five thousand," I told them.

My friends said, "Paula, no! That's insane. You're screwing up already by overordering."

Well, I failed in math, but not in logic and risk taking. I went for the five thousand.

The boys knew I was working on the book, and gradually they were getting as excited as I was. One day, the print shop called Jamie and said, "We've got three books ready, hot off the press. Want to come and see them?"

Did we! On the way, walking down the street holding hands, Jamie said, "Betcha fifty bucks you're gonna cry!"

I said, "I'll bet you fifty bucks I ain't! I'm so glad to be shed of this book."

He took about three more steps, then stopped again and said, "I'll bet you one hundred bucks you're gonna cry." Right there in the middle of the street we turned to each other and shook hands. I said, "I ain't goin' to be cryin', son."

We went into the printer and they handed us the books. When we opened the book we smeared the ink—it was that fresh off the printin' press. Jamie said, "Turn to page four."

It was a tribute to me from my sons. Now, I never left my business for anything, but that day I had to go home and go to bed, that minute. This is how page four read:

> *Our mother, Paula H. Deen, is a true symbol of strength and perseverance. This book is a product of her twenty-four-hour workdays. It is her third "child" and she has nourished and cherished this book just as she has cared for her two sons, in a way only a mother could do. This book spans many years and many jobs, from homemaker to bank teller to restaurant owner; our mom's dreams for the future have come true.*
>
> *Thanks to our mother, these are now the best days of our lives. We have more pride in this lady than can possibly be imagined. She has our undying adoration and our commitment to follow in her direction. Mother is a remarkable lady. We hope you enjoy her wonderful cookbook.*
>
> *We love you, Mom.*
> *Jamie and Bobby*

Jamie won his bet. I cried like a bloomin' cow. I don't think I've ever read the tribute but one more time since because it makes me bawl wildly every time I lay eyes on those words.

My children and I had been having such a hard time with our relationship because I was such a slave driver. I didn't care about anything except survival. Of course, they were older than I was when I lost my parents, but I didn't want them to suffer the devastation I bore if something ever happened to me. I wanted them to cry, then laugh, and, most important, carry on everything we had built together.

Honestly? I thought I had done permanent damage to our relationships. I had said things out of anger that I didn't mean, but still I knew they wouldn't forget those harsh words. Then to see that they understood, and they still loved me? That page in the book meant everything to me.

The next day I set the cookbook out on the credenza in the dining room of the restaurant.

Just as I thought, there were some exciting things finally beginning to happen in downtown Savannah. John Berendt had written his wildly successful book *Midnight in the Garden of Good and Evil,* and Clint Eastwood had come to town to make the film. It was very exciting to see all these cameras shooting all over our city. Some of the old Savannahians, the blue bloods of Savannah, might not have liked the book because it brought so many curiosity seekers and tourists, but it did so much for the city's economy. I will forever be grateful to John Berendt for writing his book, and then for later writing the introduction to my book.

So, here was my humble little book settin' out on a table. It sold for $16.95. We sold about twenty-five copies in the first month. We had 4,975 left to go.

One day a violent rain came up just out of the blue, and a woman from New York just happened to be walking down the street with her boyfriend. When she got to my place it started lightning and thundering. The woman stopped into my restaurant to get in out of the rain. She had never heard of me, the restaurant had not been recommended to her.

Ever hear of a word called synchronicity? It means a coincidence that is too meaningful, too wonderful, to be just coincidence. It happens when seemingly unrelated things are linked together and create an extraordinary other thing. I think the fact that I had a cookbook just sitting there, dying to be read by millions, and a rainstorm and a woman who could change my life all just happened to be in the same place at the same time—well, God was making sure Paula had a whole lot of synchronicity working that day.

Her name was Pamela Cannon. I didn't know it then, but she happened to be an editor from a New York publishing company called Random House; she'd been in town because of John Berendt's book, which had been published by Random House. I served her and her boyfriend chicken and biscuits and hoe cakes. She was the publishing girl, I was the hoe-and-biscuit girl. She did not tell me then who she was, but I spoke to her and her boyfriend and welcomed them as I did all my other guests, and went on with my work.

This is the funniest damn thing. One day soon after the rainstorm, the phone rang. It was Pamela Cannon. She said, "You don't remember me, I was in the restaurant a couple of weeks ago to have lunch, and the lunch was quite delicious. Did I see a cookbook in there?"

Thinking fast, I said, "My goodness, yes! My little book's been out only a month and it's doing so good."

Good was twenty-five copies.

She said, "Well, I did not buy one, but if I give you an American Express card number over the phone, can you send me a few copies?"

I said, "I'd just be delighted to do that for you."

I hung up the phone and went and found Jamie. I said, "Jamie, I just got a call. Do you know what Random House is?"

Jamie looked at me, and he shook his head and said, "You cannot be my momma. Momma, Random House is one of the top three publishing houses in the country. What did she want?"

"Copies of the cookbook," I answered.

You could see the color draining from his face. He literally ran and got three cookbooks, and he ran to Mail Boxes Etc. and got them in the mail within twenty minutes after her call.

"Well, we'll probably never hear any more about that," I told him.

I was wrong. Pamela Cannon called again, and she said, "Hey, Paula, I just want to say congratulations. Your cookbook has merit, and Random House would like to publish it."

I remember when we got that call. I was sitting there in the dining room with Jamie. It was around 5:45, and we only opened up at night for private parties, so we knew how much food to cook, and how much money we were bringing in. Jamie was the waiter that day, and I was the only cook because it was at night, and I had let all the staff go home. Everything was ready. We were just waiting for the people to get there. We had flickering candles on all the tables.

After that the phone call, I started jumping up and down, and Jamie and I hugged and kissed and danced all around that dining room floor.

Random House was going to pay me an advance of five thousand dollars. To myself, I thought, *Oh, my gosh, that's a lot of money*, but by that time I had *businesswoman* written in my heart, so I got up the guts to call New York and say, "Pamela, that is going to be very hard for me to accept—just five thousand dollars."

I was so afraid I was going to blow the deal and they'd tell me to go screw myself. "Call you back," she told me.

Well, she called back and said, "Okay, your advance is seventy-five hundred dollars, and that's as high as we're going. That's the deal—take it or leave it."

I said, "I'll take it."

In the contract, they had given me until March 31 to sell the books I had in stock because my little self-published book should not be there to compete with the new edition. I didn't know how I'd manage that, but, you will not believe this, on March 31 we sold the last book. A girl walked over from the *Savannah News Press* and bought the last one.

And you know what? I wish I could buy every one of them back. There was one for sale on eBay a month or so back that sold for like $271.

It was so easy to write that first cookbook because I had no food police and no publisher police doggin' my steps. I'd say, "Cover some bones with water, bring it to a boil," and I'd never say how many bones, or exactly how much water. I'd say, "Put in a can of cream of celery soup," and never mention how big a can.

But the Random House version took one whole year to rewrite. It was so much harder. The wording had to be specific. The amount of ingredients down to the last grain of sugar had to be so freakin' exact. Pamela told me I had to assume that the person who was going to use the recipe had never before walked into a kitchen. Does that sound logical to you?

I came to know she was right because one day around eleven-thirty in the morning, the lunch crowd was about to come in and I was so busy in the kitchen, but Bobby told me there was an urgent phone call for me. The lady was desperate and I had to take it, he said.

"Miss Paula," said a voice I didn't recognize. "I'm truly sorry to bother you while your restaurant's open but I'm having the hardest time trying to make this squash casserole from your cookbook recipe. I want to make it so bad but I can't figure it out. I keep taking the squash and pounding it down in the measuring cup because the recipe says use two cups of squash, and I'm having all this trouble pushing the squash into the cup. Can you tell me how to get these bleepin' long yellow squashes into the cup?"

I forgot to say *"Slice up the squash."*

I started screaming my head off laughin', and before you knew it, both of us were laughin', and I said, "I'm so glad I took this phone call because you have just made my day and driven home a point with my cookbook. Now go into the kitchen and cut those sons of bitches up and *then* measure them." I know y'all are not going to believe this story, but it happened.

Anyway, writing the book the professional way was extremely frustrating; it took up so much of my time and I was almost insane by the time the book finally came out.

And it sold, it sold, it sold! America was ready for Southern country cooking, it seemed. People were asking for my autograph. Can you believe that?

One day I happened to watch QVC, long before it became so popular. I called Pamela and told her I'd love to take my book on QVC.

"What's QVC?" she asked. When I told her it was a home shopping network, she got interested and went to do some talking to whomever editors talk to when they want to make books fly off the shelves. Next thing I knew, she called back and said they'd booked me on QVC in Philadelphia.

Now, I'd been on national television once before. It was *Good Morning America* and the host was the most adorable, kind man—Spencer Christian, the weather person. He came down here to The Lady & Sons to film part of the segment; he brought his whole film crew right into the restaurant and everyone ate up a whole storm—there were no profits that day! We had a big old wonderful time with the crew, all my family, and even some of my buddies. After that, I was scheduled to go into the New York studio to do a little cookin' for the rest of the segment, and I was so scared, I liketa die. You shoulda heard me talking to myself:

Paula, Spencer's not going to let you die, he won't let you die, he won't let you die, grow up Paula, it's going to be good, Spencer's your friend, remember how he liked your fried chicken so much?

And then I said the Serenity Prayer to myself and cooked hoe cakes for the New York television audience. When the segment aired, I could hear the quiver in my voice, and I could see my hand shake, but I was never again scared on TV after that.

By the time QVC came into my life, I felt like Julia Child. Since I am a born ham and was by then an experienced television star with my appearance on *Good Morning America,* QVC was a piece of cake. I felt like I was just talking to my own customers, not thousands of TV watchers. I'd tell them that a recipe was really just a startin' point and they didn't have to stick to no recipe, even mine, as if it was the word of God. I encouraged them not to take food so seriously and to experiment in cooking; if a dish didn't come out, they could always give it to the dog. They'd only be in trouble if the dog came up to them, burped, and said, "Now, *that* was *tough*." I'd tell my readers to make double the amounts and put half away for another day when they spent time fixin' a recipe. It's important to befriend your freezer; a lady's got a life to live.

Bottom line is this: it don't take much money to eat good. Even rednecks can eat like kings. I consider us all rednecks, by the way, but maybe *refined* rednecks.

Well, honey, the response was *huge*. I sold seventy thousand books in one day. Since then I've been on QVC more than fifty times and I've loved every minute.

Now I got a whole new publisher called Simon & Schuster, and I love my editor and every one of my copy editors there to death even though they're even fussier than the last ones about getting every darn word exactly right. What happens if you put an editor in front of a stove and ask her to fry up some chicken exactly right? Someday I'll find out.

It's all still a mystery, this publishing business, even though I've now written three more cookbooks. All kinds of friends call me regularly to say, "Paula, would you please help me? I've got a book that I'd love to get published. How do I do it?"

And I usually answer, "Hell, I don't know. Open a restaurant, and pray for rain."

Biscuits and Sawmill Gravy

If you ask me *really* how you can get a cookbook published, make sure there's a cookbook editor in your friend's kitchen when you bring over your offering for a potluck supper. This is the recipe that will definitely seduce that editor into publishing your cookbook, because it is so divine. I promise!

BISCUITS

Makes about 1 dozen

> 3 cups all-purpose flour
> 2 tablespoons sugar
> 2½ teaspoons baking powder
> ½ teaspoon baking soda
> ½ teaspoon salt
> ½ cup vegetable shortening
> 1 to 1¼ cups milk
> ¼ cup melted unsalted butter

1. Preheat the oven to 450°F.
2. In a medium bowl, combine the flour, sugar, baking powder, baking soda, and salt. Cut in the shortening with a fork until it looks like cornmeal. Add the milk, a little at a time, stirring constantly until well mixed.
3. Turn the dough out onto a lightly floured surface. Knead lightly two or three times. Roll out the dough with a floured rolling pin to ½-inch thickness. Cut with a 2-inch cutter. Place the biscuits in a greased iron skillet. Brush the biscuits with half the melted butter. Bake for 12 to 14 minutes, or until golden brown. Brush the hot biscuits with the remaining butter. Split the biscuits in half and ladle Sawmill Gravy (see page 136) over the hot biscuits.

SAWMILL GRAVY

1 pound ground sausage
4 slices thick-cut bacon
½ medium onion, diced
2 cloves garlic, minced
3 tablespoons all-purpose flour
1 teaspoon salt
2 teaspoons black pepper
2 cups half-and-half
2 tablespoons butter

In a large skillet, combine the sausage, bacon, onion, and garlic. Cook over medium heat until the sausage is browned and crumbles. Stir in the flour, salt, and pepper; cook for 1 minute, stirring constantly. Gradually stir in the half-and-half. Cook over medium heat, stirring constantly, until the mixture is thickened. Stir in the butter until well blended.

Chapter 11

LOVE ON A TUG:
MICHAEL

I was hot as a June bride on a feather bed.

It's one thing not to trust that good fortune will hang out with you all the time; it makes you more grateful every day for what you have. But early in the new century, when everyone else was celebrating the millennium, I was a total emotional mess. Okay, by this time I had a couple of cookbooks under my belt, my business was on its way to being fabulous, I had money in my pocket, and financial security, but I was still struggling with a long, dead-end relationship that was suckin' the joy from me. I was so disappointed in myself because I craved a love that was fine and trustworthy. I wanted somebody my whole family approved of, someone I didn't have to hide, someone who could make me laugh.

And I was ready for passion; lovely *returned* passion. Just because there's snow on the roof doesn't mean there's no fire in the furnace. No one knew how I felt—even my children, who could no more imagine their momma's feet pointed up to Jesus than they could imagine me deserting them. Children want to think their birth was an immaculate conception; they don't want to picture their mommas and daddies with lust in their hearts. *These old folks?* they think. *Why would they want to do* it?

But intimacy is one of the greatest gifts that God gave us, and it doesn't have an age limit. Doesn't always mean doin' the dirty, either. It can mean holding and caressing each other. Snuggling. Remember necking? Nothin' better. Of course, it is nice when you can consummate great love—it completes the intimacy. Listen, I was so ready. Starving. Just starving. Waiting for the telephone call of a married man I didn't even like that much anymore was getting to me, but I was not strong enough to tell him to go freak himself.

But my days and nights were chock-full of work, and when I wasn't working I was involved with family. I don't do bars, and even church was out of the question because Sunday was the one day I could not leave the restaurant. I tried to figure out how to zap up my personal life, but everywhere I looked, I saw only a dead end. I was living downtown and all my neighbors were either older couples or single men who would have liked my brother better than me. I felt that if I could meet someone who was decent and available, I could take total responsibility for myself, but for the meeting of the man, I needed God's blessing.

This was a problem I'd have to turn over to God.

So I did just that. I added a sentence to my nightly prayers: "God, please send me a neighbor." He'd know what I meant, I figured.

I know about prayer. Aside from my family, it's the only thing in my life that's bigger than food. You can pray anytime, even when you cook. You can hold a person's name in your heart as you stir the fixin's for a hoe cake, or season the chicken. You can ask for God's help when you pepper, salt, and sift. So that's what I did. I thanked Him for every blessin' and asked for one more. That neighbor.

Then I got pretty busy on my brother's behalf. We'd recently had some news that really shook me. After being married nineteen great years, as Bubba puts it, the twentieth turned out to be a real loser. No one knows what really happens behind others' closed doors, and it's probably better that way, but I was shocked to hear that Jill was leaving my brother and they were planning a divorce. Somehow, I thought that marriage would last forever.

I've always been very protective of Bubba, and I was so devastated from his sadness that I began to badger him to move to Savannah. Looking ahead, I figured, very correctly, he'd be great in the restaurant business, and there was always room in my business for my baby brother. Early in the new millennium, Bubba called me and said, "I'm ready to leave Albany now; I want to come live in Savannah." I was thrilled that he and his daughter, Corrie, were thinking of moving near to me.

"Come on," I said. "You can stay with me in the meantime, and we'll find you a place to live."

So, we went looking for a house for Bubba, but who ends up buying a new place? Me! I'd gotten a wild hair that I wanted to live on the water, so one day the real estate agent brought us into Turners Cove on Wilmington Island, a new waterfront community under construction. It was gorgeous—and out of Bubba's price range—but I loved it. Every unit but one had been sold and I piped up and said, "I'll take it."

I looked around and said, "Was that my evil twin sister? I didn't say that, did I?" But, just like I signed the restaurant lease on Congress Street without a second thought, I bought this three-bedroom condo. It was a row house designed after the row houses in downtown, and it even had a square with fountains, and dolphins jumped in the lagoon in front of the condo. I got to pick out the paint colors and the appliances and I busied myself with the move. In the meantime, we'd also found Bubba a wonderful place. Things were looking up—now I had my baby brother and his child with us all the time. My niece, Corrie, really became like the daughter I never had. I loved having that beautiful, funny young woman around so much. We spent hours together laughing, talking, watching television, creating a bond that will never break, never even stretch.

I still said my new prayer every night: "God, please send me a neighbor."

On January 19, my birthday, I loaded up my cat, my dogs, and my birds and I moved to Turners Cove. Moving day, I was so tired—I'd been working my tail off in the business, preparing for a major move—and when I walked into my new home, I found out my children and Bubba had gotten together and called my two best friends in Albany, and everyone was there. It was wonderful.

As soon as I moved in, I started on my third book, *The Lady & Sons Just Desserts* for Simon & Schuster, and I took a short hiatus from the restaurant. There was no way I could work on this book and be at the restaurant every day because I had a serious deadline. I put on my baseball cap, then started testing recipes and writing.

My household had grown to include a one-eyed cat named Popeye; Ladybird, the macaw; Dixie, the umbrella cockatoo; and two precious Shih Tzu dogs, Sam and Otis. Because I was afraid the dogs would run away and get lost in this new neighborhood, they were not allowed to roam freely outside. When they needed to relieve themselves, they would come over, scratch on my leg, and we almost always went out the door on the water side; we'd take a right, go into the square, they'd do their business, and then we would come back. I had never even been to the left of my house; I didn't know what was down there in that direction.

This one particular afternoon, around the first of August, the dogs came over to signal me. We got up, went out the back door as usual, but this time they turned around, looked back at me, then in a jailhouse break they whirled left and just hauled ass. They ran like the devil, barking crazily all the way. I saw they were in a race to get around a big old tall wall near my condo where there was about a foot that you could maneuver around before you fell into the water. They were still running and barking, so happy to be out of the house. I'm in hot pursuit, beggin' them, *beggin'* them to stop.

But Otis's head is harder than my arteries. He is so damn stubborn. He will not stop for nothing. So, I shimmy around that wall after them, and then I see what's caught their interest.

They're heading straight for this man who's propped on his chain-link fence talking on his cell phone. And my first thought was, *This could be the neighborhood pervert. Or an ax murderer.* The guy was mean- and shaggy-looking, with gray shaggy hair, a gray shaggy beard, and a gray shaggy mustache that covered his mouth, and he didn't look very happy. He was a dead ringer for Ernest Hemingway, just back from a month at sea without catching no fish.

And I was frightened. Of course, the dogs run straight up to him and immediately start pooping there in his yard, right under his nose. And there I am, looking at this shaggy man who does not look happy, and I'm saying, "Oh, my goodness, I'm so sorry. I'll clean it up. I'm sorry they've done this." And he mumbles something like, "That's all right. I like dogs. It's people I ain't crazy about. People I don't trust."

He sounded like a loon and it didn't surprise me. I told him I was his neighbor, I had a restaurant in town, and I was home writing a book.

"I'm so sorry the dogs have disturbed you, *suh,* and now we've got to get back home." I get these dogs loaded under my arms, and as I'm walking back, I'm saying to myself, *God, that ain't my neighbor, is it? Is* that *who I'm praying for? Nah! That can't be him. Please, God, that ain't what my neighbor's supposed to look like.*

The guy had muttered something in a low voice about having a drink together when I was finished with my book and I said to myself, *Over my dead body!* So I go home, and I tell myself with a giggle that I thought I might have just been asked out on a date by an ax murderer.

Two weeks later, damned if those dogs didn't do the identical thing. This time, I know where they're going. I'm running behind them one more time in my baseball cap, my dirty shirt that's got gravy stains all over it, and these ugly-ass stretch Wal-Mart jeans. I'm chasing after them, begging them to please stop.

And it was the weirdest thing: it was like that man had not moved away from that fence in two weeks. He was propped on it in the same spot talking on that same stupid cell phone. The dogs start pooping again. It was like déjà vu all over again. He got off the phone, but this time he didn't seem so scary; he seemed kinda nice, actually. I decided I would talk to him. He told me he'd lived here all his life, and I thought that was a good sign. I asked him if he knew anything about boats. If he had lived on this water all his life, he probably knew something about boats.

The fact was, I had me a boat.

When I moved to this property, I would not shut up about getting me a boat. Talking to my closest and dearest, I was like a woman on a mission, just crazy with the idea that we had to have a boat for the family. I knew nothing about boats, but that didn't stop me one bit. I would not get off Bubba's back. I told Bubba I wanted a boat that I could jump in and take out myself without having to ask anybody for help. We wound up buying a gorgeous twenty-seven-foot, preowned twin-engine Blackfin fishing boat. I just loved it. It had a top that covered a fly bridge and you could drive it from there, way up high over the water. On the move, the wind just hit you in the face, and you had a clear shot of the dolphins down below. But listen here, I had insisted that we have a boat, and I could not even crank up the engine by myself. The only thing I could do with that boat was turn on the CD player, and at night when I would get through working, I'd get on that boat and turn on that CD player. I'd just sit there waiting for maybe another boat to come by and break a wave so that I could feel like I was moving and going somewhere.

That's why I asked this shaggy man, whose name was Michael Anthony Groover, a fifth-generation Wilmington Islander, "Do you know anything about boats?"

He chuckled and said, "A little bit."

I said, "Well, what do you do for a living?"

He said, "I'm kinda semiretired."

I said, "Well, what do you do?"

He said, "I'm a harbor docking pilot—which is a kind of valet parking for big ships." Later, much later, he teased me that he was sure I'd found him so attractive that I'd done the research on him and already knew he was a docking pilot. He said he thought I was setting him up for the kill so I could get my hooks in him.

It wasn't the truth.

Then I said to him, "Look—I've made a mistake here. I have a boat I can't crank, much less drive. Would you mind taking me out to see if you can teach me how to drive this boat?" He said, "Yeah, I can do that." We made a date for the next day.

I took special care with a shower, my makeup, and my hair. His beard had not been groomed, but he'd certainly had a shower and put on a fresh shirt. I believe we were both thinking that we wanted to put forth a little better foot than we had on the first two meetings. A neighborly foot, of course.

So we got on my boat, and it was clear he'd done this once or twice before; he just melted into the captaining. He took me out to Wassaw Sound and, oh my goodness, we were flying through that water. It was a brisk, breezy day, and a rough kind of ride, the water was foldin' in high waves like I like it. I was laughing and screaming and it was just wonderful. We saw the porpoises diving about, and he turned us around before we went into the real ocean. Then he drove us back into the most magnificent sunset I've ever seen, and that boat was still just pounding hard; it was a *passionate* ride.

We were almost home, almost to my dock, when I looked hard at him. You know what? At that moment I knew that my life was never going to be the same again once I got off that boat.

I invited him into my house. I was on a low-carb diet because I had eaten so many sweets while I was making that book. I don't know how much weight I gained, but there were some serious pounds involved. I had no food in the house. I never wanted to see another dessert as long as I lived.

So he came in and I fixed us a diet drink and we sat down.

I was sure he thought I was pretty cool and sophisticated. Wasn't I a restaurant owner? The truth is I'm a bawdy woman with a loud laugh and colorful language; but I am all talk and not much do. The do had happened early on, but I didn't have nearly the experience that people might have thought I did. So I was a little nervous about how to start talking to this interesting, docking pilot guy. On my coffee table, I had a great little book, the *If . . .* book. It's a wonderful way to get to know people, so I picked up the book and read, "Okay, if you were stranded on a desert island, what would you bring with you?" "If you could meet anyone from olden times, who would you want to meet?" It worked; we sat on the sofa for hours and hours, just talking and "if-ing" and finding out about each other. Being a good hostess, I asked him if he would like a snack or something.

And Fat Boy's sitting there thinking (he later told me), "I can't wait to see what her snack is." He knows what my business is, he's expecting great food. I go to the cabinet, and I pull out a box of microwaveable pork rinds. They have no carbs in them. That's what I was living on. I'd dip 'em in cream cheese for real excitement. The look on his face! I could tell he was disappointed. He was nice and said yes, he would like some of those, but inside I knew he was in shock.

We sat there eating pork rinds until about ten at night, when he finally got up and said, "Well, I need to go home. I need to check on my children. I need to say good night." And I thought to myself, *Dad gum it! This is the moment I'm dreading, my least favorite part of the day.*

But I barely knew the man. How do I say good night? How do you thank somebody for teaching you something big? I was so grateful that I now knew how to run that boat. My instinct was to stick out my hand. Michael told me later that he thought I wanted to kiss him, but he was wrong.

I did not want to kiss Shaggy Man because that afternoon, as we were hitting the waves, I dipped extra low in my seat because I was very curious to see what he had in his mouth (remember, his mustache came down to *here*) and I could see nothin' in there. So when we were saying good night, I'm thinking, *This man has got no teeth or he's got a mouthful of rotten teeth.*

I couldn't figure out which was worse. So we go to stand up, and he looks like he's about to make his move. He's gonna ruin a perfectly good night. He thinks he's gonna kiss me, and I try to act real worldly and cool, like I've been around, when indeed I have not been around a whole bunch. So, we're standing up there and his mustache is covering his mouth completely.

He goes to make his move, and I cover my face. Then I had to say something.

I said, "I am so sorry, but I've never kissed a man with a beard and mustache before." And he looks at me with that smart-ass smirk on his face like a lot of Southern white boys can get, and he says, "Well, thank God, 'cause I ain't neither."

So, finally, I said to myself, *This man has taken his time to take me out on that boat.* I knew I had to give him a little peck good night.

"I am so sorry," I said. I grabbed his hair and lifted his mustache and then laughed with joy because, thank the Lord! My neighbor had teeth!

Michael says now that when we met, his idea of a long-term relationship was about thirty minutes, so teeth were not real important to him. Actually, he says, he was looking for a woman who owned a boat and specifically had no teeth. He told me that after a long, bad marriage, he was happily *un*married and that his goal was to get any woman with whom he had a short-term relationship to keep her toothbrush at her own house. He'd made a vow never to marry again, and whenever a woman started to talk serious to him, he'd definitely do something to piss her off.

But then, when he's not kidding around, he admits that we were a match made in heaven. Our first meeting was because of the dogs—we both love animals—and as we started talking, we realized that we had so much in common—family, the water, food—that he really knew it was clicking from the very beginning. Oh, of course there were some differences, and as time went by we discovered them. He was raised Catholic and I grew up Baptist, but it never did matter a bit because we honor the same God. More important, what did matter was that I was a child of the sixties and I loved my romantic Motown music and those Platters and, oh my God—Sam Cooke and Otis Redding and Barry White and the Temptations. But, when Michael, who came up in the seventies, put his junk on my CD player—Led Zeppelin and Ozzy Osbourne and Black Sabbath and AC/DC—I remember saying, *"Who the hell is that and what are they screaming?"*

Let me say right now, we were growing so close. We didn't care about anything but being together. We began to love being in bed; we came to realize how much holding each other meant to us. I'm not talking just about sex but about cuddling, nurturing, whispering, telling secrets, getting to know each other real well. Night after night, we'd lay up in that bed and talk and listen to his music, then my music, and sometimes, sure, we'd play hide the sausage—and then the music was great, whatever was playing.

Grace, pure and simple, had poured into my life, and there was no room left to be lonely anymore. We started in dating seriously. By now, I was on him like white on rice because, oh, he was a breath of fresh air. For starters, he was available 100 percent of the time except when he was on the ship. This seemed strange and wonderful to me, being used to dancing to that other guy's married-man schedule. We could be seen in public without worrying that an angry wife's friends would spot us. We could go to dinner in a restaurant. We could go to a movie. It was all right if we touched or kissed in public.

Weeks passed and it got so we didn't go anywhere without the other one, and my staff at The Lady & Sons was the happiest crew in the state of Georgia because I had gone from bitch to drooling teenager.

I was hotter than a two-dick dog. You know that's *hot*. I had been leading a very unhealthy life for the last ten years, and now I'd turned the corner at a 180-degree angle.

Happiness shows.

One night, before Michael entered the equation, I'd drawn my life as a pie on a blank sheet of paper. Up at the top of the pie I'd actually written "Paula's Life." Then I started trying to slice this pie to give me something visual to connect to: I wanted to see my life spread out in black-and-white. I saw it all right. In one huge piece of the pie, actually, seven-eighths of it, I'd written "work." In the tiny sliver that was left, I'd written "family," "worship," "love," "fun time." No matter how many times I looked at this drawing, I couldn't honestly give any more space to family, worship, love, or time for fun. So there was my life: a huge slice of work and a tiny slice for everything else.

No wonder, I'd said to myself that night. *No wonder I am so tired. I'm really a very sick girl.* It was clear my life was very unbalanced.

Enter Michael. He entered laughing, and he made me laugh so hard I thought I'd break. He was this big old virile guy, different from anybody I had ever been with. Michael didn't have the prettiness that I had always been attracted to, as in Jimmy Deen, but he had something that was far more than pretty. He was sexy—he was his own man. He knew who he was, what he wanted—and, my stars, he seemed to want me. Still, this is not to say he wasn't a little rough around the edges, not to mention stubborn and hardheaded, but all that made him irresistible. Best of all was his *wicked* sense of humor. I can't say it enough—it was so important to me—*he made me laugh!* Michael is very soft-spoken and you have to listen to him hard so that you wouldn't miss his zingers because he kind of mumbles, but those zingers—priceless! This son of the sea was literally a breath of fresh air: when he entered the room, I found myself gasping with pleasure. He was no longer Mr. Shaggy Man; he was somebody I could talk about with my friends and family. I felt so proud of him; he was the *manliest* guy I ever met, and he was so very divorced. I could bring him into the restaurant and show him off. We could snuggle together without me feeling guilt. We could make passionate love together. My days and nights all of a sudden became very healthy. I loved him so much.

Wasn't long before we settled into a very comfortable lifestyle. He and I stayed in my condo, just a stone's throw away from his house. My tiny dogs, Sam and Otis, were in heaven, because now they had Cody, Michael's big old black Labrador, to bully. Michael's children were pretty grown. Michelle was nineteen and lived in his home, as she had all her life, a very responsible young woman who was really concentrating on getting her nursing degree. Anthony, Michael's sixteen-year-old son, was away at military school. I loved that my neighbor was in daily contact with his children and was completely in love with them, just as I was with mine.

Then disaster almost struck. We were that close to ending it all. God, life *is* a roller coaster and words can hurt like the devil.

We'd been together every night for a month or so, and one weekend, my best friends from Albany, Susan Dupree and Ann Hanson, were visiting and staying in the upstairs bedroom. I was so proud to introduce Michael to them. One early evening, after dinner, we all said good night and went to our rooms. Michael and I were lying naked on our bed and just talking—that slow, easy, confidin' kind of talk. We felt so close, so tied together, that it seemed it was the right time to tell him about this long dead-end affair I'd been having. So, there I was, making nervous chatter, trying to get into confession mode big time, talking and talking, trying to explain why I'd stayed in a terrible relationship for ten years. I hoped Michael was hearing how desperately I wanted him to tell me it was going to be different with us. He said nothin'. So, I asked him, "This friendship you and I have started, is it going anywhere? Is there hope we can build a solid, lasting relationship? Would you like me to totally close the door on this married man?"

Well, let Michael tell you what he heard.

"I thought you were asking me," says Michael, "if you and I should continue to date even if you were still seeing this other guy. I didn't hear you asking me if you should cut it off completely with him. And I'm thinking, *Here I am lying in bed with this woman who has to know I feel something deeply or I wouldn't be coming back every day. Why would she even ask me that insulting question?* I *wanted* to say, 'Yes, it's damn foolish to date a married man, much less ask me if I think it's a good thing.'

"You put me in a terrible position," Michael says. "I knew I felt love for you, but I also felt that if you didn't know the answer to that awful question before you asked it, your feelings might not be as real as mine."

So Michael answered my question about what he thought I should do.

"I don't give a shit what you do," he said.

I was heartbroken.

"Oh," I said, and got up and got dressed. He also got up, dressed, and left.

That, I thought, was that. I couldn't catch a break. So, I did the only thing that seemed reasonable, which was to gather up my girlfriends and go out to the mall and shop. And cry and cry and cry.

"What happened?" they wanted to know. *"Where did he go, that wonderful Michael?"*

Well, it *was* wonderful, I told them, but he does not give one plug nickel about me. *"Why do you say that?"* they asked. Because, I answered, he told me so just before he left an hour ago.

Then my cell phone rang and it was Michael.

Oh, I was so happy, I just bubbled into the phone, "We're shopping, but we're coming right home now. Oh, stay right there, darlin'!"

When we got back, he was waiting for me at the house.

"I like a little competition," he said, "and I think I would win over any married guy." That's all he said. We didn't talk about it, except he promised me he'd never say "I don't give a shit what you do" ever again. And he hasn't.

So we settled into this fabulous life. We had the water, we had our animals, we were eatin' good, our kids were well situated in their own lives, and I had him pretty much all to myself. The scene was set for true love.

But now I had to deal with the married man I thought I loved before I knew what true love was. For the last couple of years, I'd been living for the crumbs that the other man threw my way, the crumbs that the pathetic sop of a woman I was thought were all I deserved. Before I'd started making my nightly prayer for a neighbor, I'd also prayed for the strength to end this relationship that could only hurt a lot of people. Truth is, I had long been uncomfortable with the man and the whole situation. I wasn't raised that way. It was not in my nature to be with a married man even if he protested that his marriage was terrible. But my selfish needs overrode everything else because I'd so craved adult time with a partner even if it was just stolen moments here and there. Frankly? I secretly always felt this man really didn't care for me, but he stayed around because I was convenient. I helped him out on occasion. I was a good friend to have because I always stand by my friends. At the same time, I knew that if the man had to make a choice, he would rather I be out of his life than his wife.

So, even before Michael came on the scene, I'd quit calling him. There was silence on his part.

And then Michael came to me.

Soon after we moved in together, and Michael said he didn't give a shit what I did, and I found out he really did give a shit, my phone rang.

"*Hello,*" said the man.

"*Hello,*" I said.

"*What's his name?*" he said.

How did he know? I guess because I'd stopped calling.

"*Michael,*" I said.

"*What does Michael do?*" he said.

"*He's a harbor docking pilot,*" I said.

"*I'll go home and get my things and move in with you—in less than an hour,*" he said. "*I want you,*" he said. "*I've been a fool. I thought you would always be there. I'm heartbroken,*" he said. "*I'll get divorced,*" he said.

"*I'm so sorry, but it's too late,*" I said.

The man kept calling me, maybe six times a day. He told me that Michael, who was ten years younger, was far too young for me. Another time he told me Michael was probably a pauper out for my money. Then I heard he did a background check on Michael, and I'm sure he saw that my love wasn't out for my money, because Michael had plenty of his own.

I was shed of the man at last. What I did for what I *thought* was love. Now, praise God, I had the real thing.

It was coming up on our second Christmas together, and I was dying for a ring, but I thought this shaggy river man don't know nothin' about no diamond rings. I confided in my niece, Corrie, "You know, I'm almost hoping for an engagement ring. I'd so wish I'd get that for Christmas but I know he would never do that."

And Corrie said, "Well, you *don't* know that."

And then I said, "Well, don't tell anybody that I've said that wish because I don't want people to even dream that I am thinkin' that way."

But I was. This is the way it was with me. Although we were so happy living together, I seem to have just needed Michael to propose and let me know that his intentions were honorable. It almost didn't matter if we got married. I deeply wanted him just to ask, so that I knew he was in there for the long haul, so that I knew he was committed. I needed that like I needed to breathe.

So, on Christmas Eve I noticed at the back of that overflowing tree of gifts there was a new gift and it was a big box shaped like a house with a white tag on it. The tag said "Paula" in real big letters.

That gift has just come into this house, but I'm going to pretend like I don't see it, I thought.

The next morning, all the family shows up. Michael and his

children have spent the night there with me, so we're already there. Then my children come piling in as well as Bubba and Corrie. Nick, Michael's brother, and *his* children come in. I was talking and laughing and seeing if anybody wanted something to eat, and finally Michelle, Michael's daughter, came over and said, "Listen, you've got to start opening your gifts. I've got to get to Momma's."

I said, "Me open my gifts? *You* start opening *your* gifts. I'm not worried about my gifts." But I thought, *Well, that was real strange*.

Before I knew it, they'd sat me down in a chair; they knew I'd be the last one to open gifts because I'm always seeing to everybody else. The room got quiet. I thought, *Why is everybody looking at me? Christmas is for children*.

Well, I wanted everyone else to open their gifts first as was the custom in my family, especially because I'd bought Michael a magnificent Rolex watch and I couldn't wait to see his face when he unwrapped it. "No one has ever given me a thing in my life," he'd once told me, "maybe not even bought me a meal." So, I was focusing on him and his present and I could barely contain myself.

But Michelle would have none of that. Although each person had a few gifts waiting, she ignored the others with my name on them, went to get the intriguing house-shaped box, and set it down before me.

"*There*," she said. "We're waiting for you, Paula."

I looked over to where Michael was propped on the frame of the wet bar. Ernest Hemingway was just standing there grinning.

Well, I opened this box that said Paula, and in it was another box surrounded by all my favorite candy that I could just eat by the pound: Hershey's Kisses, Snickers—stuff like that. And in a third box, it was the same thing.

Corrie said, "Paula, there's a message in each box. Read it."

So, I went back to the first box, and it said, "Paula." The next box had a message that said "I." The next box said "love." The next box said "you." I opened the next box, and it said "Will."

When that durned box said "Will," I said, "No! I mean yes!" I knew what was coming, and so the entire message—it took nine boxes—said, "Paula, I love you. Will you be my wife?"

That last, ninth box held a diamond ring. I'd found a man who gave diamonds? I couldn't believe the ring . . . it was simply magnificent. How could this rugged river man have such an eye for jewelry? Oh, that ring. I haven't taken it off since.

It was the most wonderful proposal, so romantic and so like Michael. He devised this extraordinary way to do this thing in front of all the people we love, and he never had to open his mouth. *He never had to open his mouth*. They were all in on it, by the way. Corrie had even seen the ring.

It was a blessed Christmas.

From that point on, we really fell into a comfortable relationship. I was happy as a clam. You couldn't slap the smile off my face because this man whom I had grown to love so deeply had made a commitment, and I was fine with that. It didn't matter to me if we never got married, although people started asking me about a marriage plan. So, we settled in, not making any moves to set a date and pick a place for the weddin'. I didn't know when, didn't care. It didn't matter. He'd committed.

In a century, in five centuries, I would never have guessed what would happen next—that thousands of people I didn't even know would come to our weddin' when it finally happened.

Shaggy Man Split Pea Soup

So when Mr. Shaggy Man came to my house for the first time, I made him those microwaveable pork rinds, which didn't impress him none. If only I'd known that his favorite soup in the whole world was a great split pea, I'd have had a pot of the stuff simmering away. On a rainy night—which actually happens here in Savannah more than you'd think—this is what Michael craves. Serve this with corn bread.

½ stick butter
½ pound thick slab bacon, diced
1 large onion, chopped
2 celery stalks, very finely diced
2 carrots, peeled and grated
3 quarts chicken stock
2 tablespoons House Seasoning (see page 96)
1 teaspoon salt
1 teaspoon black pepper
½ pound Smithfield pork sausage
One 1-pound package dried split peas, soaked and drained
Instant mashed potatoes (optional)

In a large pot or Dutch oven, melt the butter over medium high heat. Sauté the bacon, onion, celery, and carrots together. Add the chicken stock, House Seasoning, salt, pepper, sausage, and peas. Bring to a boil. Lower the heat and simmer for approximately 2 hours, covered. If the soup is too thin, add a handful of instant mashed potatoes to thicken.

Serves 4 to 6

Chapter 12

HOW I GOT MY OWN TELEVISION SHOW, AND IT WASN'T NO DESPERATE HOUSEWIVES

They wanted me to wear an apron on television.
It made me look fat, well, fatter than usual.
I told them I was going to drop that apron crap.

Now I had it all: a fiancé, a popular restaurant, cookbooks, workin' kids, money in my pocket, and three dogs. At least, I thought I had it all. I'd had a run of bad luck and it was one for the records, but, been there, done that. Now I was finally in a run of great luck, and it wasn't over yet. This gray-haired over-fifty lady with an ample and over-fifty bod, this formerly agoraphobic, algebra-flunking cheerleader from Albany High School, was about to become a television star. God works in mysterious ways.

Carol Perkins was a Victoria's Secret model in her day. She lived in New York, and she traveled in business circles—circles that never crossed my path. After a certain age where no perky-breasted Victoria's Secret model ever tread, she moved to Savannah to make a new home and start a designer-dog-accessories business she called Harry Barkers. She'd often come into The Lady & Sons to get her balanced meal without the hassle of cookin' it.

Naturally, anyone who'd been a Victoria's Secret model and ended up with dogs was a woman after my own heart, and when she'd come in, I'd go over, sit at her table, and we'd talk and laugh. One day in 1999, she said, "Paula, do you know Gordon Elliott?"

I knew of Gordon Elliott: he was that Australian television star and I remembered seeing him on different American shows, like *A Current Affair, To Tell the Truth,* and a crazy breakfast show called *Good Day New York* in which, on live television, Gordon barged into New York homes before the sleeping occupants had opened their eyes to the light of day. I remember seeing the one in which he surprised Bill Cosby with what I later learned were the 101 voices of the New York Choral Society singing the *Hallelujah Chorus.* He made me laugh big-time, that Gordon Elliott, and now Carol tells me he's her dear friend and is coming to Charleston to shoot an episode of the Food Network's *Door Knock Dinners.*

"I've told Gordon that there's a woman here in Savannah that he really needs to meet," said my friend. "Would it be all right if I asked him to come over for lunch so you two can chat?"

I told her I'd adore it, thinking it was the last I'd hear of Gordon Elliott.

In a week, Carol comes in and says, "Gordon is going to be here tomorrow. Are we on for lunch?"

Were we! I'm game for anything fun! Well, my Aunt Peggy and Bubba were here visiting and I got a table up in the corner for us all to sit at. Of course, lunchtime was so busy I couldn't sit, but I'd keep going back and forth to the table because the moment that Gordon walked in, he and I looked at each other and we laughed and clicked. Turned out we've both got the same sense of sick humor. I'd work the room and then come back over and talk to him for a minute. I knew my Aunt Peggy had him in her scope, so it really wasn't necessary for me to be there; she would be able to figure out everything. So, when I finally got a chance to come back and sit at the table, he looked up at me with those big old eyes and that big old grin, and he said, "Would you do a guest shot on *Door Knock Dinners*?"

Now, look here: I didn't have time to watch much TV, but I knew that show so I asked Gordon, "Is that the show where you go knocking on people's doors, and you have to cook whatever they've got in the refrigerator? You can't go to the store. You have to make a meal out of whatever you can find."

"Yes, darling," he said.

"Is that the truth? No cheating?" I asked.

"No cheating," he said.

"Well, I'll tell you right now, Gordon," I said, "I'm as green as a Granny Smith apple when it comes to talking in front of a TV camera, and I'll be scared to death, but I will do it. You got to know, though, I can't come without my boys."

So, Jamie, Bobby, and I flew out to Las Vegas—my first visit ever. I'd told the boys to bring only casual clothes because they didn't have to do anything; I just wanted them to be there with me, and to watch what was going on.

I don't have to tell you how happy I was to go to Las Vegas. I luuuuuuv the gambling life—for a couple of days, anyway. Gordon showed us the most wonderful time: I will never forget Gordon and me screaming and laughing at the craps table till five o'clock in the morning.

The first night we were there, Gordon took us all to dinner. Bear in mind that I had been to New York only twice, first when I was eighteen, and then again when my cookbook came out, to do a spot on *Good Morning America*. That was the extent of my city sophistication. Gordon wanted to take us to Le Cirque at the Bellagio hotel, the fanciest restaurant in town. His people make his reservations, so the restaurant owner knew that the big shot Gordon Elliott was coming.

My people—well, one has on a button-up shirt and khakis, and the other one has on a golf shirt with nice jeans. We walk in, and the first person we speak to is this maître d', and his head is all bent to the side and he's talking in a fake fancy French accent, and he says, "A jacket and tie is required." Gordon turns around and looks at the boys. Gordon doesn't have on a jacket either. The maître d' says in his prissy French accent, "I have jackets and ties for those in need of them."

Well, Bobby Deen gets so mad that he can't see straight because there he is wearing a golf shirt and he's definitely in need of the Frenchman's jacket. I'm getting tickled, and he's getting madder by the minute. Bobby was twenty-eight and inside he really cared about how he looked to other people. They take him back to the little wardrobe room, put a tie around his neck and over his golf shirt, then put him in an ill-fitting jacket. By that time I could see the muscles dancing in his jaw, he was so humiliated.

Lord, I prayed, *please let my son keep it under control long enough for us to have this damn dinner without embarrassing me.* Jamie had on a button-up shirt, so he put on the jacket and tie without a problem. Gordon also had to put on the restaurant clothes.

And there they were, the three guys, all in black restaurant ties and black jackets. So, we get to the table, and I look over at Bobby in his golf shirt with that silly tie, and I just start laughing my head off. The more I laugh, the madder I can see him getting. Well, Gordon just says to the waiter, "Feed us whatever is good. We're not going to order anything."

So, they bring the first course, and I'll never forget it—a tall slender glass that climbed into a tulip shape, and it was filled with blue ice. One oyster on the half-shell sat on top of that ice, and on the oyster was a spoon of heavenly sauce. We each picked up our oyster and put it in our mouths. I looked over at Bobby. His eyes had rolled back in his head, and he was smacking his lips. At that moment, he didn't give a damn what he was wearing as long as he knew he was going to get the rest of the courses, which so far tasted pretty good.

Jamie and I still laugh about it to this day.

The next day we started knocking on doors. Our goal was to find a family who was willin' to let a bunch of strangers come into their house and cook a meal that would be shown on television. We had knocked on about three doors and had them all shut in our faces. I was getting pissed. Gordon will tell you that he's never before had a chef take over his show, but I'm used to taking charge and I said to myself that Vegas had pretty good restaurants, but Gordon is getting nowhere quick on the door knocks. We all loaded back up in this big old van and started hunting the neighborhood for the next door to knock on. It turned out to belong to a young housewife with two little boys.

"No," she told Gordon, she didn't think she wanted us to cook no meals in front of no cameras in her house.

This time, I kind of squirm up in front of him, and I get to talking to her. I said, "I'm the cook and I promise you it will be so much fun—we'll just have a good time." Her little boys ran to the front door to see who was there and I said, "Oh, my goodness, y'all are so cute! You remind me of my two little boys, but look how big they are now."

I was workin' that door-knock lady.

"But my hair and my face," she said. "I look so bad."

"We'll put some makeup on you. You'll be just fine," I assured her.

I had no idea what that woman had in her refrigerator, but, with little children, I was banking on her having food in there—something I couldn't do if a bachelor had opened the door. I really wanted to get into this woman's house even though she was not thrilled to see us and didn't appear to be real outgoing.

I got in, and Gordon and the cameras followed, and there was plenty of food.

Now, I was fast getting into my actressy mode. The only experience I'd ever had on TV besides *Good Morning America* and QVC was when I was fifteen. I was the chalk-it-up scorekeeper of a local game show at WLB-TV, kind of the Vanna White of my day. They'd put me in my high school dance costume, which was seductive, with fishnet hose and real spiked high-heel shoes. I had never done anything of the Gordon Elliott magnitude before.

But, oh, you know it, we had a wonderful time with this lady. With a few Paula flourishes and pronouncements of *"Yummy!"* I saw that she had chicken, ground beef, and tomato sauce, and I could make a wonderful spaghetti casserole. I found stuff to make a salad, and there was some apple-pie filling in her pantry and some canned biscuits in the refrigerator. I made my grandma's fried apple pies. She had vanilla ice cream. I served those hot pies with the ice cream.

Looking at the tape later, I couldn't believe how crazy I looked—like a butch Aunt Bea from Mayberry, if you remember that show. I had just let the color grow out of my hair, and it was so damn short, it made my neck and chins just appear to go on forever.

When I saw the tape, I said, "How would anybody in America like a cook that looked like that?"

But it worked. The ratings for the show were high. Gordon was very pleased and he called me back to ask if I would do another *Door Knock Dinner*.

I told you I was game for anything and just asked, "Where are we goin' this time?"

"Rutgers University up in New Jersey," said Gordon. "This time you're going to be in a sorority house."

That sounded safe to me. I knew about those prissy sorority girls who like pretty stuff and good food to eat. This time, I took Aunt Peggy with me. We get in the van, and we go to Rutgers and come to find out there's going to be another chef, a guy. They have decided to change the plan and give me the fraternity house and give this guy the sorority house; they thought that would be clever.

I was so mad I could puke fire! I did not want to be with the frat boys. The guy chef should have drawn those guys. I should be with the girls. I raised boys. I know what they do: they eat crap.

So, first we went to the sorority house, and we all went in. I could not believe it—they had a kitchen with more food in it than my restaurant. They had one double-wide reach-in cooler just for cheese. *Just for cheese.* There was every kind of cheese you could ever hope to have in that big old cooler. I'm seeing all this food and getting more ticked off by the minute.

So we get the guy chef situated, then load back up in the van, and we set out to find a frat house. Well, the first frat house we go to that we're hoping we can film had a party in it the night before. It had been one of those soap parties where they fill the house up with soap, and they walk around up to their middles in bubbles. You could see the bubble stains everywhere. I would not have let my dog spend a night in that house. No one was in this frat house now, it was beyond belief, a shack that you would think needed to be torn down immediately for unsafeness. So, we're riding all around the campus, and we see another big two-story frat house, which doesn't look too bad from the outside. We knock on the door, someone opens it, and there are beer and liquor bottles everywhere, also from a party the night before. Here, we apparently are waking up the occupants. They're coming down scratching their crotches, those class acts, totally hungover. Not one fraternity brother had better than green beans or English peas for brains.

So, I say, "Take me to your kitchen," and—what a surprise—it was horrible. There was a big old silver disposable pan filled with an unidentifiable dish from Friday, when the frat house cook was there. The whole place was nauseatingly unkitchenlike. I walk over to this piece-of-crap refrigerator. I open the freezer. There's one smushed-up frozen pot pie. In the refrigerator, nothing. So, I turn to these boys who are still looking dazed, and I say, "Where is your food?"

They look at this door with a padlock on it, and they say, "Well, it's in that locked room right there. We don't have a cook on the weekends, and they feel they can't turn us loose with the food, so they lock it up so we'll have some for Monday when it's time for the cook to come back to work."

I say, "Okay, future Einsteins, can you tell me what *would* be in there if we could get to it?"

They say, "Yeah, there'd be some chicken and some lettuce and tomato and pasta."

So I say to the crew, "What are we gonna do here, guys?"

And Gordon says, "We're going to have to go to the store and duplicate what that locked room probably holds. There is absolutely nothing else here, and we can't bust the padlock."

I want to do this fair, so I make a list of the things that they said could be in the padlocked place and I go to the grocery store, trying to stick as close to the list as possible. I buy some chicken, canned biscuits, and tomatoes, and I fry up for those Einsteins the most delicious chicken fingers and put them on some kind of wacky-looking paper dish on top of the stove.

I've got two frat guys now who are gonna be my assistants, and they're gonna be on TV, so their mommas will be proud. They're half dead but I've got 'em standing up there helping me with the food. Finally, I'm flouring the chicken fingers, and I look over at one of these zombielike guys, and I just pop him square in the face with my floured hands. I leave a flour print on him. I say, "Wake up, son!"

That kind of gets his attention. Then I take those biscuits and tomatoes, and I make darlin' little tomato tarts. Oh, and I bought dill pickles and ham because the guys said they usually had lots of sandwich meats. So I just spread a little cream cheese on the dill pickle and wrap the pickle in the ham.

And there, that was our meal.

Then it was time for us to take our food over to the sorority house because everybody was going to sit down and eat together. Well, the guy chef had prepared a great-looking meal from frozen breaded chicken cutlets in the freezer. Imagine—he had all that wonderful food, and he chose the frozen chicken. My head just about blew up. Still, he had some pretty china. Mine may not have looked as good because let me tell you what I had to serve in: a few paper bowls, some plastic silverware. Period. When I walked into that frat kitchen, the only thing I found to season with was dry basil, some salt and pepper, and some water. Period. My meal was chicken fingers, tomato tarts, and wrapped pickles. Dessert? Ain't no way I could have plucked dessert out of nothin'.

We filmed.

When it was over, I said, "Gordon Elliott, you owe me!" He still apologizes for that show. It took me almost a week before I could smile again.

I didn't know it, but I was being judged. The Food Network had somethin' in mind for me, but I had to prove my mettle.

A few months after that, I guess they'd had some good feedback from the show, and they called and asked if I would come up to New York and appear on another show called *Ready . . . Set . . . Cook!* "I'm in," I yelled! I liked this television business.

This show was sort of a contest, with two chefs in front of a live audience. There was a time clock, and when a bell rang, the chefs lifted their domes and found a big old platter of different kinds of foods. Then they had to prepare the best meal they could from the foods they were given to work with. Three people were pulled from the audience to judge the food each chef prepared, by the presentation, the flavors, and the uniqueness of each dish. They wouldn't tell you whom you'd be competing against until like five minutes before you walked out onto the stage.

I never had a thought that I was being observed by some hidden producers; I was just tryin' to have a good time on television.

Five minutes before we go out, they tell me, "You're competing against Chef Ludivic Sump'n Sump'n Sump'n." You hear that? Five minutes before we're supposed to go out they also tell me that he's listed as one of the top fifty chefs, not in the United States but in the world.

I thought, *I am screwed.*

I realized why they didn't give you any warning, because if they had, my ass would have gone home. I wouldn't have been there to put myself up for this kind of humiliation.

He was from France, a young good-looking man probably in his late twenties with the most beautiful eyes. I called him Lulu because when they told me his real name, I could not say it. I have to work on words to pronounce them when they're not like normal words. *You* just try sayin' Chef Ludivic Sump'n Sump'n Sump'n.

"Sorry," I said on camera. "I just got to call you Lulu. That's yo' name. Tell yo' momma."

Well, we got out there. I was trying to have a good time, looking relaxed and playful with Lulu. The bell rings, we lifted our domes, and I didn't recognize a damn stick of food underneath that dome. Not none of it did I recognize. They had a team that came in during the break to answer any questions.

Questions? "What *is* all this damned stuff?" I asked. And they had to tell me what everything was. If it was completely foreign to you, they would tell you, this is best sautéed, this is best fried, this is best grilled. So, they had to tell me how all these foods were generally prepared.

We go out there, and Lulu whips my ass. He blows me off the map. I was a good sport, though, but I took a break between that and the next show and went out on the streets there in New York on the corner. And I smoked me a cigarette, and I said to myself, "You have just let some kid use you as a mop. Now, you get back in there, girl, and you make up for that loss."

It wasn't easy. We did four shows. During the second show, I'd put something in the microwave, and I was so intense on getting my stuff ready, not knowing none of these ingredients, and what do you think this French Froggy boy, Lulu, did? He'd snuck over and turned off my microwave so my food wasn't cooked right.

But good triumphs over evil. I think it was the third show that we did, we lifted up the domes, and I started cackling like an old hen. Under that dome was canned biscuits, black-eyed peas, grits, some ground beef. It was all Southern food. He did not have a clue what to do. You could see this very perplexed look on this boy's face. Under my breath, I say, "Well, Lulu, look who's screwed now!"

So, I'm keeping my eye on him as I'm putting my meal together. I look over there, and Lulu has got those canned biscuits. *And he is using a can opener on them.*

I say, "Lulu! Stop! Stop! They're gonna blow up on ya!" Well, he looked over at me and kept on going. He thought I was trying to sabotage him. And about that time, those biscuits blew out of that can and hit him in the face. And I laughed my butt off.

Come to find out later, they said we were one of the highest-rated shows that had been on *Ready . . . Set . . . Cook!*

I told you Lulu and I had four competitions. I won three. He won one. Don't screw with me, Lulus of the world.

The winner got a gold medallion like in the Olympics. They'd put it around your neck like you were this world champion.

I went on to do four more shows for *Ready . . . Set . . . Cook!* The next time, I was up against a great, big black chef out of N'Orleans, a giant of a chef. He was huge, and he was N'Orleans, and he did cooking classes for all the folks who came to visit the city. When the bell rang and we went to run to our domes, he got down in a football position and wouldn't let me get around him to get to my food. He blocked me.

I said, "Oh, my goodness. This one ain't gonna be easy either."

But we had a great time. So, after that, Food Network sent the people from the show *Food Finds* to see me. This was a wonderful show hosted by my friend Sandra Pinckney. The idea of the show is to track down the long-lost favorites of America's past—like kettle potato chips, homemade jam, or smokehouse sausage—by visiting small-town shops, mom-and-pop stores, and local vendors who take pride and pleasure making food the old-fashioned way. It's so strange because that show is now Jamie and Bobby's show. Sandra moved on to another network and *Food Finds* wanted to jazz up this very successful show. What Jamie and Bobby are doing is just like *Food Finds*, but they've changed the name to *Road Tasted*.

So, Food Network was just trying me out, exposing me to different television food experiences and looking hard at the way I handled them because that doll Gordon, aiming to push me into the big time and maybe even my own show, had introduced me to his agent, Barry Weiner. (Barry is better known to my family as Barry Cuda. Perfect name for an agent.)

I'll never forget the day I first laid eyes on Barry in the Greater Sheraton Restaurant. I was in Philadelphia doing QVC for my cookbook, and we made arrangements for Barry to drive from New York over to Philadelphia so we could chat in between shows. I never will forget when he walked in because when I had talked to him on the phone I could tell that I was talking to a smart New York Jewish man. Well, I was blown away when I saw him and realized he was Asian by birth. He had been adopted as an infant by a Jewish family who lived in like a seventh-floor flat in the Bronx. The man who walked into that restaurant in the Greater Sheraton with his fabulous Italian suit and fabulous Italian shoes just blew me away.

"You're just not what I pictured," I managed to say.

"I know," he answered.

Barry and Gordon felt like there was a show somewhere inside this Paula character that could be very successful. They probably courted Food Network for two years trying to push me at them. Food Network kept saying, politely, "Call us later."

Look—I didn't cook or look like their other fancy chefs, and they didn't think that America, in the throes of a health-food diet mania, was ready for this strange-talking, middle-aged, feisty, butter-wielding, mayo-spreading woman.

Gordon had come down and he shot a pilot in my kitchen at Turners Cove. It was so stinking bad that Barry would not allow the president of Food Network to see it. They had me in cashmere and pearls and high heels and this sleek hairdo. My stove was against the wall. It was a traditional stove, just like your stove at home. I've never seen a TV show that worked when your back was to the camera all the time, facing the stove. My niece, Corrie, was on the pilot with me, and she looked like a deer caught in the headlights because she was so scared. It was forced-looking, and Barry Cuda almost died when he saw it.

The president of Food Network at the time was named Judy Gerard. Barry and Judy were good friends, and he told her, "You cannot see this pilot; you just have to trust me on this one."

So Food Network never saw the pilot.

Then, one day, something terrible, terrible, terrible happened in this country, something that devastated the whole world, not just New York. And that was 9/11.

We were literally shaking here in the South, shaken to our bones. Our hearts were naked, knowing the tragedy that our northern neighbors were going through. It made me very aware that one moment I could be laughing and on top of the world, and the next minute I could be gone. It was a very, very scary time. Think back: Did you ever want to get on an airplane again? Nine out of ten people would say no. Would you ever want to get on a crowded train? No. It had us all frightened at every turn. How could they get us? We fixated on our water systems. We fixated on our transportation and national treasures. We became conscious of every way that we could have been gotten.

After a while, Barry and Gordon went back to Food Network, and they said, "Listen, this country's scared. We are all scared. We need comfort in our lives. We need to feel that safety again that we felt when we were home with our momma and our daddy with our feet under the table and we didn't have a care in the world. We all need to feel that again. And this woman, Paula Deen, can make us feel that way."

We never made another pilot. I got my show.

Paula's Home Cooking was born. It would launch in 2002.

Georgia Cracker Salad

One of the most popular dishes on *Paula's Home Cooking* is Georgia Cracker Salad. People are always surprised that it's made out of saltine crackers, and we get so much mail from the Georgia Cracker Salad show, we need to have our own postal delivery person just for the one show! I've modified the dish I make on the show and in the restaurant by adding shrimp, which makes it positively irresistible.

This is a wonderful summer lunch or an easy summer late dinner, but you want to stir it all together and eat it immediately, or else your saltine crackers will get soggy. As soon as you fold the ingredients together, put the shrimp cracker salad on those lettuce leaves and sit down and enjoy!

1 pound shrimp (do not peel)
1 sleeve saltine crackers
2 cups mayonnaise
1 large tomato, finely chopped
3 green onions, finely chopped
1 hard-boiled egg, finely chopped
1 head Boston leaf lettuce, washed, dried, and separated
  into leaves
Pimiento slices, for garnish (optional)
Cucumber slices, for garnish (optional)

Boil up the shrimp for 2 to 3 minutes in salty or seasoned water in a pot; you can use crab boil if you like. Next, peel and clean the shrimp, removing the tails. If they're large, you can chop them coarsely. Crush the crackers, combine the mayonnaise, tomato, green onions, and egg, add the crackers, then immediately fold the warm shrimp into the salad and serve on lettuce leaves. Garnish with pimiento and cucumber slices, if desired.

Chapter 13

BACKSTAGE SECRETS AND A WEDDIN' TO BEAT ALL

There are spitters and there are swallowers.
I'm a swallower.

They were going to give me my own cooking show! I couldn't believe it. But before that even happened, I got a phone call that was almost as thrillin' as being a TV star.

It was the middle of lunch at The Lady & Sons on 311 Congress Street, and we were working furiously. I wasn't doing as much cooking in the kitchen as I had in the early years, but on that day in 2002, I was back there frying chicken because we had gotten slammed with guests and I was trying to help everybody get the food out. Girl, we were busy. Rance Jackson, who was now our manager, had his cell phone clipped to the waist of his pants and it rang, and he answered it. Something about his manner made me stop and pay attention, and then I heard him say, "Yes, please, just a minute."

He handed me the phone, saying, "Paula. For you. It's Oprah."

Now, I'm standing there with flour and goop on my hands, frying this chicken, and I look at Rance and I say, "You just get the hell out," and he grins and stutters, "No, Paula, it really is the *Oprah* show."

Our kitchen was insanely loud, crowded, and tiny. You couldn't have a private conversation in that kitchen if you were a deaf mute. I said hello, and, of course, it wasn't Oprah herself but a member of her staff.

They had heard about me, she said. Oprah was doing a show on women who started successful businesses in their homes and she would like to invite me to be on the show, but before that could happen, they wanted first to interview me over the telephone. I thought I didn't hear them right, so I asked them to wait a moment and took the phone into a quieter place. We made a time and a place to talk when it wouldn't be so blasted noisy, and the next week, sure enough, a producer called with some questions about my life. Then another producer called with some more questions. Finally, they called me back for the last time and told me, "We definitely want you on the show." Whoa! *Oprah!* She was my hero.

It was explained to me that five different businesswomen would be in the audience that day. Two, possibly three, of us would have the opportunity to come up onstage and sit with Oprah.

I couldn't breathe, I couldn't sleep, I could think of nothing else for days. I wanted so much to go meet this woman, look her in the eye, and see if she was the woman who America thought she was because, to me, the eyes are the windows to the soul. It's hard to be tricked by somebody if you're allowed to see into their eyes. She'd become one of the most powerful people in the world, and in order to do so she had to overcome so many obstacles. I sure knew from my own experience that to be a poor little black girl growing up in the South in the fifties was a tremendous challenge. Oprah had survived incest, rape, prejudices, many, many forms of heartbreak, and I'd always admired her.

The day of the taping, in Chicago, the other women and I took our seats in the audience. During a commercial break, one of the producers came over and whispered to me that I was the third one chosen to go up on the stage to talk with her, but they didn't know how much time we were going to have. I almost screamed.

We were all seated in the first row, right in front of Oprah. The three of us who were going to get to go up and sit next to Oprah went one at a time. We didn't have to compete with one another. Oprah gave each of us time to share our individual stories. That's the kind of woman she is.

Well, when I got up on that stage, I felt that she and I immediately bonded. Look, I'm not terribly impressed with celebrity, and I'm not a groupie type of person. We all put on our britches the same way and we all pull 'em down the same way to go to the bathroom. But when I got up to that stage, I took her hand, and I think I kissed it—do you believe it?

I said the first thing that popped into my mind.

"I feel like I'm meeting the queen," I stammered. She laughed and answered, "No, honey, I was with the real queen the other day."

I knew she didn't mean Elton John.

"And let me tell you," she finished, "I ain't a queen."

How could you not be comfortable with someone like that? Yup, I decided in about two minutes that she was the woman America loved. I think she truly cares about other people, and you know what? Crazy as it seems, in that short time on her stage, I sure felt she cared about me. I have seen Oprah without makeup, and she kind of reminds me of myself, because we're not at our prettiest without Maybelline magic. Oprah's skin was just as smooth as a baby's butt, the color of milk chocolate. Delicious. Her hair was fixed so nice and she was smaller than I thought—not skinny, not chunky, just voluptuous. She's the kind of woman I cook for, sexy and sensual, not that pencil-thin type.

I felt so proud. Jamie, Bobby, and my Aunt Peggy were sitting there in the second row, their faces grinning with excitement, and I'm sitting up here by Oprah and thinking, *Only in America could this happen. I'm sitting up here to the right of the queen even if she doesn't think she's the queen.*

She said, "So, you can cook."

I said, "Well, I didn't get this way by looking at the pictures of cake, Oprah."

She liketa fell out of her chair. The audience went nuts. Right at the first, we hit it off. We laughed together, and we teared up together during the interview. I probably had only ten minutes with her, but I quickly gave her a short version of my life story, and I told her that at forty-two, I took complete responsibility for my life, and God had not missed one day blessing me for doing that. I could see the tears forming in her eyes. I really felt connected to this woman.

And then I did a smart thing. Grass don't grow under my feet, honey, even when I'm with the queen. I announced right there on *Oprah* that shortly I was going to have my own cooking show on the Food Network.

Do you know how many people watch *Oprah*? About ninety zillion. My restaurant had been doin' real well and usually had a waiting line, but after *Oprah,* it seemed like people were coming from all over the world. Everyone was asking when my show was starting. I was amazed that Oprah's arms were so long and they stretched out so far. The Lady & Sons became a destination trip for many people. Fact was, I couldn't fit any more people into the restaurant no matter what show I was on because I had just so many tables, and that's when I started thinking about moving to a much bigger place.

When I got home, I wrote Oprah a note even though I knew she'd probably never get to read it, the note being among thousands she gets every week. But I still wanted to write. "Girl, I want you to come to Savannah," I said. "I want you to put your feet under my table and let me feed y'all. I'll protect you. I won't let anybody know you're here." So far, she hasn't come, but I'll never forget my time with Oprah Winfrey.

Paula's Home Cooking began very quietly. We just starting filming, with me cookin' and chattin', and from the beginning it was a huge success. People were incredibly receptive, I think *because* I was not a size 2, but instead a sassy, roundish, white-headed cook. Women could identify with me. I reminded them of their aunt or their mother or their grandmother or their best friend who lived next door. I could be them, and they could be me. I even ate like them, which brings me to the very first show that I taped.

We taped the show in Gordon Elliott's home kitchen in Millbrook, New York, for the first couple of years. Because it was my first show, I was rightly a little scared. I got through the first dish, and I pulled me out a fork to taste it. Of course, I tasted it with the same robustness that I would have done in my own kitchen. Maybe a little bit dripped down from the corner of my mouth onto my shirt. Usually does. So what?

Gordon jumps out of his director chair, his arms in the air. "Paula, dahling, dahling, dahling! You must take princess bites," he directs.

"What the hell is a princess bite?" I asked.

"It's that little, teeny, delicate bite that lets you taste the food but still allows you to talk coherently. You can't take huge chunks of food in your mouth on television."

"Get the hell out," I answered him. "I ain't takin' no princess bites. I'm gonna do it just like I do it."

And he turned around. It was so funny. He said like a little boy, "Oh, okay, so freak me and freak the Food Network." And he went and climbed back into his director's chair and never said another word about no princess bites. And it wasn't *freak* he actually said.

Let me tell you something. I bet Oprah don't take princess bites. She's a *real* woman.

Now here it seems appropriate to say some more words on cursing, even though I briefly dealt with it right in the start of this book. I must admit I'm loose with four-letter words, not on television, of course, but in the privacy of my own home. Still, there's one that I do not use in a curse. I never say GD. I try to never take my Lord's name in vain unless like I stump a toe or somethin'. And then, possibly, I forget.

When you work in a kitchen in the restaurant business, you become the best curser in town because you're constantly dealing with a tremendous amount of frustration. You get very, very, *very* good at four-letter words, and there's even a chance that with the different cultures in your kitchen, all those diverse people coming together, you'll even learn some new four-letter words. So, you burn your hand bad. You're not gonna say "Shoot." You're not gonna say "Oh, my goodness." You're gonna say *"Shit!"* When you burn yourself or you drop this whole tray of food that you've got to get to the guests who are waiting in the restaurant, you're not gonna say "Oh, my gumdrops." You're just not gonna do it. So, if you are offended by four-letter words, don't ever get a job in a restaurant and certainly don't own a restaurant.

Look, I understand how people can be offended by the particular kind of colorful language that usually employs some four-letter words. Sometimes, when I have been around people who are constantly using four-letter words in a mean-spirited way, I almost want to wipe myself down after being in their presence, because those words are said in a filthy or mean spirit. On the other hand, I can hear other people say the same thing with maybe a smile on their face and a lighter delivery, and I think nothing of it. So, a lot of times, the deliverer or the speaker of the bad words determines whether that word becomes dirty or not.

Still, I was the first Food Network host ever to get bleeped on TV, and that's when I learned you can't do the kinds of things on television that you can do in your home or when you're writing a book. I understand that. If you come to my house, and you want to see the real Paula Deen, it would be stupid for me to say I never use four-letter words. But I do apologize to my fans who are shocked that their Paula has this part of her that maybe they never heard or saw before from me. I'm still the same me who loves you, everyone—just maybe a *tad* bawdier than you thought.

At the same time, I'm wanting to go after a big children's audience for my show and I do want people to know that their children are safe with me. If a tray falls on my foot on television, you'll never hear me say what I say in my own kitchen. I promise you that.

You know what I suspect? I think even the most ardent church lady, in the privacy of her own home, doesn't say "Oh, my gumdrops" when she drops a tray on her foot.

My show is the best fun, second only to running a restaurant. Here are some little-known behind-the-scenes peeks at what goes on in a cooking show.

First of all, believe it or not, there's no script on my show, no set plan for what I'm going to say. It's totally ad-libbed. When you watch my little corner of the Food Network, you should know that of course I've thought about what I'm goin' to cook for that show and what I want to tell viewers, and of course everyone else on the show is totally prepared for that meal, but there are no writers involved. It's only me, Paula, talking to you as I would if you were sittin' in my own kitchen—which explains the occasional silliness. I use my own dishes and my own pans in the cooking, and my own appliances as well. Maybe other hosts do different; I don't know. I can only tell you about my show.

The first question people ask me when I meet them is, "That yellow house—it's yours, right?" And, oh my gosh, I just hate telling them, "No, it's not my house. It's Gordon Elliott's house." We taped every show up to Thanksgiving 2005 in Gordon's house, which he shares with a gorgeous, sweet wife named Sophie and three of the cutest little miniatures of Gordon Elliott you have ever seen.

Then people always ask whose dogs they're seeing on the show. I usually stand behind Michael to answer that one because the viewers literally groan when I tell them those three dogs are Gordon's as well and their names are Rennie, Gertie, and Harry. I fell in love with them from day one, especially Gertie, the yellow Lab who was always the first one to greet me when I pulled up to Gordon's driveway to start filming.

The Thanksgiving special of 2005 kicked off the filming of *Paula's Home Cooking* in Michael's and my new house, so if you're watching shows filmed since then, it's Otis, Sam, and Cody you're seeing—our very own dogs. Cody is my stepson, a big old black Lab who came with Michael, but sometimes Michael walks Otis and Sam with their rhinestone collars, and if he runs into people who recognize him, which is always, he tells them they're our huntin' dogs—all eight ounces of them.

Then there are a whole lot of people who ask if we cooking show hosts really eat *and* swallow our own food during the taping. I don't know what other people do, and I've also heard the rumors that some television chefs turn away from the camera for a moment and spit out into specially placed "spit bowls" what they've just tasted, or, even worse, force themselves to vomit afterward because they're nervous about gaining weight. Maybe they think that if they eat everything, they'll wind up looking like me. Let me tell you, honey, while there may indeed be spitters and swallowers on television cooking shows, I am definitely in the latter group. Those bites you see me taking—the definitely-*not*-princess bites—are truly and happily swallowed by Paula Deen. But me? I enjoy every mouthful of the food that's prepared, especially the food that I actually get to cook.

Another secret (that I guess is not such a secret anymore): I don't actually cook every morsel that's featured on a show. In thirty minutes, you can't produce a full meal—well, maybe if you're Rachael Ray you can. But even she can't cook a pot roast in a half-hour show. So, to me, that crew in the back kitchen is very, very important. I don't know how much training they have, but they have my recipes and they're out of sight, making three of each dish because we have to have the beauty shots for the start and finish. Then we have to have a backup, in case anything happens to the dish that I've prepared as you watch me on TV. Finally, we need what we call swap-out dishes ready for me on the set.

Look, the camera's on me, I put the roast in, you see a commercial, and two minutes later I come back and say, "The roast is ready." Did I fool *anyone* on the planet into thinking the roast I put in is the one that's ready? I didn't think so. Actually, by the time they get the commercials in, you have only twenty-two minutes to prepare all this food. So, you need the swap-outs.

Another thing: food temperature counts. I'm very easy to work with, but I insist that the food has to be hot if it's supposed to be hot, or cold if it's iced tea or watermelon, just as I'd serve it to Michael. I cannot fake the "yummy" look if I chunk down into cold mashed potatoes. Sometimes that happens. Once in a great while

I'll say, "Ooh, this is just delicious," but I can't help wrinkling my nose in horror because the swap-out dish is either seasoned poorly or the wrong temperature.

Invariably, there's a great yell of *"Cut!"* from backstage and Gordon or someone else will run out and say, "You don't like that dish. What's wrong with it?" And we have to reshoot that piece of the show.

Who comes up with the show theme? Well, Follow Productions, owned by Gordon Elliott, will come up with themes like a summer brunch, a Valentine's Day dinner, a birthday barbecue. Then my staff works on going through all my personal files to pick out just the right dishes for the themes.

I'm always asked what happens to the food we cook on the show. Usually, we all dig in and eat it right after the show. Sometimes, people who work backstage in the kitchen take the food home, especially if they live close by. But I'm telling you, I think nobody enjoys the food more than Gordon Elliott. I'll never forget the day I was doing hamburgers, and I was cookin' what ended up being called a Beau Burger, which was topped with a fried egg. Actually I wanted to call it a Sambo Burger. It came about when this motorcycle-driving, long-haired lawyer named Sam told me about his favorite little hamburger joint owned by a guy named Beau. When Sam was out tooling along on his cycle, he'd stop off for the best burger in town, topped with a fried egg, some melted cheese, a load of grilled onions—out of this world! One day, Sam was on my set because we were doing a show about motorcycles, and we were standin' around talking about these burgers and I told him, "Sam, I am going to do that burger on the show. We'll call it after you—the Sambo Burger. You know—Sam, Beau. Sounds great, doesn't it?"

Well, my producers said no—I had to find another name, because some people associated the name with an old children's book that was insulting to black people. So we called it a Beau

Burger after the guy who owned the joint, and I made that hamburger on the set during the cooking show, took one bite out of it, and my eyes rolled back in my head, it was so stinkin' good. All of a sudden, Gordon yells *"Cut!"* and he runs up there with his big old size 15 shoes, those big old feet just *clomp, clomp, clomp* running up there, and he snatches that burger out of my hand and says, "You don't need that, Paula," and he gobbles down the whole thing.

Sam, I haven't seen ya since that day, but I just got to tell you, if you're reading this book, you were right on with that burger.

Lots of things can go wrong in a shoot, but you usually don't see them. Sometimes, if you're working with as loony and brilliant a director as Gordon Elliott, some mistakes don't even get cut because he thinks they're funny—and they probably will embarrass you forever. For example, when I was a kid, I used to love Creamsicles, a confection of vanilla ice cream covered with orange ice on a stick. One day, I told my crew that for a great dessert we could reproduce the flavor of Creamsicles by layering orange sherbet and vanilla ice cream in a dish, freezing it, and then slicing it. We'd call it dreamsicles. Well, this was just going to be so simple because I was using store-bought sherbet and store-bought vanilla cream. I told the kitchen staff, "You will need to line the dish with parchment paper to come up on the sides before you put in the cream and sherbet. That way I'll be able to grab that parchment paper and just flip out the dreamsicles."

On camera I pull my backup dish out of the freezer—the one that had already been frozen and set—and to my horror I see that the crew had cut the parchment paper just to fit the bottom.

"All right, I can do this," I tell myself, and with a fixed smile I take a knife and run it around the edges. I flip this thing over, and it ain't budging. And I have no paper to grab on to. There is a monitor in the back kitchen so that the kitchen staff can see what's going on and run in with what I need if something happens. So,

I'm looking at the camera and I'm saying, "We'll try that one more time . . ." No one is running in to help me. I'm struggling with this ice cream, trying to keep cool and trying to figure out how I'm going to get it out of the pan. I take a warm rag and rub the bottom, just trying to get out this damn dreamsicle in one take so we don't waste footage. I struggle for probably three minutes, trying to make small talk and work this dreamsicle out of the container, and all of a sudden I hear the kitchen staff just giggling because they're standing back there watching me struggle.

So I say, "You buncha son of a bitches! Y'all didn't leave me no paper to grab, on purpose!" And everybody was laughing, and of course Gordon was telling the cameras to keep rolling. And it made it to the air that way, with "bitches" bleeped out.

People are so into the shows. They think every speck they see is real, just as it happens. Of course, the food is real, but there are so many cuts and edits in there to make it flow smoothly, make the time work out and give the poor cook some paper to grab to get her dreamsicles free.

When my show first aired, I was told that there was a fan board that people could go to on Foodnetwork.com, and they could open up viewer conversations about the show they'd just seen. Well, I was just amazed, and a little insulted and hurt, when people would make comments like "Did you see Paula lick her fingers while she was seasoning that meat? How nasty!"

Listen, if there's a person out there who works in her kitchen that doesn't lick her fingers while she's cooking, I'll lick yo' heinie!

Someone would write, "Did you see that? She didn't wash her hands." Or once I read, "She walked in with those herbs from the garden and didn't wash them—did you see *that*? How could they let this woman behave that way in a restaurant?"

My answer? This show is called *Paula's Home Cooking*. It is not called *Paula's Restaurant Cooking,* and there's a big difference. Rest assured, I do not feed the folks in my restaurant what's been cooked on my show. On television, I'm representing a woman in her home, not in a restaurant kitchen. Even so, there are edits that you don't see when I'm out back there, washing my hands. There are edits after I taste something, when I'm changing spoons, or washing herbs that you don't see.

Every now and then, someone will say she's so upset that I'm wearing my diamond engagement ring on television. I once read, "Why does she have to show off that bling when she's cooking— it's so *unsanitary*!"

Well, you know what? That ring was a gift from the love of my life and I've never before had anything like it. I'm not going to have it sittin' in someone's pocket even for thirty minutes. If I were home cooking in my kitchen, it'd be on my finger, just like ya own ring doesn't leave ya finger when you're cookin' up eggs. Right?

What makes it all okay in the end is that, in contrast, I have so many people come on that fan board sayin', "Paula, don't ever stop licking your fingers. Don't ever stop enjoying your food. I love seeing that big old ring shining on your finger." Most people *get it,* they know me.

Every now and then, we have a special on *Paula's Home Cooking*. The most incredible special of all time was filmed in March 2004.

Michael and I hadn't yet set a date and one day I received a phone call that forced us to get moving. The Food Network was asking if we'd consider getting married on television. Would we invite America to the wedding of my dreams?

I was game; it sounded like fun, and I knew they'd do a great job and be as unobtrusive as possible, but it was up to Michael. He wasn't used to being so out and upfront with his personal life, and if it made him uncomfortable, case closed.

"Michael, something wonderful has happened," I said to him

one day, "but if you have any reservations, just say so. They want us to get married on my show."

He looked at me and grinned. "Sure, why not, I've never done that before." What a sport! Wedding wheels were set into motion. We'd be married on March 6, 2004, and a one-hour wedding special would be broadcast in June 2004.

For several months before the wedding, I was feeling overwhelmed. It's true, I felt like Cinderella, but the preparations turned out to be intense. I had to swallow my pride—me, who always could tackle and handle anything that was thrown my way—because it looked like I needed a wedding planner who could smoothly put a million details together for me. Michael and I had decided on an intimate ceremony of 75 family members and close friends (because we couldn't see them, we wouldn't even think about the zillions of people who would be at the wedding via television), and afterward we'd have about 650 guests at a reception at—where else—The Lady & Sons. We'd always loved the tiny Whitfield Chapel at Bethesda, which is the oldest working orphanage in America. The chapel holds only a hundred people and so it was perfect for the ceremony. Set on acres of rolling green grounds, the charming chapel has time-worn wooden benches and pews where thousands of orphaned boys have prayed their hopes and dreams. I'd felt peace and wonder in that chapel and I could just visualize our loved ones flanking a canopy-covered aisle with white hydrangeas, French tulips, my garden roses, English ivy, and elaeagnus (small, fragrant silvery white flowers no one knows about but me and my brilliant assistant, Brandon Branch). Even Otis and Sam, our Shih Tzus, would be watching us get married. Corrie was charged with making sure those two didn't escape, like the last time, when they'd found me a neighbor.

I would rather have had a gasoline enema than do the guest list. I mean, I hated the thought of doing that thing. Getting names out of Michael was like pulling eyeteeth. I knew this was not going to be easy, and him being a typical man did not help. So, we would work on those invitations every day, and we finally got them all out.

Then we had to do another thing that was just as horrible: I had to find a dress. I put it off as long as I could because it ain't fun if you're a fat girl trying to find clothes. I can't stand to clothes shop, period. Finally, I had to go to the bridal shops. I was trying on all these dresses in all these places and I finally said to the last salesperson, "You know, it's just very upsetting. I have eaten too many pieces of chicken and too many hoe cakes and biscuits; now here it is, time for me to get a weddin' dress, and I forgot to start a diet." The wedding planner, Tricia Windon, had handled most of the other details, but no one could help that sick feeling when I walked into those wedding-dress shops. They stocked mostly size 4 gowns, except for the few outsized ones that made me look like Granddaddy Paul in drag.

Still, Michael assured me that I was beautiful. I really felt so when I ended up having a dress custom-made of crisply elegant white organza with a soft but tailored long-sleeved jacket. It was made by my friend Kate, who'd had her own line of clothes in Chicago and moved to Savannah just in time for me. She almost designed the dress as we went along. I wanted something that would remind me of my momma and what she would have loved, and it ended up so pretty, I had just that beautiful dress, all alone, painted on the wall in the guest room of my home.

Now that I had me a wedding planner, I also needed a special cake maker, and of all the people Tricia came up with, Molly Stone was my choice. When Michael was a little boy, his mother used to bake his favorite cake in the whole world for him, a banana nut cake with cream cheese icing. Molly and I decided to surprise him with that very same cake as his groom's cake. Following tradition, the single women would each take home a little piece of that cake in a tiny box to put under their pillows and dream about the man she would marry. Our wedding cake would be a pound cake made with sour cream, almond, and orange extract. It would be frosted with a pale-yellow buttercream icing and finished off with fresh flowers like the groom's cake.

I knew I had to plan the food for the reception stayin' true to my traditions. We'd have a station for shrimp and grits, which would be served hot in martini glasses. We'd have very traditional tomato sandwiches, okra sandwiches, steamship rounds of beef, crab-stuffed shrimp, and white-bread handle sandwiches, which are drumettes of fried chicken wings tied with leeks. There would be fruit trays with fresh cream, a raw oyster bar, and the only thing that wasn't really Southern would be the wontons I loved—but we'd stuff them with collard greens and cream cheese to make them Southern, different, and delicious.

Before the wedding my friends threw a bridal shower for me, which was also taped by Food Network. It was a riot. Jamie and Bobby showed up as bridesmaids in long, gorgeous dresses.

"I feel beautiful," crooned Bobby. A couple of years later, in June 2006, when Bobby was voted by *People* magazine as one of the most gorgeous and eligible bachelors in the country, I was real pleased they didn't find a photo of him in his bridesmaid dress.

Jamie did not feel so beautiful. "I think this whole bridesmaid-dress thing—which my brother talked me into—is going to unhinge my personal presidential campaign one day," he noted.

The day of the wedding finally dawned magnificent. Bubba informed me it was the last time he was givin' me away. We rented a horse-drawn carriage to take us to the church: I felt like Cinderella just praying twelve o'clock would never come.

I looked at my white-bearded, seagoin' Michael and giggled with happiness through much of the ceremony. I was still a little worried about his comfort level bein' married on television, and I was hoping he wouldn't pass out on me. I will never forget when Bubba walked me down the aisle that Michael's face, when we got to him, was as red as a Coca-Cola cup. I said to myself, *Lord have mercy, if I had a blood pressure pill, I'd pop it in his mouth.*

I'd met my soul mate at last, of that there was no doubt. Two middle-aged lovers were madly in love, walkin' back up that aisle feeling such a wave of joy that had never been felt by no twenty-year-old. I just knew that.

We were going to be great together, I knew that too. Michael says that he thought for many years his mother had been telling him to marry a "kook." He couldn't figure out why she was saying that, and years later he figured out she was saying "cook." After he'd come to know me, he figured he couldn't go wrong: "I married a kook who turned out to be a cook," he loves to say.

Funny thing—we never saw a camera during that whole wedding; the Food Network cameramen were so discreet. Our good friend Tom Edenfield, an attorney and a judge here in town, married us. Michael's brother Hank, a Catholic priest, led us in prayer in his white robe. We were so *in* the moment. I remember feeling like my feet were not quite touching the floor and someone would have to slap me hard to get the silly grin off my face. I'm so thrilled we decided to get married on my show, because now I have wedding pictures the likes of which no one has ever had before.

Mrs. Groover's Banana Nut Delight Cake

From Michael's momma's memory and my cooking smarts, we reconstructed Banana Nut Delight Cake, his supreme favorite dessert, for his groom's cake at the wedding. It turned out to be delicious, but not *exactly* the cake he remembered so fondly. Imagine my own delight when, a year later, we found Mrs. Groover's original recipe box and the true Banana Nut Delight Cake recipe written in pencil on a little card in her own hand. Here it is. Now we have to have the weddin' all over again with this exactly right groom's cake.

CAKE

> 2½ cups sifted cake flour
> 1⅔ cups sugar
> 1¼ teaspoons baking powder
> 1¼ teaspoons baking soda
> 1 teaspoon salt
> 1 teaspoon ground cinnamon
> ⅔ cup vegetable shortening
> ⅔ cup buttermilk
> 1¼ cups mashed ripe banana
> 2 eggs

1. Preheat the oven to 350°F. Grease and flour three 8-inch or two 9-inch cake pans.
2. Sift the dry ingredients into a large mixing bowl; add the shortening, buttermilk, and banana. Mix until all the dry ingredients are dampened, then beat at low speed for 2 minutes. Add the eggs and beat for 1 minute. Pour the batter into the prepared pans and bake for 25 to 30 minutes. Cool for 10 minutes in the pans, then turn out on a rack to cool completely before frosting.

Banana Nut Frosting

One 8-ounce package cream cheese, at room temperature
1 stick unsalted butter, at room temperature
One 1-pound box confectioners' sugar
1 teaspoon vanilla extract
1 cup chopped pecans

Combine all the ingredients except for the pecans and beat until fluffy. Fold in the pecans, and frost the cake. If you love lots of icing, you can make 1½ times this recipe. Remember, this is not banana bread but a stacked cake, so be sure to frost between the layers as well as the outside.

Chapter 14

BLEND. DON'T MIX, STIR, OR BEAT

Kiss the nuclear family good-bye, y'all.

*I*f y'all are marrying for the second time, and either or both of you have children from your first marriage, kiss the nuclear family good-bye. No more is life going to be a dreamy picture of one momma, one daddy, and their kids. It's not even going to be just yours, mine, and maybe ours, if you're young enough. Take it from Auntie Paula. We're now talkin' yours, mine, ours, theirs, their in-laws, and maybe one hundred thousand other cousins, uncles, aunts, and pets.

I read a statistic saying that of all the reasons for breakups in a second marriage (and about 60 percent of remarriages end in divorce), the failure of the new family to blend without shaming or blaming one another is number one. I wanted our blessed marriage to succeed more than I wanted to breathe. But the truth? It damn near came close to failing.

It doesn't matter that the blended family is becoming increasingly common and that about one in three Americans is now a stepparent, stepchild, stepsibling, or step*something;* it's *still* hard to get right. Since nuclear families fail about 50 percent of the time, is it any wonder that the new, blended families are so hard to get the hang of?

When you think about a stepmother, which I had become, what comes to mind may be Cinderella's warty witch of a stepmother, or Hansel and Gretel's stepmother, who threw those blessed babies to the wolves. Well, most stepmothers are not warty witches, but stepmothering also isn't anything like they promised in *The Brady Bunch,* and it sure ain't *Yours, Mine and Ours* or any of all the other feel-good blended-family movies you see out there.

Fact is, you cannot force a family to blend. You cannot take two separate families and force them to like each other, and then force them to create something they don't feel. Making a real family takes time, not force. When his and her families first meet, they don't have history together so they have to be willing to go slow enough to form memories together. You have to be able to get to a point where you can sit around a table and say, "Do you remember when we all got lost in Disneyland? Remember when you cooked me the soggy grits?"

We all got to have patience. We live in a world of instant. We want that thirty-second meal from McDonald's. We want that million-dollar payment from that lottery ticket. But, deep down, don't we know that the most important, treasured things are those that you have to wait for to get? And, for sure, family is the best treasure you can have, and it takes waiting.

I learned that some people can do it better than others. Taking the Groover and Deen families and trying to make them one happy loving group was among the greatest challenges I ever had. When kids in a second marriage are older, as ours were, with the courage of their own convictions, they're as set in their ways as your ninety-seven-year-old grandpa.

Thank God, in the end I figured it out: successful family blending is kind of like making a delicious but delicate blueberry muffin. You don't want to stir it hard and you certainly don't want to beat it. You want to take that spatula to gently fold the butter, milk, eggs, flour, sugar, salt, baking powder, and those fragile blueberries together until each ingredient is just wet enough to absorb the goodness of the other ingredients. A blending of two families is kinda like that. You can't overwork it, trying to make a perfect single family who fall in love with one another and blend effortlessly. If you vigorously mix, stir, or beat the ingredients together, those berries—those people—will mush and crush and never blend.

This is the way it was with Michael and me. On my side, I had my two sons who were very, very protective of their mother. They were so wary that a man would walk in and bamboozle their mother not only out of her heart but also out of her money. So, on one hand my children wanted me to find companionship, but on the other hand they saw the dangers a new marriage could bring to the table. They are savvy enough to know that there are people out there who will do anything for financial gain, people with no morals or ethics.

On Michael's side there were two almost-grown children, Michelle and Anthony. My sons weren't pushovers, but let me tell you somethin', girls are *tough*. I was a girl—I know. I was nineteen years old when my daddy died. My mother was thirty-nine years old, a beautiful woman with a lot of life still ahead of her. She met this older man, on the country side in his personality. Curtis was not nearly as dynamic or energetic as my daddy, but he was a good, soft-spoken salt-of-the-earth guy. He loved my mother and gave her company and comfort.

Well, I acted like the biggest bitch. I never will forget the day I went over to my momma's, to the house I was raised in, and Momma and Curtis were sitting at the table. I think I'd tapped on the door to just let them know that I was coming in, and Curtis said, "Come in."

It was me who knocked, but I still said to myself in fury, *Why the hell is he telling me to come into my own daddy's house!* I was twenty years old, so full of anger, and I came in that door and slammed the hell out of it, about slammed that door off those hinges. How dare this man be sitting in my daddy's house and be giving *me* permission to come in! I marched around to the back of the house to Momma's bedroom, so self-centered that the only world I cared about was mine. I never wanted that new marriage to happen.

And it never did.

Michael's daughter, Michelle, had been living with Michael and her brother in Michael's home ever since her momma and daddy got divorced. When I met her I kind of understood her pain and the threat I represented. I'd been in her shoes. But although I *kind* of understood, I didn't understand completely, not by a long shot. It was not that she thought I was going to try to replace her mother, with whom both kids had a very good relationship, it was the fact that I was going to take her daddy away from her. Michelle was very young to have worn so many different hats as her daddy's girl, but wear them she did. Michael and she had an extraordinary relationship. While I worshipped my daddy, he didn't count on me to keep the wheels of our lives turning. It was just a straight-out "I love you—you love me."

But Michael counted on Michelle for so much more, and she knew her daddy needed her. Part of her loved that and depended on it for her sense of safety. It was a great responsibility. Michael probably relied on her too much, because she had so much more sense than most girls her age. She would help him pay the bills, do the cleaning, and make important decisions. You know, even when her folks were married she took on some of these responsibilities. She helped raise her brother, Anthony, and teach him life's lessons.

But when it came to dealing with me, she was nineteen, about the same age as I was when I turned on my momma's gentleman friend, and she was not acting much different from the way I had acted.

I felt her pain, partially. But bein' the adult, I knew that she needed to learn to love her daddy not any less, but develop a relationship where she didn't feel so responsible for his welfare. She needed to feel like she was a nineteen-year-old girl. If we could all hang in there we'd be okay.

But I'll tell you what: from the beginning I suspected I was headed for trouble coming up against this headstrong, angry, jealous young woman. In the end, though, I was to learn that every family should be so lucky to have a Michelle, with her sense of loyalty. I learned that if trouble came your way, you'd want this girl on your side because she would absolutely take a bullet for you. I was to learn it—but honey, I sure didn't know it yet.

Michael's son, Anthony, was all boy. When I came into their lives, his daddy was pretty fed up with Michael Anthony Groover Jr. because he was not performing well at school. At the time, Anthony's heart was sad because his father had made a decision that was very hard for both of them—to send his son off to military school. It was so important that Anthony know Michael was not doing it to get rid of him but to build character and pride into this young man. Apparently, it was clear to Anthony that he wasn't being sent away as a punishment, because it turned out he came home every weekend. He did well, just as Michael hoped, and he graduated with plans to follow in his daddy's footsteps as a harbor docking pilot. Because Anthony was not living at home, we met at the end of the summer, before he was to leave for Camden Military School. I instantly saw he was this precious, precious boy, and I could see a lot of his daddy in him—like once you got to know him, he was full of smart-ass comments and sarcasm. From the start, Anthony was very open to me. He'd been used to seeing his sister in a very close relationship with his father, and so it was much easier for him to accept me, another of those pushy females, into his family. He embraced me immediately and would put his arms around me and kiss me and say, "I love you."

Once Anthony told me that he never felt he was forced to love me, but he did quickly fall in love with the idea of his daddy's happiness. That's what mattered most to him. He said he didn't feel negative or positive about the weddin', but was just along for the ride, and when the ride turned out smooth, he was glad.

But Michelle was a different story. In her book, I was a dead ringer for Cinderella's wicked stepmother.

Well, except for my relationship with Michelle, things finally did start to settle down. I can't tell you the relief that my boys felt when they found out that the new man in my life was financially secure, had a very good job, and did not need my money. I was adamantly against a prenuptial agreement, which I knew was popular, but, in my mind, kind of unsavory. To me, asking somebody to sign a prenup almost makes you feel like you're going into a marriage expecting it to fail. You are discussing how you're going to handle things if the marriage fails instead of talking about how you're going to make it succeed. Look—I'm no dummy—I was going to protect my boys' money and I was going to see to it that nobody was going to take what was rightfully theirs. I knew I could do this through lawyers, setting up special trusts, for example. Michael and I made an appointment with my attorney, and we wrote our wills. We made sure that should something happen to the other, each of us would always have a place to live. But

Michael's money would go to his children, and my money would go to my children. At the time of both of our deaths, our four children would come together and split the property and share equally. I did not want to start a marriage off saying, "Listen, you son of a bitch, I don't trust you." I can understand why Donald Trump would want a prenup, but it was not for me. In no time, my children came to have a lot of respect and love for Michael. Of course they love their daddy, Jimmy Deen, but there was enough love inside them that they could allow another man to come into their mother's life. The same with Anthony.

But that daddy's girl! That Michelle.

Michael was definitely caught in the middle of two women whom he loved more than anything in the world. It was a very uncomfortable situation for him because the bottom line was that his daughter and I were both jealous of each other, and jealous of the power that each had over the man we loved. Meanness passed between us too many times. I didn't quite know how to handle it, but I knew I'd better learn because I was trying to be the grown-up in the situation. In many ways, I was startin' to love Michelle because her daddy loved her and he'd told me so many wonderful things about her. But the truth was that I didn't like her, and she neither loved nor liked me.

Michael and I had looked high and low for a house to live in, but we couldn't find any land that was prettier than the property on Turners Creek that he owned. He had four floating docks, which he rented out, and one dilapidated dock house that he'd converted into a home for him and his family, and in which the children had grown up. Finally, Michael convinced me that the best thing to do would be to tear down the old house and build exactly the house we both wanted in its stead on his property right on the water. This was the plan: while Michael's house was being torn down, Anthony, home from military school, and Michelle would move into my house with Michael and me. We planned to create wonderful new rooms for them in the new house. I was so excited thinking how I would spend any amount to please the children of the man I loved.

But when the kids moved in with us, I also remember thinking to myself that first day, *I need some control here. I'm going to get this girl who dislikes me to understand that this is my house.*

So Michelle has a load of dirty laundry and she says with real attitude, "I would like for my clothes to be washed separately." I remember replying, "Well, I *don't* want them washed separately. We might not have a full load, but when we throw yours and Anthony's clothes in, we can get a full load."

What difference did it make if she wanted to do her laundry separately? Why could I not have been kind enough and generous enough to say, "Okay, darlin', that's fine with me"? Why? What was in me that I could not do that?

One day, she and Anthony came in, and Michelle was spittin' angry, and I had no idea why. Michael and I were working on Anthony's room. I'd just excitedly said to my stepson, "I'd like to do so and so and so and so here," when Michelle turned to Anthony and asked, "Is that the way *you* want it?"

It was clear that she was letting her brother know that if he didn't want the room the way I was designing it, she would fight me. She would go to battle for him.

I turned around and walked away and left the three of them in that bedroom. I was trying to choose my battles, and if it meant the way a room was decorated wasn't to my taste, I wasn't ready to fight. So I came back downstairs, trying to think and calm myself. When I turned to go back upstairs, Michelle was walking down the stairs, and I was hanging over the lower balcony when she said, "I would like to have a meeting with you."

It sounded awfully smart-ass, and so, in my own best smart-ass tone, I answered, "Well, yes, ma'am. When would you like to hold court with me?" I was about at the end of my rope.

She looked at me and said, "You are such a bitch. You've ripped my family apart."

Then she stormed out. My heart about broke.

It finally dawned on me that the house we were tearin' down was the house she had been raised in with her mother, her father, and her brother. Beautiful new rooms in a beautiful new house didn't count for nothin'. It was *her* house she wanted, and as she stood and watched it being knocked to the ground, it knocked the breath out of *her*. I was decorating the hell out of *her* home. It was worse than knocking on the door of your own home and having a stranger say you could come in. Looking back, I'm disappointed in myself that I was not more understanding and more compassionate.

It sure looked as though this family was never going to blend. Michael had told me on many occasions that it seemed as if Michelle actively tried to find something specific wrong with me—a reason to justify the fact that she didn't like me. That was pretty obvious. She came up with nothin' in the specifics department, he reported, but she didn't fall in love with me anyways.

I remember one awful night, before Michael and I wed, I'd finally broken up with that married man, and I had some things of his that had to be returned. He asked if he could come over to retrieve his stuff, and I told Michael, who didn't seem too happy to hear that I was going to see that man again. Michael and Michelle planned to have dinner at a restaurant, and when I'd finally said good-bye to my old lover for good, I jumped into my car and headed straight to that restaurant. I was so thrilled to be starting my new life with Michael, totally unencumbered by my past.

I rushed into the restaurant and I saw that Michael and Michelle were wholly engrossed in each other. When they saw me, guess what? They completely ignored me. *Ignored me. Like I wasn't there.* Michelle, it was clear, was not one bit happy I'd shown up to take away her daddy's attention. And as I stood over the two of them, I could see that they were not about to let me into their little closed circle—not one inch.

I felt mortified.

"I've made a horrible mistake here," I told the two of them. *I've just formally, completely, and totally ended a ten-year relationship, and was so excited to rush back to the two of you and be embraced—and now, oh my God.*

I ran out and home and couldn't stop weeping.

When Michael finally came home, he explained that he'd felt horrible about my seeing the man even one more time. *She's back from her date,* he thought when I rushed into the restaurant. I don't know what Michelle thought—she must have been happy to see me ignored by her dad. The bad feelings between Michael and me passed as soon as we talked about it, but Michelle and I never exchanged a word about that terrible scene.

About a month before Michael and I were to be married, I was miserable; it had gotten to the point where Michelle and I, living in the same home, weren't even speaking to each other. It was so upsetting to me that I actually started having heart palpitations. I went to my doctor, and told her, "My nerves are almost shot. I dread going home. I just want to stay at work all night long and not go home."

"Paula, you cannot continue to operate this way," the doctor told me. She started me on Zoloft. I had to get a little help because I could not allow myself to jump on every roller coaster that came by. I had to keep myself level and grounded. Here I was, all the wedding details had been arranged, we were going to be married on television, and I was ready to back out. The truth was, though

I loved Michael, I just didn't think it was going to work. I thought Michelle would see to that.

Lord, what am I going to do? I prayed. *This marriage is going to end before it ever gets started.* But because of all the work that everybody, including the people on the Food Network, had put in, I could not let 'em down. I decided that I would go through with the wedding, and if I had to come out later and say it didn't work, I would just deal with it.

You know, I always wanted a large family. I remember begging my mother when I was in high school to please have another baby. When I married Jimmy Deen I would have loved to have had five or six kids even though I knew I couldn't financially take care of them. Mother Nature took care of that, and I'm lucky to have the two that I have. But I wanted a large family because when a family gets big, it's more interesting; there are more personalities, more interesting psyches that go into the mix. That's what I hoped for when I met Michael and his two kids.

In my own defense, I have to say that I never have been one to hold a grudge. I think the person whom a grudge does the most damage to is the grudge holder. It will eat away at you like a cancer. But I still would not let my guard down. I felt like even if I were to get a full day of peace with Michelle, it would be short-lived. Strange thing is, at this point, we weren't fighting. We simply ignored each other.

So Michael and I were married, and for a long while it was still tense between this child and me. I knew that if there was a big blowup, Michelle was so full of emotion, she'd be so hurt that the damage might last forever. Michelle's a little teapot: you know it's fixin' to boil and that little cap's going to come up and it'll start to whistle. Well, Michelle can go for so long and hold all these feelings back, and then they have to come out. Then she starts whistling, and she ain't whistling Dixie.

I finally saw this just after the wedding when she and her

daddy had a very, very *lively* conversation in the front yard. I stayed in the house, too frightened to move; I didn't want to be part of it. Michelle was wild with anger. When her daddy tried to reason with her, it just didn't work: she needed to get everything out and cleanse her soul and she wasn't paying him any mind at all. She was wild with anger. But that was the turning point. Her father very firmly but lovingly explained to her that I was his wife and partner, and that we so wanted her to be our daughter and friend and play a huge role in our family. If she chose not to, we would both be heartbroken but we'd understand.

The next day she apologized to me. I told her that I certainly accepted her apology, but I don't remember saying I was sorry. I have to give Michelle credit because even if I was the grown-up, Michelle has always been the one who is first able to come up and make amends.

I had not behaved exactly in a way that made me proud of myself either. I didn't necessarily misbehave, but I didn't act the way I wish I had. I *reacted* instead of acted.

One day not too long ago after Michael's heated argument with Michelle, Michelle and I had a wonderful conversation. We were sittin' in my bedroom talking. I was feeling pretty desperate, but I knew I had to keep the conversation going if I was ever going to reach the true heart of this child.

I said, "Michelle, hon, I just feel that I have to tell you that you have the ability to break up this marriage. I'm fifty-nine years old. I spent twenty-seven years fighting in a marriage, and then I fought to start my business. I'm done fighting, and I will walk off if there's fighting ahead, because right now in my life, all I want is peace and contentment."

I think she realized at that very moment that she certainly didn't want to be responsible for the breakup of this marriage. Deep down, she wanted to like me. She wanted to love me. And I wanted to have a daughter. I wanted Michelle.

As I write these words a year later, Michelle is lying in my bed with her head on my belly. The dogs are curled up on *her* belly. Anthony is sitting at the foot of Michael's chair, leaning back against his daddy's legs. My sons, Jamie and Bobby, watching television, are a lot older than Michael's kids—Jamie is old enough to be Anthony's dad if he'd made a mistake—but they have a world of love and respect for their new sister and brother.

Thanks to the Lord, now we have memories together; we're truly a family. The other day I read something that gladdened my heart. After five years, said a researcher, stepfamilies are more stable than first marriages. They experience most of their troubles in the first two years—and then they rise above them.

The things that are most worth having are those you have to wait on, and my relationship with Michelle was definitely worth the wait. I want the world to know that today there's not one thing on this planet I would change about her and maybe not one thing I'd even change about our early time together, because although the way she reacted to our relationship hurt me, it also says what kind of person she is and how much she values family. Coming to understand and respect each other just took a while longer than either of us would have liked it to. So, she's my daughter, and Anthony is my precious teenage sometimes-pain-in-the-ass son (because his room is a mess and he won't shut off a light or pick up a shirt if he had *twelve* mothers telling him to do it).

I've told an awful lot of private things about us, but creating a happy family was probably the most crucial element to Michael's and my happiness. Family is our currency; the love of family is what moves this family. Even if we have bad arguments, we know we'll be together in the end. It's all for one and one for all. And, listen, y'all—it's okay if we talk about it ourselves, but damn sure nobody else better talk about us. I'd like to give some space in my book to what Michelle has to say about a blended family—our family, to be specific. I've offered her the rest of this chapter with the promise not to edit her comments.

Michelle says:

For so long after my parents' divorce, it was Anthony, my dad, and me—just the three of us. Then when Anthony went away to school, it was just Dad and me, and we grew extremely close. Dad had never planned on getting married again. We just never thought that would happen. But I remember the first time he said, "I've met someone who's become a good friend of mine, and I want you to meet her."

So I met Paula, and we all went out on the boat and it was wonderful. How could you not like her? But it wasn't long after that when Dad moved in with her, and their relationship started looking serious, and that's when it began to get harder on me. I was in Savannah's Armstrong State University Nursing School, nineteen years old, and Anthony was off at high school in South Carolina. I wanted to stay in our family home, so when Dad moved in with Paula, I was alone in the house. Going from a family of four to a family of three, and then a family of two, and then, well, I was all alone. I missed my dad something fierce.

I know I was jealous of Paula because I always had my daddy wrapped around my little finger like a piece of string, and suddenly he'd broken that tie. Before, when I wanted something, or if I was lonely, I could cry and cry on the phone and get whatever I wanted. In fact, if Daddy heard me crying, he'd come home from wherever he was in ten minutes. But when Paula came into the picture, it was the first time ever that I didn't come first in his life. It was an awful position for him because here he was being pulled in two different directions by two people he loved. Look,

I never hated Paula. But from the time that I was seventeen and things in my family began to change in a major way, I learned that it takes me a longer time than anyone else to adjust. Change is difficult for me—that's just a part of who I am. It was my resistance to change that was telling me to reject the new woman in Dad's life. If she left the picture, we could all be alone and together again.

Initially, what really freaked me out was that my family home was being torn down. I remember Anthony telling me, "Michelle, you can always have your memories, whether the actual house is there or not." But I spent many hours shedding tears over that. It was mainly because I thought I was never going to have a home or my family again.

Well, anyway, it took time, but I finally realized that Paula was all about family. That helped me kind of jump the jealousy hurdle with her. I started spending the night once in a while over there in her apartment. We started having big parties together— her friends and mine, her family and us. It takes me a while to let someone in, to show them who I am, and Paula seemed to finally get that. She wasn't trying to rush things anymore. I can't remember how long Paula and my dad had been dating when I finally looked at the two of them and realized, *Wow, what a match! How happy they both are, and how happy they make each other. Maybe this will all work out for me, also. Maybe.*

It could have been so much worse. It could have ended badly. And Paula, after everything we've gone through, is still able to empathize and understand and love me for who I am, and treat me as if I'm her own daughter. I just think that says so much about who she is.

We worked at it, I promise you. It took time before we could give to each other what's called unconditional love. You know, a couple of years ago, we all went on a cruise together and it wasn't all fun. This past year, we went on another family vacation, and it was a blast, just terrific. I started to feel about Paula and Jamie and Bobby as if they were my own blood and not only connected through marriage.

One of my biggest hurdles was getting to actually *love* Paula, not just respect her for everything she's achieved and for what she's brought to my dad. See, I'm also extremely close to my mother. I had to see that loving Paula did not mean a minute's less love for my mother. I now believe 100 percent that a person can have many mothers. When I accepted that is probably when I did open up my heart. And although Paula is often like a rock star with the attention she gets from her fans, she never created a situation where it was a competition between her and my mom. And here's my secret: I had a little therapy to help me work through everything too. It taught me how I could open up and love my two mothers. I recommend it highly for anyone who's in a blended family.

My mother was great too. She has always been very open to my dad's remarriage, and she's helped me to accept it. There were times when I heard myself be so downright nasty to Paula that I didn't know who was saying the words coming from my mouth. Never saw *that* girl before. I think back on some of those things and *whoa!*

But here's the thing: Paula never stopped loving me, never shut me out; she only shut out the meanness coming from me. She just opened up her arms to me and wanted to know about my day. She never quit trying.

That's when our relationship started developing as more of a friendship than as my dad's wife. Honestly, I don't even consider us a blended family anymore. We're all one natural family. We love to be together and there was a time I would have never thought it would happen.

I'm engaged to be married now, but when all the trouble with Paula started, my fiancé, Daniel, and I bought a house about a mile from here. Now, I know that even though I have my own house, there's always room for me here in Paula and my dad's home. It's no different from what it used to be with my daddy. It's just that there are more people around the table now.

Paula has been helping me plan my wedding as if I were her own child, which now I am. It's been a stressful time, but having her be able to share in my happiness and help me plan things has been so helpful.

My big wedding crisis came when I was figuring out how my two moms would walk down the aisle. I wanted Paula to have just as much a place in this wedding as my own mom.

The wedding coordinator said, "Your own mom needs to go down the aisle first."

And I said, "You don't understand. I've got *two* mothers. At this point, my feelings are no different about Paula than about my natural mom."

So, we worked it out; I think Anthony will go get Mom and hold her arm on one side and then go get Paula and hold her on the other, and they—Anthony and my two moms—will walk down my weddin' aisle together. And then my daddy will give me away.

That's how I want it.

It's me again, Paula. There are no guarantees, but I think the Groovers and the Deens stand more than a fair chance of being close forever. We'll always have to work at it. We know that. I feel that so much of our future togetherness is my responsibility because, frankly, as my business success grows, I find that my words hold even more weight than they ever did. It's only fair, now that I think of it: after all, next to Aunt Peggy, I'm the matriarch (although she'd tell you she's still the queen and I'm only the princess). It's true that I seem to have the strongest ability to hurt or to set the togetherness tone.

I'm plannin' on togetherness.

The Best Damn Blueberry Muffin You'll Ever Eat

Here in Savannah, we love our muffins, and I especially love these delicately blended, delicious blueberry babies. This is my favorite blueberry muffin recipe.

2 cups all-purpose flour
2 teaspoons baking powder
½ cup sugar
1 stick unsalted butter, melted
1 egg, slightly beaten
¾ cup whole milk
1½ cups fresh blueberries
½ cup granulated brown sugar or white sugar

1. Preheat the oven to 350°F. Grease and flour 12 muffins cups.
2. In a bowl, combine the flour, baking powder, and the ½ cup sugar. In another bowl, combine the butter, egg, and milk and blend well. Pour the wet ingredients into the flour mixture and, with a spatula, stir until just combined. Do not beat or overmix; it's okay if there are lumps in the batter. Gently fold the blueberries into the batter.
3. Spoon the batter into the muffin cups, filling each cup about two-thirds full. Bake for 10 minutes and remove from the oven. Sprinkle the tops of the muffins with the granulated brown or white sugar and return the muffins to the oven to bake for an additional 10 to 20 minutes, until the tops are golden brown and a toothpick inserted into the center of a muffin comes out clean. Cool for about 10 minutes in the pan before turning the muffins out.

Makes 12 muffins

Chapter 15

FOOD, GLORIOUS FOOD,
SOUTHERN STYLE

I'm not yo' nurse, I'm yo' cook.

After Michael and I got married and Michelle and I ironed out our problems, it was back to real life and work. I'd lie awake nights thinking more and more about the philosophy of Southern cooking, my cooking, my momma's and my Grandmomma Paul's cooking—in short, how Southerners have cooked since the stars first fell on Alabama. I wanted the food in my restaurant to be authentic. I wanted to give my customers the best of the South. For years I'd been taking for granted what my momma and her momma did in their kitchens, but now that I was a professional, it was important that I understood the culture and the heritage of the cooking I understood and loved, so that I could faithfully dispense it. Southern plantation cuisine was my style. *Country cookin' makes you good-lookin'* was my motto.

For starters, y'all, I knew there are but four ingredients that signify Southern cooking: the pig and all its parts, butter, mayo, and cream cheese.

For years I'd been hearing every now and then that those four ingredients so close to my spiritual and emotional heart were likely to hurt my physical heart, not to mention my breasts and my colon (one body part to which I can honestly say I'd not paid too much attention). Once, I got real testy when one of those food police asked me why I didn't cook healthier, and I told him I was his cook, not his nurse.

Not one Southerner I know threw her butter out the window when we heard our food was going to send us all to an early grave. As the diet gurus threatened early death to Southern cooking lovers, the old Georgia farmers who put cream in their cereal instead of milk continued to live to a hundred muttering, "The fat makes mah arteries so slick, the blood glides right on through."

Butter and cream are not killing us off like flies. How could all that good stuff be bad for y'all? Sure, fatty foods are fattening and it isn't a good idea to be obese, but the point, it seems to me, is to give up gettin' nerves whenever you see butter. The point is to find a way good-tastin' food fits into your life. Don't live scared of food pleasure. I guarantee, y'all, one of these days the health police will finally stop wringing their hands over butter and bacon. One thing I've always known is that food is not supposed to be measured out in dry and boring increments. Food is meant to be enjoyed because science changes its mind every five minutes about what's best for us. In the meantime, I continue to follow my own advice that two sticks of butter is good, and three probably better. Now, you puritans who've been eating mostly granola and lettuce, you'll be sorry, one day, that y'all missed my butterscotch delight cake made with three cups of heavy cream all these years.

Back in the early nineties, when I started thinking through the concept of Southern food, first I decided I never wanted to be in competition with other chefs and what they were doing all across the country. A gourmet chef is not what I wanted to be, and I didn't have no worries there: it was certainly true that down-home Southern cooking is not what's ever called "gourmet" cooking. It's poor man's food. It's what you grew up with if you grew up in Memphis or Charleston or Atlanta or Albany, Georgia. Kids don't have to acquire a taste for it—they're born lovin' it. Cooking memories are part of everyone's life, the common denominator among people. If you're Jewish or Baptist, French or American, the food of your childhood usually makes you feel safe, and as far as I'm concerned, Southern cooking makes you feel safest. It has little to do with health or diet: it's just down-home good eatin'.

In my neck of the woods, food connects us to others. For some reason, at almost every party, everyone usually congregates in the kitchen. In the South, people spend a whole lot of time in the kitchen sharing recipes, passing down traditions. Food brings everyone to the table. Perhaps at a hoity-toity dinner party in Los Angeles or New York, people gather at the table to talk about the fascinating ways of the world, maybe they stare at the trendy foods in front of them to try to figure out what's happening on that plate, but in the South, you have your mashed potatoes and your butter beans and your fried chicken, and you're not talking about the food or the politics—it's all about coming together to have a conversation about your day, and, by the way, to eat mighty good.

Southern cooking is nothing but Southern—we don't fly in our ingredients or menus from distant points in the world. What's in our pots and on our plates is all home-grown. You won't find kiwi fruit or foie gras at a Georgia table, but you will see peaches and pork chops and fresh shrimp. You don't need a trained, sophisticated palate to love fried chicken, which has turned out to be the key to my past, my present, and my future, God willing.

Southern dishes don't need split-second timing, either: a few extra minutes in the oven isn't going to hurt that macaroni and cheese. And although our plates look pretty when they're brought to the table, we're not about to turn our food into towers. We just heap that shrimp and grits, those buttermilk biscuits, that tomato aspic with cottage cheese dip, right plunk on the plate.

Look, I know that some things I cook will make a French chef roll his eyes—like the way I make red-eye gravy with the drippings from country ham fried in a skillet, water, and strong coffee, but if that French chef takes a chance and tastes my gravy with one of my biscuits, he'll be asking for seconds real quick.

Fact is that people come from very far away for down-home Southern cooking: it's the food to try before you die.

There are four main kinds of Southern cooking.

COMFORT FOOD

> Something comforting and tasty, something to make
> you feel safe—if only for a moment.

Comfort food is the kind of food people most associate with the South. You don't even have to be hungry to eat comfort food; most people dive into the praline cookies, the leftover macaroni and cheese or pork butt roast, the hot grits or potato soup, not because we're starving but because it satisfies more than our physical hunger.

A lot of people say that when they're stressed they can't eat, but there are definitely more people like me than the ones who don't eat. I have never been in a situation that's been so bad I couldn't eat; I do whatever I have to do to help the hurt, fill the emptiness inside me, and that, girl, is always eatin'. Give me food that warms me up, like chicken and dumplings, which was my daddy's favorite meal and which my grandmother made for me when I said I needed a nerve pill. Or cookies hot out of the oven, which I ate endlessly when my daddy died.

Nora Ephron writes in her book *Heartburn,* "I have made a lot of mistakes falling in love, and regretted most, but never the potatoes that went with them." Oh, Lord, that's me. Truest thing I ever heard.

I never want to get so uppity that I forget who I am and where I came from. I'll always crave real, honest country food, and that means grits, grits, and grits. Banana pudding, spoon bread, creamed corn, a perfectly baked potato—and preferably eaten in the kitchen—that's the food with my name on it. Collard greens, fried chicken, mashed sweet potatoes. Food that is rooted in Southern history, food that Stonewall Jackson's momma might have given him. That's what I want to serve my family and friends.

I heard the greatest thing. A Chicago critic reporting on the latest culinary finds told his readers that grits and fried chicken were not only cool but worth sixty bucks a plate at the newest, fashionable "Southern" restaurant in the Windy City.

The highest compliment for comfort food in a Southern restaurant is that it's almost as good as home.

FUNERAL FOOD

> It's Death Warmed Over—maybe with a little cream
> of mushroom soup.

Southern funeral food is down-home food but prepared with company in mind. Funeral food is really serious business in the South. Although I'm sure funerals are pretty serious in other places as well, I'm not so sure the food plays such a big part.

In my neck of the woods, after the service and the cemetery, family and friends arrive at a deceased's house. This is not a party but a get-together after the burial when people reminisce and say nice things about the deceased. People bring food so that the family doesn't have to feed their guests and worry about meals after losing a loved one. Funeral meals are meant to show off the cooks' creations even as they help gentle the grief of the survivors. Mourners who are exhausted and grief-stricken by bereavement and having taken care of the deceased in the last days need nourishment; it also makes them feel good to know that their friends and family cared enough to prepare their best dishes. Funeral food is also meant to celebrate life: nothing says you're alive more than eating. Sometimes, after a funeral, I'll go into the house, and my heart breaks when I see potato salad that's been bought in a grocery store and some greasy chicken that's been picked up at a fast-food barbecue joint. Then, praise the Lord, I'll see a pot of butter beans that someone has taken the time to cook just perfect, and all's right with the world. I'm not no dummy; I know we live in a fast-paced world and we don't have the time or even the inclination to spend so much time in our kitchens like our mommas did. But there's no excuse for store-bought potato salad.

Here's the way it used to be, and still is in many communities. When someone you know passes on, after the viewing you send over to the house your best dish filled with your best recipe. If you're planning to go to the burial, you bring it over afterward, when all the food that's been brought over for the family is put out. Now, when I say your best dish, honey, I mean your best cooking on your finest plate—not those throwaway aluminum pans. This is the final act of respect you can offer the deceased, so you want it to be your very, very prettiest china, polished silver, or cut-glass dish. Plus, your name is always put on the bottom of your dish and you don't want an ugly dish with your name on it, 'cause everyone will know it's yours when it's washed and returned to you.

Some women I know even keep a casserole ready in the freezer, just in case. And it better not have soggy instant rice as a base. Soggy rice is unfit for the family and for the deceased.

That's how it is.

So, if it's like the old days, after a funeral there'll be some fried chicken in a beautiful dish, maybe a sweet potato pie and a baked ham so good you can't hardly stand it. You don't hardly see it much anymore, but a funeral dish with real roots is a tomato aspic.

In the South, when you go to a funeral you're sad, but when it comes time to eat, you get happier. Today, when a friend or family member or a loved customer passes, I'll get up a buffet at the restaurant—macaroni and cheese, biscuits, fried chicken, and corn bread, and I never forget the hoe cakes. Those buffets, I might add, do come in plain old aluminum dishes, 'cause they're comin' straight from the restaurant. No one seems to mind. Just a month ago, I lost my Aunt Jessie, my dear little aunt who lived in Eagle Lake, Florida, next to Winter Haven. We all loaded up to go down to the funeral, but I couldn't take any food because I was traveling eight hours to get there. I knew the church ladies would do right by my Aunt Jessie.

Oh, my goodness, that food was *so* good! One little lady made chicken and dumplings and I thought I was gonna hurt myself on them. There was creamed corn and a huge blue bowl of cheese grits. There was black-eyed peas, fried chicken, broccoli casserole, and there was a potato salad. There was even praline pie and pickled okra, without which, it's said, you can't be buried in that area. And yes, I spotted a beautiful plate filled with traditional deviled eggs, real funeral cooking.

It was a grand funeral for Aunt Jessie. Somewhere she was smiling with pride, because she always brought the best dishes.

CELEBRATION FOOD

> My ideal celebration would be sitting in the middle of the floor with a T-shirt on and a bushel of Baltimore crabs, extra jumbo male, gettin' my crab on.
> —PATTI LABELLE

You go, Patti.

In the South, a celebration can be a party to honor the arrival of a major celebrity, but more likely, it's a family get-together. We just love to be in touchin' range of each other, and when we are, we're usually celebratin' by eatin' because we're so happy to be gathered around the table at the same time. Families coming together are a cause for celebration as much as is a wedding or a christening. These family get-togethers can be called pretty spontaneously for almost any old occasion—a graduation lunch, a New Year's Day good-luck meal, a Sunday-afternoon football party, or an I Just Got My Engagement Ring tea. The food that's served at these shindigs can be simple, but they usually have a note of festivity inserted in the food. For example, my own boys always loved a baked potato bar at their special events. I'd put out big bowls of crispy-skin baked potatoes with a dozen different toppings to choose from and those boys would love to shovel giant helpin's of creamed seafood, chicken à la king, crumbled bacon, or steak and mushrooms on top of their potatoes. The trick is to remember that celebration food for families is usually jolly food that makes your people feel prized and pleasured! Family is precious to me and equally precious is me seeing that everyone goes home satisfied.

When our own family gets together, we often serve a Low

Country Boil (pronounced *bawl* for all of you not born in Georgia). This is about the most celebratory dish you could ever hope for. Everything goes in one pot—the crab boil, the red potatoes, the sausage, the shrimp, and the corn. Sometimes, if we're lucky enough to have been out crabbin', we'll throw some blue crabs in there too, which is just fabulous. With a French bread, a green salad, and some coleslaw, we have an honest-to-goodness celebration feast.

Some say Southerners seize on any holiday as an excuse to make celebration food and they'd be right as rain. I personally love to pull out my recipes for shrimp and lobster bisque on Valentine's Day, my strawberries dipped in white chocolate for May Day (once I was the runner-up for Queen of the May in middle school), deviled eggs for Father's Day, and even peanut butter gooey cakes to celebrate our King Elvis's birthday on January 8. Fact is, we Southerners love to entertain, and that's all about making people feel good in your presence and serving them food that honors how special they are.

I serve celebration food every day in my restaurant because it's my opinion that every day, just to be on the right side of the dirt is a celebration. When someone comes into my restaurant, I want to make him feel good he walked in my door. I want to show him I appreciate his business and that he's doing something nice for me by being there. Every bit of food I serve him is a little celebration of that customer. Sometimes I go into restaurants whose owners seem to feel they're doing me a big favor just by sending a waiter over to take my order. We invite people into our restaurant home and we treat them as though they're at a family celebration, which brings me to one of my favorite sayin's—*you'll never be lonely if you treat family like company and company like family.*

Southern hospitality means celebrating friends in bad times as well as good. When one of our friends is hurtin'—say, she's just gotten a divorce, her child scored all D's in school, or she's put on twenty pounds—we'll likely make her a celebration party so's she can remember how lucky she is in other parts of her life. One thing you'll always find at that party—or any other Southern party—are tomato sandwiches; we just love 'em down here. We trim off the crusts from some bread slices, cut round circles out of the bread with a small juice glass, and spread the circles with a salt-and-pepper-seasoned mayonnaise. Topping it all are small, round slices of succulent red tomatoes. What you'll never find at that party would be a sea urchin cocktail. We don't cotton to sea urchins in these parts, honey. Or any exotic dishes, actually.

Southern hospitality extends to business relationships also. We rarely celebrate a business deal with cocktails in a restaurant; we're more likely to invite that colleague home for a celebration dinner to show that we feel he's done something nice for us and we want to honor him with an intimate little party . . . just as you'd invite your boss and her husband over to pay tribute to a great year. The celebration food you'd serve would be special— maybe a veal loin stuffed with peppers or a glazed Rock Cornish hen stuffed with wild rice. This would *not* be the occasion to serve my famous beer-in-the-rear chicken, which is yummy, but because it calls for a whole can of beer inserted in the chicken's butt, it's not exactly grand.

Southerners know how to entertain, and they love to share their special occasions with displays of food that show creativity. Celebration food almost always involves a new way of looking at an old dish. For example, a party called in haste for, say, someone's unexpected job promotion can be the simplest supper consisting of festive margaritas and a giant bowl of spaghetti topped with a dramatic meat or shrimp sauce. What fun—it's a gala! And, if you've noticed, it's really just spaghetti. A New Year's Day soup lunch for the neighbors could involve a celebration display of six different pots bubbling over with six hearty soups—a spicy tomato soup, a potato soup with shrimp, a wild rice soup, a cream of broccoli and cauliflower soup, a French onion soup, and a beef and cabbage soup. The neighbors dip into their favorites using one of six or seven pretty soup ladles; then, they carry their soup to a table set with long French breads and rolls, and everyone eats soup and gossips and toasts the New Year with joy and anticipation and soup spoons. It's just soup—but it's a whole lot more; the presentation makes it celebration food.

Although there's no law that says you can't make a celebration feast for your own self—say, an entire junior sausage pizza just because you placed second in the marathon race—celebration food is most often about sharing. It's about gathering up all the mothers of your best friends for a Mother's Day tea where you'll serve cucumber and ham sandwiches and an enormous assortment of tiny pastries, or the members of your book club for an ice cream social featuring every possible ice cream flavor and topping on this sweet planet. Southern celebration food is hospitable and it's spirited.

Here's to celebration food celebrating the times of your life and the life in your times!

SEXY FOOD

> Nothing says lovin' like something from the oven.
>
> —FROM THE BACK OF A PILLSBURY
> FLOUR BOX

Finally, I'd like to say a few words about Southern cooking and sensuality. You can disagree with me on this one, but you'd be wrong. Every true Southern gal knows for a fact that food, sex, and desire are intertwined. Sometimes I wonder if my most sensitive sexual organ isn't back there on my tongue.

I have always felt that cooking with my man is a kind of love-making, from foreplay to consummation. You lick each other's gravy fingers; you squeeze the tender peach, then feed it to each other; you get the taste of the key lime pie he just sampled. From the quick kiss you steal; your lips, your tongue are always busy with the sucking, the sampling, and the drinking in—and then the slow, slow eating of that turn-on meal—don't tell me that cooking isn't sexy, child.

If I were going to make a romantic feast today for my man, I'd start with oysters at a table for two at home. A sprinkling of rose petals over the tabletop and a little candlelight wouldn't hurt. Some people say that oysters are an aphrodisiac, and I don't doubt it for a moment. Just think of holding up that cold, silky oyster and slipping it down your man's throat. I can't hardly stand it. After the oysters, I'd probably serve a steamed lobster dipped in butter. Yummy. You could almost rub yourself down with butter. That warm, yellow butter just slipping that lobster down his throat—imagine it.

Now, it may not seem very sexy to you, but a tater is just the absolute feel-good food of all time, and I'd definitely include it in my seduction dinner. You can mash a tater, you can boil it, you can fry it, you can scallop it, you can make soup with it, you can roast it. I might even take that lobster, split it, and make a shrimp and crab mashed potato and stuff it back into the lobster's shell. Oh, *baby*.

I think eating anything with my fingers and dipped in—yes—butter is pretty sexy. I could even get Michael Groover to eat a few stalks of roasted asparagus if I fed them to him.

Finally, for dessert, I'd wrap some puff pastry around my Michael's favorite chocolate candies (Snickers or Hershey's) and bake it until the pastry was crisp and the candy melts. When he bites into that irresistible oozing chocolate, *he's* going to melt.

Now, if that don't create a romantic response, grits ain't groceries in a poor man's house.

Food, glorious food, Southern style. I got it all straight in those early years running The Lady. I knew the food I cooked would celebrate my heritage and my joyful days.

Mrs. Dull's Tomato Aspic Funeral Food Dish

This is one of the most traditional funeral food offerings in the house. Mrs. Henrietta Dull was born on a plantation in the mid-1860s, and she conducted cooking schools throughout the South, eventually becoming the editor of the Home Economics page in the *Atlanta Journal*. She was my grandmomma's favorite chef and her tomato aspic was legendary. You couldn't hardly die in style without this aspic served on someone's very best china at the gathering after the funeral. Following is Mrs. Dull's recipe, handed down from Grandmomma Paul, as she wrote it.

1 quart can tomatoes
A half to a whole bunch of celery
One 5¾-ounce bottle of stuffed olives, drained
3 tablespoons of vinegar
1 tablespoon of grated onion
1 tablespoon of salt
⅛ tablespoon of cayenne pepper
1 box Knox gelatin
½ cup cold water

Mash tomatoes into a pulp, removing any stem pieces; cut celery thin, slice olives thin, add all seasonings. Put the gelatin in the cold water for ten minutes, then heat over boiling water until melted; add the tomato mixture, turn into a large mold or individual molds to jell in the refrigerator. Rinse the mold with cold water before pouring in the mixture so it will unmold easily.

Serve the whole aspic on pretty lettuce leaves, or if you've jelled the aspic in individual jelly glasses, you can unmold each glass and cut the aspic in inch-thick slices—then put on lettuce with a side of mayonnaise.

Remember, this aspic is not cooked at all. You can garnish with asparagus or other fresh vegetables on the side of the plate.

Chapter 16

SO YOU WANT TO OWN
A RESTAURANT?

A customer walks into a restaurant and sees a sign
on the wall that says, $500 IF WE FAIL TO FILL YOUR
ORDER. When a waitress comes to his table, he orders
elephant ears on rye. The waitress goes into the
kitchen and a few minutes later the angry restaurant
owner comes out, lays five one-hundred-dollar bills
on the customer's table, and says, "You got me this
time, buddy, but it's the first time we ever ran out
of rye bread."

*J*ust as often as I hear from people who want to publish a book, I hear from people who want me to tell
them how to open a restaurant. *How hard can it be?* they figure.

Hard. Major hard. Very, very hard.

I'm only kidding. Sure, it's hard, but you never have to be
afraid if you're fixin' to do it with all the passion and smarts that
are in you. I once heard someone say that any first-rate business-

person loves the product she's pushing. That means that if you're a successful pocketbook manufacturer, you will generally love the leather, the color, the smell, and the feel of the purses. If you are a winning publisher, you will surely love books, good paper, good stories. If you want to start a restaurant, you'll love food, of course, seriously love it. But there's one more thing in this business: you'll positively have to love people, the people who consume your product *and* the people who help you get it to their tables. I know very few top chefs or restaurant owners who are loners. As a restaurant owner, you got to be out there selling your passion for feeding people well, working the room with pleasure, greeting your guests with affection, and not from a sense of duty.

I've seen the dread in people who have to go to work at jobs they hate. It's so sad to me, because we spend two-thirds of our lives at work, and to be miserable two-thirds of our lives—how awful is that? My family and I feel blessed that we're able to make a living doing what we love, because so many don't have that luxury.

So let me tell you a little bit about my own experience.

First of all, there are different levels of success in this business. It takes a stubborn, single-minded path to have a wildly popular restaurant, and you do lose something (like a whole lot of playtime) when you're focused on that quest, trust me. Determining what's your most comfortable degree of success has to come from your honest appraisal of how much time and effort you're willing to invest in work. What's success to me (like workin' seven days a week) may not be what *you* define as success.

It was probably inevitable that I would own restaurants one day. I'm happiest feeding people, and from the first time I noticed how much pleasure I could bring to others, it was a done deal. How many professions can boast that kind of instant gratification for the owner's work? Now, if I go to a dentist, and he's fillin' my teeth, even though it's good for me, I'm sorry, I ain't goin' to say, "Thank you, that feels wonderful." But how lucky am I that I can put fried chicken and biscuits in front of someone, and watch him roll his eyes and say, transported, "Oh, God, this is so delicious"?

When I opened The Lady & Sons, I needed help, I needed financing, and, most of all, I needed sound advice. Here in Savannah, a building owner will not construct your restaurant. If you pay him a hefty rent, he will allow you to run a restaurant and make improvements in his building—just don't go looking to him for help with the cost of any renovation. You have to have a certain percentage of the cost of the entire project right up front. If it's going to cost about $150,000 for a reconstruction, you've got to have saved anywhere from $25,000 to $35,000 of what they call "good faith" or "start-up money" to offer the bank so's you can get that bank to finance the rest. I've already told y'all about the money I'd saved and how Aunt Peggy came through with the balance of the start-up money.

How much will you need? For starters, make a list called "Professional Help." You'll almost definitely need money for a lawyer, and, for me, a good accountant was key. An accountant puts the pencil to the paper, takes your expenses, and then tells you how many fried chicken dinners you need to serve to make a profit in a week. I survived two years and some months without an accountant: I had nothin' to count, so why would I need an accountant, was my clever reasoning. Then I broke down and realized I needed professional help, and, thank God, in early 1990 I found Karl Schumacher.

Probably the first thing Karl told me was that every successful entrepreneur in the restaurant business must be three types of people—and if she can't be three people, she has to have two other types of people in the business to complement her and she's got to pay them. (That's the start of the list called "Salaries.") The first type is the one with the ideas—that was me. I was the one with the risk-taking ability and the creative brain, and I had to think everything through. One of my best ideas, for example, was the buffet. It would be like eating at Momma's table, where you just knew you'd like most everything on it—but, for sure, there was something special on it just for you. We'd have the country fried steak *and* the Salisbury steak—something for everybody.

I knew I needed a general manager, an administrative person who would keep track of everything that went on and be the one who stayed behind when the restaurant closed to make sure everything got done. Dustin Walls is the general manager of The Lady & Sons. He's been with me for about ten years and he has some ideas about good managing.

"If someone is unhappy because they say they don't like the food (and that's rare), we always have to find out what they didn't like about it. Some people just don't have the palate for Southern food; the collard greens, for example, are mighty spicy. If you want to put some South in your mouth, expect plenty of butter at Paula's places. To some people, that's not pleasing to the palate. If there's a legit complaint, I try to make the complainer as happy as I can, maybe find them something else, like a nice salad. We treat our guests like they're in Paula Deen's house."

Dustin makes sure that everyone's satisfied, and that's a good restaurant policy for any owner. "It's illegal," says Dustin, "to say no to a guest's needs when you wouldn't say no to a guest in your home." If we should run out of chicken, it's often Dustin himself who gets in his car, drives like the wind to the grocery store for more chickens, and gives the customer some fried green tomatoes until the chicken's ready. Many things can go wrong in the kitchen. If a steak is not done to the customer's satisfaction, that's pretty easy to fix, but because we make food in such large batches, sometimes an entire pot of collard greens will come out too salty and then we have to recook the whole batch, which is a long process.

In cases like these, the manager or server will often talk to the hungry customer to take his mind off his belly.

I asked my general manager to tell me the most important thing a person buying a restaurant ought to know.

"You'll have no personal life for most of your adult life," he says with a grin. "You work, you get done, you go home to sleep, you wake up the next day. You are constantly thinking about that next day—what you got to do, what you got to be prepared for, what you got to fix, who's not going to show up for work. If you have to, you roll up your sleeves and get to work doing the no-show's job. I'm a general manager but I started as a hoe cake maker, and when I have to I wash dishes, just like Paula's sons, Jamie and Bobby, do in a pinch. You never can get too big for your britches. And maybe, just maybe, if you see a little bit of success, you can try to catch up on your social life."

Finally, besides the risk taker and the administrative person, I needed to add in salaries for the cooks and servers.

Next, Karl said that we had to make a "projection." That's an estimate of what you think you'll make in restaurant sales, then what you think all your costs, aside from salaries, are going to be. Put that down on paper even though your projection may not be totally accurate.

Now you need a list titled "Food Costs." You have to figure out what *your* average cost for a meal is going to be per person, then what you'll have to charge for the meal in order to make a profit. You need to know how many tables there will be, how many people will sit at a table, and how many times that table will be turned—in other words, served and emptied out, and refilled with new customers.

Let me show you what I mean: say you have thirty tables. Each table seats two people—that's sixty seats. At lunchtime, your accountant says, you must turn each table one and a half times to make a profit. So, if there are sixty seats in your restaurant, you need to serve ninety meals at lunch (sixty plus thirty) to make a profit.

Let's multiply it out: if you charge $8 a person for lunch, serving ninety meals will make you $720. Subtract your costs for the day from that $720, and what you have left is your profit.

How do you figure your costs? Karl says you must come up with a menu to figure out costs. For example, a meal of scallops will cost more than chicken, but since French fries cost less than whole baked potatoes, you can save money on your costs by offering French fries with the scallops. You have to figure out what your cost is going to be per plate for everything you've got on that menu.

Now you can estimate how much your wholesale costs for food will be. You'll need to talk to people who've been in a similar kind of restaurant business, and also talk to the suppliers. Ask them what the best food brands are and what brands you should pass on. Ask what jumps off the menu and what just lies there because it never excited no customer.

Lots of people ask how I know exactly how much to charge so that I make a profit. Takes experience, girl, but I do have sort of a formula. When I started The Bag Lady, I'd never worked in a restaurant before and I had no idea how my grandmother managed the costs at River Bend. I did have to teach myself how to charge so I could make a modest profit after taking care of my expenses. Here's how I did it: if I paid a quarter for something, I knew I had to sell it for a dollar. That's the normal percentage that most restaurants try for—they like to pay no more for the food than 25 percent of what they charge. Some restaurants pay as low as 21 percent for the food and some go as high as 28 percent. Then there are the restaurateurs who pay as little as they can get away with for food, usually by buying inferior ingredients. These restaurant owners then charge whatever they can get, and give themselves an astronomical profit.

Astronomical is not in my vocabulary. The ideal total formula for *me* now would be this:

Food costs: no more than one-third of the gross receipts (33⅓ percent)

My costs (overhead expenses like rent, utilities, salaries, insurance, equipment, pots and pans, and repairs): one-third of the gross receipts (33⅓ percent)

Profit: one-third of the gross receipts (33⅓ percent)

My goal has always been to sell my customers a good meal at a fair price. I knew I couldn't lose if I stuck to that principle, and I think that's good advice for any restaurant owner. McDonald's, Sam Walton, and Martha Stewart all knew what they were doing when they were reaching for the masses. I hadn't been raised in a froufrou world, and, as Michael says, we would rather serve one fork and a nice plate of food than eight forks and eight froufrou bites of food on fancy, shmancy plates. I never want people to leave my restaurant hungry.

It still amazes people to this day that I can serve an all-you-can-eat buffet and our food cost generally is still only 26 percent of our gross receipts. Frankly, it's pretty unheard of. How do we do it?

We make it up in volume. And we are not wasteful. If I've got a lot of unserved pot roast, my staff knows how to turn that roast into beef stroganoff, beef stew, or shepherd's pie for the next meal. That's what all Southern cooks do. Since I was little I've heard that a Southern woman could take her dirty dishwater and make a fine pot of soup—not that I was tempted to test that! And our strict motto is, *When in doubt, throw it out.* When a customer leaves some untouched food on a plate—out it goes. But if we have a big pan of unserved peas, and I look at them, taste them, smell them, and they are perfect, they'll show up in some other dish the next day.

You would think that we'd have trouble meeting our goal of a good meal at a good price. At Uncle Bubba's Oyster House, the restaurant I own with my brother, fish is simply more costly than, say, chicken, but by having a varied menu you can charge a fair market price for the more expensive fish and less for things like, say, hot wings. You might be able to bring your hot wings in at an 18 percent food cost, while with a nice piece of fish, you're at 33¾ percent. It all balances out. My bottom line? I would rather have people come to my restaurant four times a month than four times a year.

Now let's say a few words about equipment. Karl warned me that it was going to be my major cost and that I shouldn't go too cheap. When I started at 311 Congress Street, we ended up replacing most of the equipment within the first year because we cheaped out. We're talking stoves, heavy mixers, flat cooktops (which are essentially griddles), fryers—just about everything we used to prepare our meals. If you buy cheap equipment, you're going to spend more money in the long run, I discovered, like when we bought a small thirty-five-pound fryer and found that it couldn't keep up with the demand for fried food. We had to go out and buy a sixty-five-pound fryer, which meant we could cook twice as much, twice as fast. The aim was to get that food out of the kitchen and onto the plate fast and well-cooked. Another thing: if you buy too cheap and have to buy better equipment later on, you have to figure on restaurant shut-down time too. You can't just pull an old stove to put a new one in without losing a beat. Sometimes it takes new wiring and a new gas line, or a different configuration of space. For instance, that sixty-five-pound fryer holds more because it's bigger, but I lost money in the short run because I had to shut down my restaurant for a day or so while I redesigned the kitchen. But it's a delicate balance: you don't want to spend too much, either. Rest assured that people who are selling you the equipment are going to ask you to buy everything under the sun. Don't do it. There are some things you can rent, like ice machines.

Then there's dishes, silverware, and glassware, as well as serving pieces (if you're doing things family style) and water pitchers. Are you going to have flowers? You're going to need something to put them in. Candles? Ditto. You have to figure in the cost to replace broken dishes, because for sure those dishes will break. And how about tablecloths, napkins, and sometimes uniforms? As many restaurant owners do, I have usually required my help to buy their own uniforms at cost: you can be sure they'll take better care of them.

Insurance is another big cost you have to consider.

While I was running The Lady in the Best Western, I simply could not afford insurance. I would get up and pray every morning, *Please, Lord, don't let 'em choke on those chicken bones.* Well, one day my worst fear came true, but it wasn't no chicken bone that got my customer, it was hot water. I'd recruited my children and their friends so I could save on waiters. Bobby's girlfriend Sherry (whom I loved) had huge eyes, long lashes, heart-shaped lips, and real boobs like the ones from a plastic surgeon (first time I saw her in a swimsuit I thought, *Well, I'm screwed, I can't compete against that, Bobby belongs to her now*), but this sweet girl had never been a waitress before. She was nervous and unsure of herself, and the minute she started waiting on tables she poured scalding coffee on a woman's lap. The woman was wearing—just my luck—shorts. Sherry ran right into my arms crying, and all I could think was, *Please, please, don't let that shorts-wearing woman sue us.* We got her a cold rag and some medicine, and, thank God, she didn't sue. At that point there wouldn't have been anything to get. You can't get blood from a turnip.

Tables and chairs are big items too. When we started The Lady & Sons, I bought all my furniture from a buddy who owned a wonderful antique store. Jerry had picked out his sturdiest chairs and tables, but I've got to tell you, the sturdiest wasn't so sturdy. But the dining room looked so beautiful with all that antique furniture, we went for them. Now we had insurance, so I was ready for anything, and anything happened.

We'd instructed our hosts that when they saw a very, very heavy person, they had to go tell Jamie or Bobby, who would send them to a table with the sturdiest of the antique chairs.

These two women came in for lunch one day, and while they were eating, a tall gentleman came in to speak with them. When he sat down, that freakin' chair up and collapsed.

I didn't think he was hurt—except for his pride, of course—but I went running over to ask, "Well, honey, are you all right?" Yes, he nodded. "Well, have you gotten a meal yet?" I asked. No, he answered, he'd just come in to talk to these two women for a moment. Well, you'd better believe, he got his chicken dinner free.

On our first Thanksgiving, a darling older woman just sits in her chair, and it folds like an accordion. Her legs go up in the air, her dress goes over her head, and both she and I are mortified and scared. Here it is, our first Thanksgiving, and it's ruined within the first five minutes of opening. I was sure she was going to sue us for everything; that's how humiliated she was that her weight was too much for a restaurant chair. But she didn't sue us and still comes in, but we finally had to do away with all those beautiful old chairs and replace them with newer, sturdier versions. Our insurance is up-to-date now, but still, y'all try not to get hurt when you come in. We just *hate* when that happens.

Don't forget the cost of a liquor license and one for beer and wine. Those licenses are real important to a lot of restaurants, but not to mine. It's a service I wanted to have for guests who want a drink, but I probably have the lowest-profit bar in town because people know that when they come to my place, it's not to get rip-roaring drunk. No, darlin'. They come for the food, baby—and yes, the atmosphere, too. The Lady & Sons specialty is buffet, but a lot of people come in and order from the menu—a fine steak, for example—and those people often do appreciate that we offer a full bar. But okra and gin? A Jack and Coke sound good with collard greens? No, darlin'. Sweet potato pie and the finest chardonnay? I don't *think* so.

One of my expense lists is for damage control, or unexpected glitches that cost you money. Listen, a million bad things can happen in a restaurant. You can have your place all set up, your budget planned, and costs for advertising, rent, insurance, staff, and food accounted for. But what happens when equipment breaks down, insurance and advertising costs rise, food costs more than you thought, an untrustworthy employee pilfers your best roast, or you absolutely need to hire another pair of hands? Well, honey, you've got to figure on adding some more money for unexpected damage to the cost projection. How? Maybe lower your costs on one side and increase your prices on the other.

Sometimes damage control consists of fixing what you've been unforgivably careless about. When we were at the Best Western, for example, I was busier than a one-armed paper hanger on a windy day. I did whatever it took to keep us going: I did the books, I did a good bit of the cooking, I waited tables if I needed to. By this time, my wonderful Dora had come into my life, and she certainly made life better, because she had a real smart head on her shoulders. I knew that she knew about food in the kitchen. Well, because I left so much of that up to her, I'd get careless about other stuff and get so busy, I'd forget to take care of little things. Like paying bills.

Picture this: It's twelve noon. We're in the middle of a very busy lunch when Dora comes and finds me and says, "Paula, they've turned off the gas. You didn't pay the gas bill."

I absolutely panicked; I couldn't move. But Dora moved. She

loaded up all that chicken, then ran across the road to the Holiday Inn and asked if we could finish frying our chicken in their deep fryer. Those angels said yes. We kept our restaurant moving, and I don't think people ever knew we weren't cooking with gas in the kitchen.

Sometimes you've got to deal with your staff's mistakes. For example, this nice young man had just started to work in the kitchen and I told him to finish up makin' my famous potato salad. I had gotten all the potatoes ready and put everything in it except the boiled eggs. I had to leave the restaurant in about thirty minutes for one of my catering jobs (which was payin' the bills until the new Lady & Sons made a profit), so I tell this young man, "Son, I need for you to just prepare the eggs and put them in the potato salad for me." I was in a hurry, but just before I left, I go back there and I see this huge bowl of potato salad settin' on the ledge, waiting to be served to everyone in the dining room. It has got the mayonnaise, it has got the potatoes, it has got all the seasonings in it. But now it is also covered with raw eggs.

I didn't tell him to boil the eggs.

"Are you freakin' crazy?" I asked him. "How many times has yo' momma served you potato salad full of raw eggs?"

Sometimes, I'm sorry to tell you, you need to deal with plain ugly thievery, even by your staff.

In-house pilferage is a problem, and part of the cost of doing business. I've had occasions when five hundred dollars of profit or a sixteen-pound standing rib roast just walked out the door with someone I trusted. There are horror stories out there about bartenders, for example. I've heard stories that bartenders sometimes bring in their own generic brand of liquor, pour from their own bottles, charge premium restaurant prices, and pocket the difference. The next thing you know, you're operating in the red.

It can happen with food too. Stealing food is so very easy. All someone has to do is take that roll of fillet, wrap it up in silver foil, put it in the trash, and then come back and pull it out after everybody's gone. It amazes me to see the energy and imagination some people will use to pull a fast one; if they put that energy and thought into something positive, they could be anything they wanted to be. I had one young man who was passing out duplicate buffet tickets. Say there's a four-person table and they all order the buffet dinner. The waiter rings up four tickets and gives each diner a numbered ticket to redeem at the buffet. A thieving server will ring up the four tickets and then give copies of the tickets with the same numbers to another table of four who ordered the same thing. So the waiter will collect the money from both tables, only ring up the first table, and take home the money from the second table. When he was caught, he was fired. There's no second chance for thieves.

You have to learn to shut as many doors of opportunities to steal as you can. You do that with inventory systems, by having a manager watch the tables, and by just keeping an eye on the people you've entrusted to do the right thing. You have to "encourage" honesty in many ways, even through very visible surveillance cameras. It's very important that you try to build your business with people who have character and pride in what they do. Still, you have to accept the fact that a certain amount of thievery is gonna take place and there's nothing you can do about it; you've just got to hold it to a minimum.

Downtime costs you money. Perhaps you're thinking of starting a restaurant in a space that is now just a hole in the ground or even in a space where a restaurant has previously existed. You're just going to have to figure into your projection the cost of fixing up that shell restaurant space and the cost of getting your new furniture and fixtures, or your improvements in the existing restaurant.

It's not just the hard costs for the electricians, the painters, the floor, the heat, and the air-conditioning. You're still spending money on rent, but you have no money coming in because you're not open to the public. You've got people working for you, so you've got salaries to pay before opening day. If you think it's going to take you four months to get in, you'd better project seven or eight months to get into your space: you've just got to plan on the extra expense or you're going to be opening up that restaurant with no money in your pocket. No money in your pocket means you can't buy the food that you want and, just as important, you can't do adequate staff training. If you don't train properly, that means the kitchen won't cook the food fast enough and the people in the front of the house can't serve the food fast enough. Maybe I shouldn't talk—after all, I didn't even have money for change when I opened, but I was damn lucky, maybe you won't be so lucky at first.

Too often, eager new restaurant owners think they can just open the door and their restaurant is going to make them easy money. Remember, the people waiting out there to be fed want to be served in a reasonable period of time. They want good food, and if they don't get good food and good service, are they going to come back next time? No. Are they going to tell their friends how great you are? No, darlin'.

So you do need what my accountant calls a rehearsal.

Rehearsal nights are dry runs to work out some of the kinks. Close the restaurant to the public and give free meals on one or two nights to a room filled with your best friends and family. You'll learn more from what goes right and what goes wrong than you'll lose in meal cost. After the dry runs, you might have your key people sit down and write notes about what went right, and how you can build on that, as well as about what went wrong, and how they think you can fix it.

Waste and spoilage can be a restaurant's downfall and add to hidden costs. In the beginning, although I'd had some experience at The Lady in the Best Western, we really didn't know what to anticipate in terms of how much food we needed. Sometimes we'd overorder and would have to send things back. If the food was still good and the container was not broken—it had to be in the exact shape it was in when it came in the day before—*and* if we had a good relationship with our food purveyor, often this provider would take the overorder back, but that's a rare occurrence.

We very seldom overordered. I always felt it was better to be short than lose on overstock. I've had days when I've been to the grocery store as many as fifteen times because we would run out of things. I remember our first Thanksgiving. I don't know how many times I got in the car and went to Publix to buy more hams and turkey breasts. I went nuts trying to thaw out those frozen turkey breasts so that we could deep-fry them and serve them quickly. Oh, my God!

Here's a cliché, and it's said so often because it's true: the most important person in your whole restaurant business is that customer. She must come first.

To be a real success in the restaurant business, because it is a service industry, you have got to be willing to humble yourself whether you're the server, the host, the chef, or the owner. You've got to be able to put yourself in a kind of menial position—servant. If you can't do that, it will be hard for you. But I tell my staff, in order to be good, you can't think so much of yourself that you're too good to be a servant for others.

My general manager, Dustin, knows each customer is a VIP, and he greets everyone with a warm smile. The manager sets the tone for the rest of your staff. As people enter, Dustin greets them with a shoulder touch just to let them know he's happy they're there.

So, honey, I think it's clear that you can't afford to have any insensitive managers and servers or chefs with short emotional fuses. You can't have a bully or a hot-tempered person in your kitchen preparing that food. Then your servers are too frightened to go into the kitchen and stand up for the customer. You have to be strong, and if the servers are scared of that bully chef back there, they'll be willing to serve your guests something inferior rather than face the chef and say, "This is not right." Restaurant owners can't be bullies, either. Your staff must have respect for the way you want things done, but they can't be terrified of you; they have to know that underneath the firmness, you care about them.

Bubba has an interesting theory about an owner's professional relationship with his or her staff. "Servers are independent contractors," says Bubba. "They come in and 'rent' tables from us every day and they give the revenue from the meals at these tables to the owners. We furnish the electricity, the building, the furniture, the insurance, and the product, and all they have to do is sell our product. If they do a good job, they make good tips and a good salary and they haven't spent a dime of their own money. But, at the end of the day, if it's the server's fault that one guest didn't get her food till half an hour after everyone else at her table, that guest's not going to remember the server's name but she's going to be mad at Uncle Bubba because it's my name that's over the front door. If I have to comp that guest for her inconvenience, when the day's over I'm going to tell my server, 'You owe me twenty-five dollars.' If I am going to be held accountable by the bank, the city, the state, and the federal government, not to mention my sister, Paula, my servers also have to be accountable for their actions."

You go, Bubba! That sounds right to me.

When I started out, my staff now laughingly says that I was the biggest bitch, and I probably was, but only because I was fighting for all our lives and I had to get the very best out of those people that I could. At the same time, I like to think that when we were not in the middle of battle, they knew I loved them. I wanted them to succeed. It would thrill me to pieces when I would hear that a server had just made oodles of tip money on a shift.

New owners regularly ask me how I deal with mean customers. You know, I've got to be the luckiest girl in the whole world because somehow, the nicest, sweetest people in this world find their way to my restaurant door. I could probably count on one hand the people who have treated me ugly. But see, I make it hard for people to be mean to me. If you show people love and kindness and a smile, it's hard to get angry and worked up. I guarantee that customers will get fired up in a minute if you're grumpy, frowning, short, or rude. When I have people on my staff for whom I have to apologize, that's very upsetting to me because my business was built on hospitality and making people feel good about putting their feet under my table.

When a server has the bad luck to find a truly obnoxious patron, I recommend that the server respond by being as nice as she can. She's trained to offer solutions to make customers happy. Sometimes it's a freebie. I may lose on that meal, but if what's making the customer cranky is based on something we did, I'll always do the right thing. When complaints have a basis, you apologize and say you're sorry that the customer has been unhappy with his experience and you do the right thing.

An elderly gentleman said to my brother, Bubba, "Son, don't ever apologize for making a profit. That's why we're in business. That's what America was built on, that's free enterprise. That's this country's strength."

So what did I think when I read an e-mail from a woman who wrote, "Paula, you are the greediest woman I have ever heard of and our Father in heaven knows what kind of terrible person you are." Why did she write that? Because I charged more for chicken than she paid in the supermarket. What I thought was that this person had never run a restaurant!

That woman did hurt my feelings badly.

Ever wonder what it really means when the waiter tells you what the "specials of the day" are? Is the "special" the freshest, most desirable choice on the menu? Is it the least expensive? Or by *special,* do they mean the dish is so great it'll be super expensive? In my restaurants, the "special" means something different every day. For example, I may buy a load of wonderful fish at a great price and then also offer it at a particularly reasonable price to my customers because it will last for two days and still be extremely fresh. Sometimes a special might be a way for a restaurateur to raise the price a bit by adding something extra, like crab stuffing, that will make that fish just fantastic; still, when hard-to-find or expensive ingredients are involved and the dish takes more of the chef's time to prepare, I've got to charge you more. Sometimes specials are used as marketing devices: I know some restaurants that have a different "special" every day of the week—and people who have come to love the restaurant's lamb chops come in every Tuesday to get that lamb chop special. Finally, I'm sorry to say that in some restaurants, what they call a special is what is not *quite* fresh and *must* sell immediately or be discarded. In those cases, it's usually true that an owner will lower the price, but incredibly, he may also raise the price for the same dish, and to hell with his guests. So, what makes the special special? In any restaurant but my own, damned if I know. Tip: Ask the wait person why the special she's pushing is so damned special—and hope for the truth.

Some of you may be thinking of starting a family business, and I'd like to say a few words about owning a business with beloved relatives or even trusted friends. When we were at the Best Western, my sons, Bobby and Jamie, worked as employees. Sometimes, when three in the afternoon came around, one or the other of them would take off to play somewhere, leaving the vacuum cleaner they were using right in the middle of the room. I knew that golf was drawing their attention more than the restaurant. When I was about to open The Lady & Sons, my intuition told me that they'd be a whole lot more invested in the business if they owned some of it, and so I told my accountant, Karl, that I was fixin' to give them half of the business—25 percent each.

"Paula," Karl told me, "I'm a firm believer in one person having control, so let's compromise. You keep 52 percent. You give them each 24 percent."

That's what I did and that's when I decided to change the name of The Lady to The Lady & Sons.

Well, it wasn't just the name that changed. The boys also changed so much. When they saw their names out there as owners, they became dedicated to growing the business and started putting in ninety-plus hours a week. One of them was always there, sometimes both. Sure, they were. It was *theirs* now.

That was great for me, great for them, and great for my taxes because the tax burden on me was vastly lowered. My advice? It's a very good idea to make a trusted person a partner if you want that person to really commit himself to your business. But stay in control with the smallest percentage more than your partner.

Listen, I figure that even if I don't follow my own advice and I end up giving the boys a greater share, I can still outvote them because I'm still *yo' momma*. In the South, being *yo' momma* trumps all.

The only one that outvotes *yo' momma* is the health inspector, who comes unannounced every six, eight, or ten weeks. Everyone gets in a wild tizzy when that man appears, and let me tell you, when his car's pullin' up, word spreads through the building very fast. Everyone starts cleaning and shutting cooler doors. A health inspector will write you up if a hand towel's missing or a soap dispenser's empty in the bathroom. God forbid you don't have a thermometer in a refrigerated unit. I remember one time at the Best Western, the health inspector showed up; he'd seen me at my best and at my worst, but this day was more like the latter. Here I am trying to distract him while the staff's fast cleaning up the kitchen, so I say, "John, honey, come out here on the patio deck so's I can show you what's going down on our buffet line today." Well, I took him outside where a big old drum grill was just loaded down with chicken, and his face about purpled up and he said, "Paula, what are you *thinking*? You can't do this. You can't cook outside unless it's in an enclosed area." Here I was thinking I was diverting the wolf, and I led him right to the sheep. And led myself to a big old fine, too.

Bubba remembers the time when Uncle Bubba's was open only a few months and a young boy ordered our really incredible crab stew and he was sitting there quietly eatin' it when Bubba saw him reach up, nudge his momma, and loudly say, "Momma, where's the crab at?" Well, don't you know our staff had prepared the crab stew and forgot the crab? Thank the Lord there was no inspector around that day.

So, you still want to open a restaurant? Well, friend, do it! I've been running my mouth in this chapter because I want you to be clearheaded about what lies ahead for you. It takes so much work and grit and raw strength and energy, and still so many things can go wrong, but you know what? If it works, it can be the most magical business in the world.

Pan-Fried Corn

This is my momma's recipe. I never published it in any of my books before, and I don't know why, because it's pretty delicious and everyone just loves it in my restaurants. This is the recipe I use when I prepare pan-fried corn at home; for the restaurants, I have to modify it a bit because there isn't a frying pan big enough for those crowds.

You start with a dozen ears of Silver Queen corn, which is kinda like white corn. First, wash the corn. Next, grate those ears with a corn grater to get the kernels off. Then put a little butter in a cast-iron skillet and fry up about 3 or 4 strips of streak o' lean, which is pork but minus the fat (you can find it in packages next to your hams in the grocery store or order it on the Internet). In a pinch, you can always use bacon or fatback, but I personally love streak o' lean for the ultimate piggy flavor with my fried corn.

When the streak o' lean's nice and brown, take it out, add a stick of butter to the streak o' lean drippings, and then pour in your corn kernels and stir and fry them until done, about 5 to 8 minutes. Then I chop my meat, whether it's bacon, streak o' lean, or fatback, and throw it back in the corn. Season it with salt and black pepper.

It serves 6 to 8 people and is great served with ham or fried chicken.

Chapter 17

SCENES FROM A LIFE: GROWTH, CAMERON, MR. JIMMY, BUBBA, AND ME

Taste makes waist.

The Lady & Sons, at 311 Congress Street, was filled to capacity every night, and I started to think: *Dare I take yet another risk? Am I arrogant to think I could expand to something bigger, much bigger?* The restaurant had eighty-five seats and we'd maxed the space: lines of friends, neighbors, and other locals circled the block two and three times nightly, so there was always a wait of from one to three hours to get in. We'd long ago stopped bothering to take reservations from groups under ten people—it was "Get here and we'll get you in, somehow." But it was the tourists I had on my mind now. Savannah was growing by leaps and bounds, and I felt I had to accommodate all those people who'd heard about us from Oprah, my cookbooks, and our show on the Food Network.

We knew that eventually, the lease at 311 West Congress Street would end and the landlord would raise our rent. It was time for me to be my own landlord. To do that, I needed to put some money where my mouth was.

Now was the moment for some serious but calculated risk-taking. I borrowed money from the bank and started purchasing property that would make me a real, grown-up landlord.

On October 25, 1999, I bought 108 West Congress Street, which was about the same size of the space we were renting. Although we were still under our lease at 311 West Congress, I wanted a place my restaurant could move to when the lease expired. The luxury of 108 was that it had a tenant who could help pay for the property until we could renovate the space and move in.

Then, miracle of miracles, 106 West Congress became available; thinking ahead but with my heart in my throat, I realized that I also had to buy this building too. An adjacent building would give us the room to eventually expand The Lady & Sons. The property didn't have a tenant, but we tightened our belts, and on June 21, 2000, we bought it and managed to pay our mortgage on time.

All good stuff comes in packages. When 102 and 104 became available, I really flinched at the price, which was almost a million dollars. I was on a roll though, and I bought them on December 20, 2001. Now we had a whole lot of property—and no income. Good work, Paula.

Was I nuts? No. I was a budding entrepreneur. I was becoming the Paula Deen I always wanted to be—not exactly fearless, but cautiously brave. We moved up our plans, and decided to borrow some more money to plunge ahead and build our big, beautiful new restaurant—even way before our current lease at 311 ran out. Following Karl's advice, I calculated that the additional revenue we'd see from a vastly expanded restaurant would pay for the new buildings, their improvements, and also our rented space at 311 until the lease ended.

We were right.

In 2003, excitedly, we moved from 311 Congress to our new home just days before Thanksgiving. It had taken fourteen months to get the new space ready. We owned about half the block now, and went from an 85-seat restaurant to a 250-seat place in a four-floor building that contained a banquet room, a huge bar area, offices, and a state-of-the-art kitchen. On Thanksgiving Day, we served more than fourteen hundred people. Loved my life! Did I need *another* restaurant? Not really, but Bubba did.

BUBBA'S STORY

How did I get into the restaurant business? My sister's dreams reach far. Let me first say that for me, Paula's the alpha and the omega, the beginning and the end, and there ain't nothing ever going to separate us but death. Not to say she don't aggravate me on occasion, but that big sister has saved my hide more than once. And, she was about to do it again.

I'd been doing very well in a landscaping and lawn maintenance company I'd started in Albany, but when my wife left me, Paula got mad and called to say, "Sell everything, and move over here." In a few months, I called back to say, "You know what? I think I'm ready."

My kids were grown. Corrie would live with me in Savannah, but for now she was off at college. Jay was on his own in Atlanta but would remain my son and close to me forever. I knew Paula was going to the top however she had to do it—and I felt like I had something to offer her. Her two sons had worked so hard, but I knew I could give them some guidance and take some of the stress off my sister. When I moved to Savannah in 1999, they didn't even have an office; Jamie used to pay the bills in the mornings on the dining room table. I truly wanted to help

Paula, Jamie, and Bobby get their business to the next level. So, for about two years, I worked at The Lady & Sons, learning the business—you might say I went from lawns to prawns. In the meantime, I started looking around for another restaurant because there were too many of us to be in just the one place. Frankly, we both thought we'd open another Lady & Sons.

One day I walked into the office, and Paula was already there. "Bubba," she said, "I figured out what we're going to do."

"Oh, shoot," I said, "let me sit down for this. It makes me scared when you start thinking."

She said, "We're already doing great Southern cuisine—the home cooking that we were raised on, and here we are living in this beautiful coastal city. Let's open up a seafood restaurant."

It was an obvious idea but it took Paula to think of it.

So that was the plan. Not another Lady & Sons, but a different kind of restaurant, one that I would be mainly responsible for. We started looking at property and found some gorgeous land on Whitemarsh Island on Turners Creek. One day, again, I walked into the office, and she said, "Bubba, I figured out the name of our new place."

I thought we would call the new restaurant The Lady & Her Brother or The Lady's Brother, but she said, "No, we're going to call it Uncle Bubba's Oyster House."

I was thrilled. It was a real Southern name. It was my name. Made me feel good.

Paula and I decided that she and I would be partners in Uncle Bubba's because Jamie and Bobby were already her partners at The Lady & Sons. If something happened to Paula, Jamie and Bobby would get her share of the interest. The main goal was to keep everything in the family. Family is what turns us on.

We opened the doors to Uncle Bubba's just before Christmas 2004. There's a creek running out back, koi fish swimming in the pond by the front door, and irresistible smells pullin' in the people. We have an old Southern tradition that says if you cook a good dish, you gotta get slapped. Our char-grilled oysters are so good, as Paula says, they'll make you want to slap yo' momma. Just a taste will give you a Southern drawl. There are a whole lot of family pictures in the entranceway of Uncle Bubba's; one them is of Paula and me with her tweakin' my left nipple—we call it the *titty-twister photo*. She has an evil grin on her lips and she's clearly enjoyin' the tweakin'. I'm shrieking in despair and dismay and horrible pain. That picture is a prime example of how she's approached me all my life, with a lot of aggravation and a lot of love. She always aggravated me with love.

And that's no frickin' lie.

So now it was 2005, I had a husband, a blended family, and two restaurants to keep me focused. I wasn't bored, y'all. Then I had an experience my momma and daddy would have been crazy proud of, given all the bad report cards they had to sign.

On a Thursday in March 2004, two days away from my becoming Mrs. Michael Groover, I got a message from Cookie, my office manager, that someone named Gail from Paramount Pictures had called and would like me to call her back. And I said, "Well, why the hell is Paramount calling me? I can't cater chicken that far from Savannah. That chicken would be rotten by the time I got it there." Very funny joke, I thought. Then I forgot about Gail and Paramount.

Michael and I were married that Saturday. It was a crazy time and we decided that because there was so much going on for us, we couldn't afford the time to go on a real honeymoon. We spent the night in a wonderful downtown B&B, Planters Inn. The next day, we had lunch with all our friends who had come for the wedding, then we drove down to a fabulous resort called The Cloister on Sea Island, about sixty miles away. We took the little silver 350Z Nissan convertible that Michael had given me for a wedding present, and we left the top down all the way to Sea Island. We checked into a room and literally collapsed on the bed; we were both so exhausted. We were only going to spend two days there because I had to get back to Savannah. On the second day, the weather's wonderful, we're riding around with our top down, we're looking at all the pretty houses, when Michael looks over at me and says, "Hey, Paula, did you ever call Paramount Pictures back?"

"Shoot," I said. "No."

"Well, I think you should call 'em," said my new husband, who had the number in his wallet. I called and asked to speak to Gail Levin, who I later discovered was the head of casting for Paramount Studios.

Gail proceeded to thank me for returning her call and then she said, "I was home recently, recovering from a minor illness and channel surfing, when I caught your cooking show. Well," she continued, "I'm working with Cameron Crowe and Tom Cruise on a movie about a Southern family. I've really had a problem finding the perfect woman to portray the character of Aunt Dora. She's the glue that holds the family together, she's always in her kitchen, and she loves to feed people. You look like Aunt Dora to me."

"Gail, do you know I'm not an actress?" I slowly asked over the phone.

She just laughed and said, "Well, you're further along than you think, Paula."

I was flattered, but I knew she could hear the hesitation in my voice when she said, "Tell you what, let me have Cameron call you. He's the writer, director, and one of the producers, and I want you to hear what a fine man he is."

The next day, Cameron Crowe called me. Within three minutes, I was in love with this man on the phone. You could hear the kindness, compassion, and thoughtfulness in his voice. He was a mixed breed—half Southern, half West Coast—so he *got* me. Well, every good thing you thought you could not say about a Hollywood director applied to Cameron Crowe. He turned out to be one of the most special people I've ever met. He told me about the character of Aunt Dora.

I gulped hard and told him, "Well, Cameron, I'm not an actress, but I will come out there and do the very best I can not to embarrass you. But if you see when I get there that I'm no good, you gotta promise you'll put my butt on the bus and I'll go home and fry chicken."

So I went to Hollywood and walked into this big old warehouse on a set on the Paramount properties, ready for a first rehearsal. When I first arrived, I saw this beautiful young man who turned out to be Orlando Bloom, who was the star. There was a script I needed to follow for the most part, but Cameron allowed me to say my part in words that felt good to my tongue. He would feed me little lines, but I could ad-lib a lot and be myself.

We practiced and rehearsed all day. At the end of the day, the shuttle bus took us back to the hotel. The next day, I think I'm going back to rehearse some more but the bus takes us to another part of Paramount Studios and we walk into an office building.

I learn that the whole script is fixing to be read by the entire cast. I walk into this room, and on the right-hand side are all kinds of yummy breakfast foods set out. To the left is a huge conference table that seats probably twenty-four people in very comfortable chairs. You better believe that I'm feeling a little out of place at this point, a little unsure, and a *lot* out of my league. I'm seeing all these faces that I have stood in line and bought movie tickets to see in the movie theater. I look over there at the big table, and there's a thick script at every seat. On the top piece of paper it says *Elizabethtown,* and in huge bold black letters, on each script, is written names—Susan Sarandon, Orlando Bloom, Judy Greer, Kirsten Dunst, Cameron Crowe, Tom Cruise, Paula Deen.

Paula Deen? On a movie script? It was a staggering sensation. So we sit down, and I'm introduced to Tom Cruise, and he takes me in his arms and hugs and welcomes me—that wonderful smile; those bright, shiny eyes.

I muttered something dumb. I was sitting at this table next to Kirsten Dunst, like country come to town. I'm in shock. These famous people start reading the script, and they're fabulous. The script is coming alive, and I'm in a trance. My part, I knew, was about two little lines. I'm listening to this story unfold as these people are acting out their parts, and I was so enthralled with the company and the whole scene and the story that when it got to Aunt Dora's two tiny lines, I just sat there. The casting director, Gail Levin, reached over and shook me, saying, "Paula, that's your line."

Well, shit! The whole reading had gone on without a miss, and I got these two little stinking lines and I messed them up. Eventually, I got into the swing of things and Cameron even added some more lines for me. Must have been my Greta Garbo presence.

The movie, *Elizabethtown,* was such a sweet movie, actually based on an event from Cameron's life. Cameron Crowe's mother was from California, and his father was from the rolling hills of Kentucky. The daddy fell in love with this California woman who wanted no part of the South, but Cameron's daddy would come back to Kentucky once a year and visit his big colorful family. Orlando Bloom played the part of Cameron Crowe, and I was Cameron's Aunt Dora.

It was kind of like my real-life role. In the end, I had no problems with the whole thing, I wasn't acting, I was bein' Paula, keepin' everyone in line.

And then came the movie premieres. I hadn't been to a whole lot of those, let me tell you.

Had to buy a dress, first. Girls, you ain't lived until you've gone shopping in New York City with two handsome, hip gay men who know their stuff. My assistant, Brandon Branch, and the famous stylist David Evangelista had me inside these boutiques, and they was snatchin' and grabbin' clothes off all the racks, shoving me in the dressing room, saying, "Put this on, Paula, no, *wrong, honey,* put that on." The dress that David and Brandon finally chose for me was in a black accordion-pleated style; it had a fancy, soft matching top with a stand-up collar and it was drop-dead gorgeous.

Before I knew it, they'd got me all decked out and I had these fancy duds and the three of us were walking down Fifth Avenue with a million packages, just as happy as clams. To make matters even more glamorous, Food Network had decided to do a one-hour special called *Paula Goes to Hollywood,* so I had a camera following us everywhere.

The film was going to have two premieres, one at the Toronto Film Festival and one in New York. So first we go to Toronto. I'm wearing my new black tuxedo suit. I pull up in the limo, look outside at the throngs lined up, and say to my sons, who were along for the ride, "These folks have no more idea of who I am than as if I was a monkey's uncle."

At the New York premiere, I wore my new gown. I took most of my family up to New York for the big opening. Michael was there, and Aunt Peggy, Bobby, Jamie and his new wife, the gorgeous Brooke, my niece, Corrie, Bubba and his girlfriend, Dawn Woodside. It was beyond exciting. We were all tarted up in our fancy duds and no one dreamed our roots were plain.

I get out of the limo and I actually get to walk the red carpet. Would you believe that? Little Paula Hiers was the cat's meow, walking the red carpet. It's really red, but shorter than what you'd think, probably not more than twenty-five feet long. So many people are crammed under this tentlike thing with this red carpet and photographers just stacked on top of one another. People shoved handheld microphones at me with every step I took.

Unlike in Toronto, when I got out of that limo in New York, many people actually knew me! They were clapping and hollering, callin' my name, and I said, "Oh, my goodness! I have died and gone to heaven. This is too exciting!" The photographers were just fighting to get their shots. My publicist at the time walked the red carpet near me, and I remembered seeing him on television on another red carpet walking with Leonardo DiCaprio who starred in *Titanic*. Now it was my turn, and it was just as Titanic.

As I was walking down the red carpet, I had forgotten something that my publicist had warned me about. "Now, Paula," he'd said, "as you walk the red carpet, photographers will say things that sound very abrasive and may shock you, but that's how they get your attention so that you will look at their camera and they'll get the shot that they want. Pay no attention, look straight ahead."

But I forgot. This fifty-nine-year-old woman from Albany, Georgia, who had as little exposure to life as you could think of, is floating down the red carpet with people clapping and lights flashing, and I'm just so happy, I'm grinning, and all of a sudden this voice yells out, "Paula, shithead! Paula, shithead!"

I turned, stunned. I see the photographer it's coming from.

I said, "You called me a shithead. You've called me a shithead." I was mortally hurt.

I looked back at this man, and when he saw that I had taken it personally, he took the time to lower his camera and miss his opportunity for other pictures to tell me, with the biggest smile on his face, that he didn't mean it like that. But I hated that moment. And the result? The pictures that they got of me were with my eyes and mouth wide open, looking shocked. Anyone who sees those pictures knows I was upset. Now, *that's* an example of mean cursing.

The person following me down this red carpet was my favorite, favorite person—that precious Cameron Crowe. He called my name, I turned around, and he does like this: "Come here."

So, I go back to the start of the red carpet, and, of course, lightbulbs really go double crazy because now I am with Cameron Crowe. He gives me a hug. This talented, generous man—well, I don't know if he saw the whole thing, but I think he did. Now he's just giving me a loving hug, like that. I got to back up and start again. There were better pictures for my scrapbook from that redo.

By the time I got to the end of that red carpet, I thought, *That carpet was not long enough. I'm an older girl who's never done any of this. I would like to kick those young girls off, say "Get out of my way, it's my turn again, I started late!" and have me walk it again, by myself.* That didn't happen.

When I came back from doing the shoot, the tour, and the red carpet, I knew my life had been so enriched from the experience and I had people saying, "Paula, you were a natural. Are you gonna do it again?"

My answer to that is, "I don't know." Since that time when I took responsibility for myself and started The Bag Lady, so we could eat, it seems like God has always had a hand in seeing that I was in the right place at the right time. It's not something I'll seek out, but if it finds me, I would love to give it another try. If Cameron Crowe called me today and wanted little Paula in another movie, I would be there tomorrow with a platter of the best fried chicken he ever et.

There was plenty of excitement on my own Food Network show. In the first year, I rode motorcycles and a Vespa scooter and flew in a hot-air balloon. The balloon part really tested me. Picture the chunky, white-haired old girl trying to crawl gracefully into the balloon basket as she desperately attempted to keep her catfish-white belly from peeking out under her shirt and onto the television screens of thousands of Americans. I won't bore you with the sordid details except one: the line on the hot-air balloon, which was tethered to the earth, snapped, and you could hear me screaming my lungs out in Timbuktu as Gordon raced across the field trying to catch the line and pull me back to safety. Thank God that man is six feet seven; otherwise, I was going to be a star in the heavens, all right. After he finally caught that rope and pulled me down, I hyperventilated off-camera for an hour—that part my television audience didn't see.

One show in particular ranks high in the most memorable scenes of my life. My guest was President Jimmy Carter, who came from Plains, Georgia, about thirty-five miles away from my hometown of Albany.

We met when I was told by my producer that I needed to find a peanut farmer, because we had to go visit a peanut field. Michael told him, "Well, we've got the most famous peanut farmer in the world right here in the state of Georgia." So we start making phone calls, and it was agreed that I could go to Plains and interview Mr. Jimmy. I took my children and I said, "You've got to be there with me, because this is like history—yo' momma walkin' arm in arm with a president." So, we go to Plains, and I'm like a little girl who's standing back of her daddy again, in awe of who I'm lookin' at. When I first laid eyes on him I fell in love with him; he smiled and you saw all these teeth and those twinkling blue eyes.

Mr. Jimmy was gonna take me on a tour of the stores on Plains's Main Street, which is only about two blocks long. Plains has gone through very little change other than the big railroad sign saying HOME OF JIMMY CARTER. Brother Billy's service station still stands across the street. It's in disrepair, but it's still there. They did restore one of these buildings on Main Street and turned it into a B&B. We stayed there, and I understand that Mr. Jimmy even built one of the beds himself.

When he walked into the Carter home and we were introduced, I asked him, "Do you mind if I touch you?" He said, "No, I don't," so I hooked my arm through his and asked, "What may I call you?"

He said, "Call me Jimmy." Now, in the South, you always teach your children to put a Mr. or a Miss in front of a person's name when you're too close in age to call them by their surname, but not close enough in age to call them by their first name. So President Jimmy Carter is always Mr. Jimmy to me. Now, I consider Mr. Jimmy and me new friends, but we have not once, to this day, ever spoken of politics. Our relationship has to do with family and roots, and this great glorious state of Georgia—his and mine.

The whole town came out for the show. All of us gathered in the back of Bobby's Peanut Shop with Mr. Jimmy and Miss Rosalynn, and we had lunch. I had something in common with the man with the blue eyes. Mr. Jimmy is, to me, the epitome of a Southern gentleman farmer. He's down-home folks, my kind of people. There was a woman there in town who Mr. Jimmy just loves, who has the little restaurant there across the street from the downtown area, and he calls her Mom. She runs a buffet just like I do, and she was to bring us all lunch. When this elderly little black lady walked in, you saw Mr. Jimmy's face literally light up—that's how big a part of his life she is. We dug into the food she brought, but there wasn't quite enough chicken for all of us.

Only Mr. Jimmy realized I wasn't eating. He took his chicken wing, and he ripped that wing in two and gave me the piece that he had not eaten off of.

I was overcome with gratitude to be able to talk with him and find out about his childhood and the foods he ate. Ever the home-town booster, Mr. Jimmy told me with his famous grin, "I feel the

Paula Deen show's gonna put me on the map. A has-been politician all of a sudden, back in the limelight."

The show was a huge success: I got a thank-you note from Miss Rosalynn saying that it had done more for Plains than anything since Mr. Jimmy won the White House. And I got an invitation to come back.

Sometime later, Gordon Elliott's company, Follow Productions, made arrangements for us to revisit Plains. Well, scheduling got complicated, and even after all the steppin' and fetchin' and maneuverin' to get us a time when the staff and I and the Carters could be together, we had to cancel the arrangements. Everyone was disappointed because Mr. Jimmy and the town of Plains were looking very forward to us coming back.

So, a few months later, I was in the kitchen right in the middle of filming a cooking show and Brandon comes flying through the front door with his phone in the air saying to the director, "Paula *must* take this phone call." Brandon would never in a trillion years interrupt in the middle of the show while the red light's flashing.

I started to panic a little as I tried to think what it could possibly be that would induce him to interrupt a show, but they kept the cameras rolling, and I took the phone.

"Hello," I said.

And this familiar voice, with those buttery vowels, and that Southern accent even stronger than mine, answered, "Hey, Paula, honey, this is Jimmy Carter."

Holy camoley, I thought. *Mr. Jimmy is calling me on my phone on my show.*

"We sure were disappointed that the show was canceled out. Plains is so looking forward to y'all comin' back because it means so much to the town here."

"Well, Mr. Jimmy," I stuttered, "I don't know exactly what happened, and I'll tell you what: I'm standing up here looking at the producer of this show, Gordon Elliott, and I'm going to pass the phone to him."

Well, those cameras never stopped rolling. Gordon Elliott could have swallowed his tongue. He wished the floor could have eaten him alive because, he said later, he felt that I threw him under a bus. Here was a president of the United States on the phone and Gordon had to tell him we didn't have time for him. That big old silver-tongued devil Gordon Elliott got to spittin' and a-sputterin'. When he got off the telephone, I could almost see little beads of sweat on him. So, he rescheduled it again.

Lo and behold, but Follow Productions called me soon after, and said we couldn't do it on the new date. This time, it was kind of Mr. Jimmy's doin'.

He'd called me to say that he had to go and meet with some world leaders but asked, "Paula, how late could you film Tuesday night?" I said, "Well, Mr. Jimmy, I am there until the show is complete. I can work as long as I have to."

He said, "Good, because there's a world crisis going on but I am so looking forward to your coming to Plains again, and since I'm going to be flying back on Tuesday around four-thirty, I wanted to know if y'all could stay later."

I told him I would work as late as it took, as long as he and Miss Rosalynn were not too tired. Then I called the production company. Gordon had a hissy fit. He was so upset because he'd allotted a certain time for filming this show, and there was so much to consider in putting it together. Mother Nature can be your biggest enemy. We can use fake light, but without the right natural daylight, lighting can be a very tricky, tedious process to get it all perfect. And, filming after four-thirty in the afternoon and into the night? Gordon said, "Paula, we are going to have to just reschedule."

I said, "Well, okay, but the reason Mr. Jimmy called me was

because that was the last thing he wanted to have happen. This is important to this man and this town, and it ain't going to be me who tells him no."

That awful job fell to one of the assistant producers. She called Mr. Jimmy's scheduler and told him *we'd* have to reschedule because we didn't have enough daylight to film. Well, Mr. Jimmy was very, very, *very* displeased.

So my phone rings again, and I say, "Hello," and this voice again says, "Paula, this is Jimmy Carter." I say, "Hey, Mr. Jimmy. How are you?" He says, "I'm not doin' good at all."

I said, "What's the problem, Mr. Jimmy?" and he said he'd just gotten word that the company wanted to cancel the shoot and reschedule yet again. He was not one bit happy.

I said, "Mr. Jimmy, I'm so sorry that you're unhappy. I have talked to the production company, and they're very concerned that your schedule isn't going to give us enough time to do the show. But I'm going to do what I can to see that the show does not get canceled."

I call up Gordon and say, "Gordon, I don't care how you do it, but you cannot tell this man no. This show must go on. We've got to figure it out because I'm not gonna be the one to tell this man that we're going to reschedule. I'm not gonna be the one to disappoint Mr. Jimmy. If I have to go buy me a movie camera and go to Plains by myself, *somethin's* going to be filmed."

They knew I meant business. I don't pull the diva thing too often, but, I mean—this was Mr. Jimmy.

Well, they got it all worked out. The next time I talked to Mr. Jimmy, I was able to say, "We're coming." Of course, he was just as sweet as could be and said he sure did appreciate it because that trip I had made to Plains earlier meant more to them than the Nobel Peace Prize he had won. Well, I'm not so sure of that, but it was downright grand of him to say it.

So back we went. Mr. Jimmy had gone overseas, had his big world leaders' meeting, monitored the Palestinian elections, flew to London to make a speech, and at four-thirty or five o'clock that Tuesday afternoon he came in ready to put on an apron I had made for him that read "Hail to the Chef" and stir a pot of grits on *Paula's Home Cooking*. It was a *scene*—lights set up everywhere, cameras, crew members, and the kitchen people getting everything prepped. Then in walks this eighty-one-year-old man with a briefcase and a topcoat draped over his arm, just smiling to beat the band to see all these folks piled in his kitchen.

"Is this my house?" he asks.

The Carters live in the same house they've lived in most of their married lives, a very humble ranch-style home, comfortable but not pretentious at all. The small kitchen is particularly simple, wall-papered in a blue-flowered print, and it had the house's original 1961 cabinets repainted white. There's a Kenmore dishwasher, a GE side-by-side refrigerator covered with magnets holding photos like the one of Miss Rosalynn catching a fish and one of Mr. Jimmy building a house for Habitat for Humanity, and a couple of rusty beer-can openers that look like they date from his brother's Billy Beer era. A window over the sink looks out on an overgrown holly bush. Still, your breath is taken away when you walk in and see all these pictures of Mr. Jimmy with every world leader you can imagine hanging on the wall. Looking at those photographs, you immediately know you are standing in the presence of history. This is the man they asked me to cancel on. Fat chance!

So Mr. Jimmy goes back to his bedroom to freshen up. He puts on a plaid flannel shirt, his blue jeans, scuffed cowboy boots, and a big silver belt buckle forming a horseshoe around the initials J.C. Then, ready for his close-up, he comes out and says, "Well, am I gonna need a little makeup?" It's clear he's done this before.

"You look so handsome, I can't hardly stand it," I tell him.

The makeup table had been set up in his office and he's whisked off to where the makeup girl is waiting on him.

My crew and I go back into his kitchen where my show is going to be filmed.

For the show, I've built a menu around a south Georgia classic, smothered quail over grits. President Eisenhower used to come shoot quail in these parts. I planned early green peas on the side (from a shiny can; I hold no prejudice against canned veggies) and miniature tarts called Pecan Toffee Tassies, the sort of rich dessert my momma used to make, and I'm sure Mr. Jimmy's momma also made.

We talk as I prepare the meal, with Mr. Jimmy stirring the grits every now and then. He doesn't have to be shown how to make grits. During the Depression, he tells us, his momma cooked grits twice a day down on their farm, using the leftovers to make fried grits for breakfast. Sometimes they had buttermilk and corn bread for dessert, still one of his big favorite dishes.

After we finished preparing the meal, we all went into the den, followed by the crew. We ate on serving trays on the coffee table with Mr. Jimmy telling us stories about what he fed various visiting heads of state. "The most peculiar diet we ever ran across," he remembered, "was that of the prime minister of India, who ate nothing that came from an animal and predominately nuts and fruits. The killer was when the prime minister drank his own urine."

"You get out!" I shouted. "Why?"

"For health reasons," said Mr. Jimmy.

And my producer Gordon Elliott, that rascal, couldn't resist asking in his reverberating Australian accent, "But what wine would go with that?"

I had to keep secretly pinching myself during the filming

of this show. Paula Deen, chattin' away with (in my opinion) the greatest humanitarian walking the face of the earth today. Paula Deen and the President. Had a nice ring.

Who would have thunk an Albany High School cheerleader could jump so high, so wide, so far? Girl, I was on the right side of the dirt, and then some.

Uncle Bubba's Crab and Shrimp au Gratin

This was one of Michael's momma's favorite recipes. It lives on at Uncle Bubba's Oyster House. Sometimes I serve this delicious, rich, cheesy delight in individual glass casseroles that are shaped more like a boat than a casserole. Warm French bread and a fine salad are perfect partners for this dish.

¼ cup all-purpose flour
⅓ teaspoon salt
⅓ teaspoon black pepper
2 cups milk
⅓ cup Kraft Cheez Whiz
⅛ teaspoon Tabasco sauce
½ pound cooked shrimp, peeled
½ pound cooked crabmeat
1 cup grated Cheddar or Jack cheese

1. Preheat the oven to 350°F.
2. Mix the flour, salt, and pepper with 1 cup of the milk and beat out all the lumps with a wire whisk or a fork.
3. In a double boiler over low heat, add the Cheez Whiz to the remaining cup milk. When the Cheez Whiz has melted, add the flour mixture and the Tabasco sauce. Stir until smooth and thickened. Add the shrimp and crabmeat. Pour into a casserole and top with the grated cheese. Bake for 20 minutes.

Serves 3 or 4

Chapter 18

SOUTHERN COMFORT: THINGS I'VE LEARNED

A balanced diet is a cookie in both hands.

SOUTHERN CHARM IS REAL. IT WORKS.

I don't know if Southern women are taught charm in the cradle, but it ain't far after that time. You know, I think it's genetic; comes with the goods, but it can be learned. So, the rest of you gals, don't despair. Y'all can pick up Southern charm—it's transportable. Some of the most aggressive businesswomen I know from up north are rolling in the art.

Southern charm is a woman empowerment thing, a kind of gentle flirting, and we Southern gals, we begin practicing it on our daddies. I had mine so under my spell that if I even looked like I was goin' to cry, it would have killed him.

Don't ever mistake charm for stupidity, which a lot of folks do. Sure, there's some giggling and batting of the eyes, but as my Uncle George once said when I told him I didn't know if I'd be able to tend to my business because I really wasn't smart, he took only a second before he answered, "Yeah, you're dumb, Paula. Dumb as a fox."

Southern charm knows how to make a man feel good about himself; you can get whatever you want without deballing guys. Sometimes all it takes, even with the strongest, smartest guys in the world, is a compliment that gives a man strength and power. When I tell Michael Groover, "I love you so much, I could kiss your socks," it just sets him off all grinning. Women can even use Southern charm on other women—and it's very appreciated. Tell someone—if you mean it!—that her eyes are beautiful or you love her outfit, and she'll follow you anywhere. Hey, listen, SC is not necessarily sweet—it can be edgy and witty—but it's always sincere. If you don't feel it or mean it, don't waste your time trying to use it. Won't fool a soul.

You can't define Southern charm in a sentence; there are too many adjectives you'd have to use. But if I had to choose one word, it'd be *niceness*. I want people to feel good about bein' with me, and bein' nice to them makes it happen. If you see Joe Blow in the grocery store, you can't walk by and just say, "Hey, how y'all doin?" If you're wantin' to display your SC, it takes stoppin' for a while.

Now, it's true you just can't break through to some men and women—niceness doesn't lay a finger on their hearts. But most people, if you give them love and consideration, they will return it.

Southern charm also takes listening hard to people; not trying to fix their problems, but just letting them share their problems. It takes (with me, anyway) touching. I love to touch—to grab a hand, stroke someone's shining hair. And it takes smiling (that's the best thing in the whole charm wardrobe!) and being able to laugh and not take yourself so seriously.

Finally, for me, Southern charm has a lot to do with feeding people. "The Lady Can Cook" it says on the front of my apron. You can make someone your willing servant with a fine gooey butter cake. You know how many daughters-in-law out there hate their mother-in-law's guts because their husband says, "This pot roast is not like Momma's"? I'm so lucky that Brooke, my own beautiful daughter-in-law, does not feel threatened. She can sure hold her own with anyone—even someone with a cooking show. At Christmastime, she brought over this wonderful candy she'd made from her grandmomma's recipe, and I told her it was the best candy I ever had in my mouth. And that's saying something.

"Well, it's all I can make," Brooke sighed.

"Don't you worry," I told her, "that candy is all you ever need to make."

My Brooke's got the Southern charm gig down pat.

NEVER JUDGE A BOOK BY ITS COVER

I've learned you can't tell much about a person by the way he wears his hair or the way she dresses or talks. Einstein's looks didn't inspire drop-dead respect: it's only when he started talking mathematics that you could see his mind. I'd say the same is true of Bill Gates. So someone can come into my restaurant looking like Ned from the *First Reader,* or Jackie Kennedy, and I give them the same respectful treatment.

I remember a story about the great cosmetics queen Estée Lauder, who was working her counter at Saks Fifth Avenue in San Antonio, Texas. In came a Mexican woman. She had gold teeth and wore torn leather sandals and a multihued serape. Mrs. Lauder said she knew it had taken great personal courage for the Mexican woman to even walk into the store.

The woman wistfully pointed to the (quite expensive) Super Rich Moisturizing Crème.

Mrs. Lauder went to work. She cleansed the lady's face, applied a mask and then the Super Rich Moisturizing Crème, she brushed a little blush on the woman's cheeks, finishing off with just a touch of lipstick. She spent almost twenty minutes with her customer, and all the while, three dolled-up Texas ladies waited impatiently for their turns.

The woman looked at herself in the mirror and broke into a radiant smile. She opened her sagging black purse, and it was literally overflowing with dollars. She bought two of everything Mrs. Lauder had used on her face, and the next day her relatives did the same.

I'll never forget when my very stylish assistant, Brandon, and I were in New York City about a year and a half ago. We had just flown in and I *really* looked like Ned in the *First Reader*. I mean, Ned was not pretty and neither was I. To make matters worse, I was in rumpled but comfortable travel clothes, my hair was stringy, and I think my lipstick was all eaten off. I looked a little rough around the edges, to put it mildly.

Comin' out on the street from the airport, Brandon said, "I am so sick of seeing you tote that free bag that the jewelry store gave you. It's not a purse, Paula, and you have got to throw it away."

I just hated to dump the tote—it was really thin, papery stuff and I loved it because it was light.

But soon Brandon and I, we're passing one of those high falutin', expensive Fifth Avenue stores—and he walks me right through that door and directly into the pocketbook section. Brandon says, "It is time for you to have a good purse. I want you to buy yourself a Louis Vuitton."

Now, I'd heard him and my niece, Corrie, talking about this Louis Vuitton person, and I always thought they were saying Lewis Baton.

So I say to Brandon, "I don't know if I really want a Lewis Baton." I'd heard they were superexpensive, and I just didn't know if that was where I wanted to put my money. But we walk in, and I'm looking around at everybody and the purses, and I'm also looking at the sales clerks.

Nobody looks back at me. Nobody speaks to us.

I go over to Brandon, and I say, "These sons of bitches think I can't afford one of their purses. I've been *culled*." *Culled* means something that's been picked out and put aside as inferior, like a lobster with no claws that's been culled from the catch and maybe sold for fish soup. One saleswoman looked at me, and fast looked right through me. She had already decided that I didn't have the money for a Lewis Baton. She was on the lookout to attend to somebody who looked like she would buy.

I knew at that moment that I was walking out with any Lewis Baton I wanted; maybe two of them. And I just strolled over to the case, pointed, and said to a different, very young salesperson, "I'll take that . . . and that one." And I pulled out the money and paid.

The one who had ignored me turned as red as a beet. She was dyin'.

YOU GOTTA TAKE RISKS

I think it was Eleanor Roosevelt who said, "You must do the thing you think you cannot do." Go, Ellie! That's how I live my life. Take cooking. When some people go into a kitchen and start to cook, it's very important that they have a recipe, and they will deviate from that formula not one iota. Some people go in there, find a recipe, look at all the ingredients, and then, by putting their own ideas together with the recipe ingredients, they create a great dish. They make that formula their own. Those people would be risk takers. That would be me.

You always have to run the risk that a dish you prepare might be delicious or it might be disastrous. The person who follows the formula exactly knows exactly what she's gonna get; she's not gonna gamble. I think that's fine—for the first time. In my cooking class, I always recommend that if you have a recipe you've never made before, follow it exactly so that you'll know what the creator of that recipe had in mind about what that dish should look and taste like. But the next time you make that dish, change something about it. Add one thing or take one thing out. Make it your own. Make it fabulous, not just good.

Even though my restaurant honors all things Southern, at home I experiment a little. I've made collard greens and ham hock pizza and deep-fried wontons stuffed with greens and cream sauce. My son Bobby loves it when I cook my version of Mexican food, and he thinks I make a pretty mean stir-fry too. Where is it written that you can't make, in one meal, Chinese wonton soup, okra and fried green tomatoes, Indian-style curry, and Jewish blintzes (Shalom, y'all) for dessert?

In my life I've learned that taking a risk and losing doesn't mean the game is over. I'm not afraid to be proven wrong, not afraid to fail even when people say I'm nuts and success is impossible.

But here's the thing: there are calculated risks—those that have a reasonable chance of coming through for me—and then there are dumber-than-dumb risks.

Most of us are pretty good at avoiding dumb risks, unless you happen to be reading this from a damn jail cell. But we're also mostly scared of taking calculated risks. I believe the dumbest mistakes we make in life come from *not* seizing the moment—even if the moment looks a little scary. I have learned to respect my intuition and I have flown by the seat of my britches so many times, they're stretched out.

When I first started The Bag Lady, I had no experience—none, zilch, zero. I was forty-two years old and I knew I had to do something even if it was a wrong move. So, I flew by the seat of my pants every day I got up. I went with my gut instinct. I knew that if I was to succeed, I had to do what I knew. I'd hung around with my grandmomma in her restaurant long enough to have an idea of what it took to run one. So, I took a calculated risk and it paid off.

I could not have gone and hung up a shingle that read ORAL SURGEON. I could not have become a race-car driver or a poet. Those would have been dumb, stupid, can't-ever-win risks. It so happens that the thing I knew best—feeding folks professionally—has the highest rate of failure in America. Probably the last thing a banker wants to see walking into his bank looking for a loan is somebody who thinks they want to open a restaurant. Any time you want to get rid of a banker, go in and tell him you want to borrow money to open a restaurant and that bastard will go to the bathroom and won't never come back.

When I purchased and opened the original Lady & Sons, I signed a twelve-year lease and put myself on the line. I had no money and I didn't know how I was going to get it. I was probably foolish and guilty of poor planning. Still, my gut—my intuition—told me to go for it. The risk worked out.

My handsome, fun-lovin' boys, Jamie and Bobby, are starting on a grand adventure—their own television show, called *Road Tasted*, on Food Network. Without a script, without television training, without coaches, they're hitting the road and crisscrossing the country in search of the best local handcrafted foods of the region. They'll find ma-and-pa specialty stores and family-run businesses that highlight the culinary specialties of a particular city and they'll ad-lib visits with perfect strangers. Jamie and Bobby are trekking through California, New Mexico, Tennessee, Florida, Missouri, Seattle, New York—you name it—winging the dialogue and also hanging on by the seats of their pants as food happenings explode around them. Now, I'm so proud of these young men, who by sheer wit (they *are* pretty damn funny), ingenuity, and passion for all things good to eat are taking chances every day, and with cameras following them to boot. But they know food—cooking it, serving it, and eating it—and they're having a blast.

I took a calculated risk to marry Michael. He was nine years younger than I, cared nothin' about cooking but the eating, and he'd already had a failed marriage. But, you know what you know, and I trusted my heart. It's by taking risks that we reap rewards, and Michael is some great prize and the love of my life.

Now, gambling, *there's* a dumb risk. I confess that Michael and I both love to go to casinos. Still, you'd better believe I'm never going to put my last dime down on a bet and I don't go thinking I'm going to win. I would never wager the house, utility, or grocery money. I'll only lose what I feel like I can afford to lose, but I'll put that last dollar of what I think I can afford to lose in the machine, knowing that this is going to be the big one.

There are people who don't like excitement; they want a steady, predictable life and they don't find that boring or unchallenging. I get off on stepping out on the plank and taking a risk, as long as it has a reasonable hope of succeeding. Here's what I believe: sometimes when you crunch the numbers and figure every angle, the numbers will say something bad—but your gut says go for it anyway. In the end, I believe it's stupid to take a dumb risk, but it's stupider to pass up a calculated risk with a good chance of success.

Here's what I think: you take the risk *if* you can live with the worst-case scenario you can imagine. If you write a book and it gets awful reviews, if you open a restaurant and it fails, if you go skiing and you break a leg, if you go to Italy by yourself and not one single person talks to you the whole time, if the man you ask out on a date says thanks but no thanks—will you just wither and die from disappointment or embarrassment? If the answer is yes, play it safe and don't risk what you can't live with. If the answer is no, go for it, girl. Otherwise, you might just drown in a sea of woulda/coulda/shoulda and for the rest of your life rue the day you didn't give opportunity a shot.

This is not the best advice for everybody. But for me—? I'm not about settling for mediocre just to play it safe. My whole life I've taken risks that had a decent chance of paying off, and enough have paid off for me to continue doing so till the day I die.

DON'T EVER MESS WITH CHRISTMAS

If ever I'm tempted to go to a glamorous, exotic place for Christmas—just Michael and me—just in time I'll remember the rule I made when I was very young: never mess with the holidays. Always be with the people you love, as many of them as you can round up.

After Bubba was born, Daddy always insisted we all spend Christmas together. He felt it was very important that children be in their own home and with their families at holiday time. As a result, I never saw how my Grandmomma and Grandpoppa Hiers decorated their Florida home, where they then lived, for Christmas. How could I be sure they even had a tree? It was nerve-rackin'.

So no matter what, I always got everyone nuts trying to get us home for the holidays, wherever we were: I can remember when Jimmy Deen and I had just moved to Savannah. I'll tell you, I missed my hometown of Albany, Georgia, something fierce. By hook or crook, this Southern gal was going home for Christmas: I would get me and my kids and my husband to Albany. We'd been planning to leave Christmas Eve, but would you believe it started snowing early in the day and Savannah ended up with seven inches of snow! Jamie and my niece, Corrie, had gone ahead and were waiting for us in Albany. Now, Southern towns aren't so good about preparing for snowstorms, and that half-foot of white stuff about shut down Savannah. *Nothin'* was moving—not the automobiles, which had turned into bumper cars, not even the tourists. I was heartbroken. And I told Bobby and Jimmy, "We've just got to make it. I've *got* to be home for Christmas."

All the kids were jumping for joy. When had they ever seen that much white powder from the sky? But me? I was devastated. Enjoy a Christmas so far away from my Aunt Peggy and people I loved? Impossible. But, next day, that Georgia sun came out shining, that old snow melted, and we did get home to Albany.

Afterward, I felt like such a brat. I promised my kids I'd try to enjoy snow the next time, maybe with a little powdered sugar on top.

One time, when my boys were still very little and we were living in Columbus, Georgia, we had *seventeen* inches of snow. That was really the first time I'd ever seen a snowstorm, and even I had to admit it was so gorgeous. My kids had the best time playing in that snow, and it was then I was first introduced to snow cream. I am telling y'all the truth, there is nothing better. We were all outside playing, and Ettie May, the housekeeper who lived across the street from us, hollered, "Come on over here, Miss Paula, and eat some snow cream." I scooped up the fresh, cold, white powdery stuff and stuffed it in my mouth, and it was the best treat I'd ever in my whole life tasted. The last time it snowed on the Deen family was in New York around Christmastime a couple of years ago. I was filming my show and it began snowing. I went outside with a big old blue bowl and just filled it up with solid handfuls of snow (being careful to avoid the yellow snow from the passing parade of doggies!). I added a bit of sweetened condensed milk, a couple of spoonfuls of vanilla, mixed it together, and soon the whole crew and I were eating the best homemade snow cream ever invented. It was the sweetest Christmas present on the planet! Let your kids actually make a whole pot of the stuff—tryin' out different-flavored snow, like lemon, melted chocolate, or even licorice snow! I promise you'll have created the best Christmas memory ever.

The first Christmas memory I have is still my absolute favorite. I was five years old, and Bubba hadn't been born yet. I was showered with presents. I got a bicycle and the Mary Hartline majorette doll that I wanted so badly. It makes me smile to think about it. That Mary Hartline was so cool in her blue uniform dotted with pink flowers with a pearl in the center of each flower.

In our house there were always snow-white lilies, flickering red candles, pomegranate wreaths, and balls of kissing mistletoe. There was gold ribbon everywhere. Aunt Peggy taught me to make our Christmas more fragrant than any other time of the year by preparing a mix of fresh fruit peels (apple, pear, and citrus), apple cores, and bay leaves, plus a few ground-up cinnamon sticks. We'd simmer it all in some water on the stove for hours, bringing fragrance to our holiday home.

And I remember that we often had turducken for the holidays. A turducken is a turkey, a duck, and a chicken stuffed one inside the other. You have the butcher debone the turkey (except for the legs and the wings), the duck, and the chicken. You cut 'em down their backs, then you lay the turkey breast side down, the duck breast side down on top of the turkey, and then the chicken breast side down on top of the duck. You can choose to stuff the inside bird alone or slather stuffing on top of each bird. Then you take those birds and you pin and tie them back together so that it looks like only one big turkey and roast it for the richest, most impressive main dish ever.

The Christmas stocking was always the best part for me: I loved to dig for all the little gifts in it. Sometimes it meant a ring, a bracelet, or a small doll, but it always meant fruits and nuts. Oranges, apples, Brazil nuts, and walnuts were the stocking stuffers of choice when I was young. There was no end of bubble bath, perfumes, scratch-off lotto tickets, and fancy underwear. Today, I'm a bit older, but Christmas stockings are still my favorite part of opening presents, and I love buying the small stuff for my family's stockings.

I so remember the last Christmas before I was married. I was seventeen and it was a bummer.

Momma always put up the tree one week before Christmas, and most of our presents were already wrapped and under the tree by December 23. One day, Momma went to the grocery store and I said to myself, *This is the perfect time for me to go in there and look at all my gifts.*

Very carefully, I snuck into the living room, opened every box with my name on it, pulled out the contents, and then slipped 'em back in their boxes. Carefully, and with a heavy heart, I put the ribbons back on. You would never have guessed that anybody had ever been in those boxes.

Well, when I got through lookin', I was so angry. There was nothing in none of those boxes that I really wanted. But I learned a valuable lesson: some things are better left wrapped. Some things need to be a surprise.

It was also the same Christmas that Momma went out and bought her own presents. I always knew Daddy would get Momma *something,* but Momma never got what she really wanted. So this one particular Christmas, Momma went out and bought herself everything she wanted, wrapped it, and put it under the tree. Lo and behold, this same Christmas, my daddy did a little bit better with his shopping. He'd bought her a mink stole, and a set of diamond wedding bands was hidden in the folds of that mink stole.

So, we get up Christmas morning, and I know what's waitin' for me, and that ruins everything. Momma, on the other hand, got gifts under the tree that she had bought herself, so she's pretty excited. Well, she opens the first box, and it had a beautiful green negligee set that she'd bought, and she slips it on and she's sittin' there, lookin' like a queen. Then Daddy pulls out this big box from behind the couch and hands it to Momma. She opens it, and it's the mink stole with the diamond-ring bonus. Well, you'd think she'd be happy, but Momma felt so bad because she had bought herself these gifts, and then Daddy had gone out and bought her the world. What's more, her gifts now so outweighed what her children had gotten. Still, I can remember her sittin' there in the living room wearing that negligee with the new fur wrap right on top of it.

For a lot of reasons, none of us was real happy. I had the feeling that if I only hadn't looked at my presents, they would have magically been a lot better. Momma was so embarrassed that she'd one-upped Daddy, but I must admit she still enjoyed every bit of the fur, and the diamond rings, which Jamie's wife, Brooke, now proudly wears.

I personally never again opened a Christmas gift before its time. Some things are worth waitin' on.

The last few Christmases, Michael and I have been either moving in or out of a house, so we especially appreciate Christmas with our family in our own home, just like my daddy always knew was the best kind. I do love this holiday easily as much as I did when I was a little girl, although I've got to say, I haven't gotten a Mary Hartline doll in years. Are you listening, Michael?

New Year's is a special holiday of its own, but I always think of it as an extension of the Christmas season. I don't want you to think I'm flaky and woo-woo superstitious, but when that holiday week rolls around, I can't help but be true to the memory of my grandfather Paul, who was a very superstitious man, especially around Christmastime. For instance, I was never allowed to have the goldfish I desperately wanted because he thought they were bad luck. Black cats were no friends to him, and you couldn't get him to walk under a ladder if there was the finest steak and a bottle of Jack Daniel's on the other side of it waitin' for him. And,

Lord knows, we kids knew better than to open an umbrella in the house.

Today? My whole family usually makes it to my house on Christmas, and also New Year's Day, where I burden them with some superstitions of my own. Even if they hate and despise greens, they've got to have at least one bite of turnip greens, so they'll have financial success all the next year. I always serve the greens along with rice and black-eyed peas with hog jowl, because we Southern dames are sure the black-eyed peas bring luck and, believe it or not, those hog jowls promise health.

There is just no way I'm going to mess with Christmas, especially with my first grandbaby, Jack, on his way as I write this book.

STINKIN' THINKIN' . . . GET OUTTA HERE

Finally, I'm throwin' all my stinkin' thinkin' out the window. Sometimes that old fear comes back a little—and a little is a lot. But instead of preparing for the worst and worryin' about what might happen—I'm thinkin' cool and positive these days.

My little Jackpot will be here by the time you're readin' this. Today he's in his mother's belly being prepared for entry into a complicated world. Along with his parents, I want to help give him wings, as my own grandparents did for me. I want to arm him with an education, because I could not give it to my sons. I've already got his miniature cooking set in there waitin' for him to make flapjacks. I want to give Jack not only the recipes that he'll cook one day but the recipe for a fulfilling, people-lovin' life. I want him to be in love with that life, want him to have passion for his work and respect for the American Dream and its promises.

The idea that I'd have my own television show and fans who would love me from all over the world, not just from Albany, Georgia, was a concept I wasn't even ready to grasp when I started.

Fame! It's swell. Now even Michael can't go anywhere without being swamped by fans. Sometimes when Michael and I have to go somewhere and it's a bad hair day and I look like hell, I try to hide behind sunglasses. But walkin' around with that man is like walkin' around with a turd on your forehead—you just can't stop people from starin' at him. I'm always gettin' outed by Michael.

I'm only kidding. The fact that my restaurants did succeed and offered recognition and financial security to me and my family is such a blessing. The security alone is like what a doctor's family enjoys. For this little southwest Georgia girl to think she could earn what a doctor could earn was an insane goal! To think that I'd be able to go on any trip I wanted, to think I could live by the water's edge and see the dolphins jump right in front of my porch, to think that I could buy my first grandchild a pony, which is what I'm fixin' to do as soon as I finish writin' this book—well, what's that worth?

Only everything. Even if his father yells at me for spoiling him.

Pony? Scratch the pony. My little Jack's getting a whole horse.

And, we are lookin' forward to so much. First of all, I want to meet more and more of my precious fans. I just love them and when I can hug a reader of one of my books or a watcher of my shows, it makes my day. I've never, ever had one bad encounter with a fan. They're very much my kind of people; I seem to always feel like I live their lives and they're livin' my life, right along with me.

And, somethin' else is about to happen to the Deen family that puts awe in my heart. We've started to allow our names to be put on certain great products that we love to use in our own home. My name sittin' on your kitchen counter!

Our family grows. Bubba is getting married again, to our darling Dawn. His daughter, Corrie, introduced them! Dawn is so much a part of our crazy family already and the knots in her head fit the holes in his.

Michael and I are looking forward to more grandchildren, and our two families today continue to grow and blend—not effortlessly, but steadily, because we are all mindful of the way words—both happy and hurtful words—weigh heavily.

It takes my breath away to realize that I was right in sayin' if you work hard enough, you probably can be anything you want. Our family is eternally grateful that we definitely need each other. If we had each gone off in different careers, the love would still be there but not so much the need for each other. I love the need—although it ain't always simple.

Bobby Deen said it just fine one day:

"The best thing about our business is being able to be with our family so much," he said. "The hardest thing about our business is having to be with family so much," he concluded.

We sure learned that when you're in the heat of family survival, it's like fighting a war, not just a battle. But then comes the day when you can step back and look out on what you've accomplished together and say, "This is ours, *ours,* and it feels so damn good."

Our thinkin' is sweet these days. We made it . . . so far. But I can't rest completely easy. You never can be too sure that success or happiness will last forever.

So, no stinkin' thinkin' from me, I promise y'all. Jack Deen—come on over here for a big hug from your grandmomma. You don't know grits yet about how good it gets.

Index

Index